Praise for *Thanks for the Feedback*

"Receiving feedback is a skill, and like most skills, it requires practice and a willingness to change and improve. . . . [*Thanks For The Feedback* is] the best guide I've found to learning this skill."
— Jessica Lahey, *The New York Times*

"*Thanks for the Feedback* is an extraordinarily useful book. It's full of helpful techniques that can be put to use by anyone seeking to manage an organization, lead a team, engage a business partner, or navigate a relationship. . . . Stone and Heen have done a remarkable job of showing individuals and organizations how to leverage the enormous value of feedback, one of the most powerful instruments available for human learning."
— *Strategy + Business*

"*Thanks for the Feedback* takes a 180-degree turn in the usual approach to feedback. Instead of teaching readers to deliver it effectively, Stone and Heen show them how to receive it in a way that builds self-awareness and action planning for improvement. . . . Stone and Heen describe in a meaningful way what is entirely true about the feedback process: It's a complex interchange that is inevitably influenced by the perceptions and biases of the giver and receiver. An excellent follow up to their bestselling book *Difficult Conversations, Thanks for the Feedback* provides a powerful framework for making feedback work—no matter what it is or how it is given."
— *T+D Magazine*

"This unique book addresses how to accept feedback gracefully, whether your boss is giving you a review, your kids are commenting on their meatloaf dinner, or your mother-in-law is offering snide commentary on your parenting style . . . [Stone and Heen] hit it out of the park with well-researched insight, advice, and tips."
— *Parents Magazine*

"We all need to get better at hearing feedback. That doesn't entail always accepting it, [but] it does mean abandoning the knee-jerk response of railing against feedback you consider unfair and instead trying to figure out why the difference of viewpoint has arisen. . . . The book asks a question worth memorizing: what's the one thing you see me doing that gets in my own way?" —*The Guardian* (London)

"The book isn't a manifesto for being a pushover: *Thanks for the Feedback* instructs in the art of understanding feedback and turning criticism into a kick-ass attitude. Saints needn't apply." —*Evening Standard*

"Feedback is everywhere. We may not be able to exert complete control over what someone else thinks of us but we can certainly do something about what we choose to do with the feedback. [This] is a sensible, breezily written book." —*Financial Times*

"Surprisingly little attention has been focused on being an effective recipient of feedback. Enter Stone and Heen with a well-rounded consideration of 'the science and art of receiving feedback well.' As they write, both of those disciplines are required to receive feedback in productive ways—not only in the workplace, but in personal life as well. . . . The authors do an excellent job of constraining the applications to feedback usefulness while also exploring some of the other ways we can define what 'feedback' consists of in our lives. With a culture increasingly focused on the individual and the self, this book on developing the ability to accept and utilize the input of others constructively deserves a wide readership." —*Kirkus Reviews*

"I'll admit it: *Thanks for the Feedback* made me uncomfortable. And that's one reason I liked it so much. With keen insight and lots of practical takeaways, Stone and Heen reveal why getting feedback is so hard—and then how we can do better. If you relish receiving criticism at work and adore it in your personal life, then you may be the one person on earth who can safely skip this book."
—Daniel H. Pink, author of *To Sell Is Human* and *Drive*

"*Thanks for the Feedback* is a potentially life-changing look at one of the toughest but most important parts of life: receiving feedback. It's a road map to less defensiveness, more self-awareness, greater learning, and richer relationships. Doug Stone and Sheila Heen have delivered another tour de force."

—Adam Grant, Wharton professor and author of *Give and Take*

"Imagine an organization where everyone is actually good at receiving feedback. Collective anxiety would be reduced. People would learn and grow. Impossible you say? Thanks to this insanely original and powerful book, maybe not."

—Judy Rosenblum, former chief learning officer of Coca-Cola
and founder of Duke Corporate Education

"Startlingly original advice for how to make feedback truly useful."

—Chris Benko, vice president of global talent
management of Merck

"If you want to lead a learning organization, improving the quality of feedback is job one. This book is an essential guide to making that happen."

—Amy C. Edmondson, Novartis Professor of Leadership
and Management, Harvard Business School, and
author of *Teaming*

"Learning and HR professionals aren't the only ones who will love this book. It should be required reading for anyone receiving a performance appraisal—and anyone who is striving to improve."

—B. Alan Echtenkamp, executive director of global organization
and leadership development, Time Warner Inc.

"Accepting feedback at work is important, but in families, it's vital. This simple, elegant book teaches us how."

—Bruce Feiler, *New York Times* columnist and author
of *The Secrets of Happy Families*

"*Thanks for the Feedback* places the reader in the driver's seat and shifts the paradigm on who is in charge of the learning."
—Wagner Denuzzo, director, IBM Management Development

"My management team and I are reading *Thanks for the Feedback*. We spend hours discussing it, as if it were directions to a lifetime gift of free donuts and coffee! We now have a way to set meaningful standards for productive feedback and most importantly, for developing sensible solutions with officers who are struggling. Melding your concepts with our desires of service and professionalism within our California state police agency are a perfect match. We are integrating the material into a training we hope to offer the entire department."
—J. Edwards, Jr., Lieutenant Commander
and police academy instructor

"*Thanks for the Feedback* is not about how to *give* feedback. It's a far more powerful book than that. It's about how to *receive* feedback. . . . We should love feedback, positive or negative. But we're also proud . . . that's why this book is so good. We have an image of ourselves as someone who can cope emotionally with criticism and is open minded. Yet the reality is that we're human beings, and very different to each other. The book recognizes that we each react differently. It provides us with ways to cope, handle, and grow with feedback."
—Dan Cottrell, *International Rugby Coaching* magazine

PENGUIN BOOKS

THANKS FOR THE FEEDBACK

Douglas Stone and Sheila Heen are Lecturers on Law at Harvard Law School and cofounders of Triad Consulting. Their clients include the White House, Citigroup, Honda, Johnson & Johnson, Time Warner, Unilever, and many others. Stone Lives in Cambridge. Heen lives with her husband and three children in a farmhouse north of Cambridge.

THANKS
FOR THE
FEEDBACK

The Science and Art of
Receiving Feedback Well

*(EVEN WHEN IT IS OFF BASE, UNFAIR,
POORLY DELIVERED, AND, FRANKLY,
YOU'RE NOT IN THE MOOD)*

DOUGLAS STONE & SHEILA HEEN

PENGUIN BOOKS

PENGUIN BOOKS

Published by the Penguin Group
Penguin Group (USA) LLC
375 Hudson Street
New York, New York 10014

USA | Canada | UK | Ireland | Australia | New Zealand | India | South Africa | China
penguin.com
A Penguin Random House Company

First published in the United States of America by Viking Penguin,
a member of Penguin Group (USA) LLC, 2014
Published in Penguin Books 2015

THE LIBRARY OF CONGRESS HAS CATALOGED THE HARDCOVER EDITION AS FOLLOWS:
Stone, Douglas.
Thanks for the feedback : the science and art of receiving feedback well (even when it is off base, unfair,
poorly delivered, and, frankly, you're not in the mood) / Douglas Stone, Sheila Heen.
pages   cm
Includes bibliographical references and index.
ISBN 978-0-670-01466-8 (hc.)
ISBN 978-0-14-312713-0 (pbk.)
1. Feedback (Psychology) 2. Interpersonal communication. I. Heen, Sheila. II. Title.
BF319.5.F4S76 2014
153.6'8—dc23
2013036968

Printed in the United States of America
20 19 18 17 16

Set in Agra Wile
Graphs by Julie Munn
Designed by Carla Bolte

To Anne and Don Stone,
the best parents in the world.
You taught me what matters.
—ds

To John, Benjamin, Peter, and Adelaide,
for accepting me despite my flaws,
and even (occasionally) because of them.
—sh

CONTENTS

FEEDBACK IN CONVERSATION

THANKS
FOR THE
FEEDBACK

INTRODUCTION

From Push to Pull

Before you tell me how to do it better, before you lay out your big plans for changing, fixing, and improving me, before you teach me how to pick myself up and dust myself off so that I can be shiny and successful—know this: I've heard it before.

I've been graded, rated, and ranked. Coached, screened, and scored. I've been picked first, picked last, and not picked at all. And that was just kindergarten.

We swim in an ocean of feedback.

Each year in the United States alone, every schoolchild will be handed back as many as 300 assignments, papers, and tests. Millions of kids will be assessed as they try out for a team or audition to be cast in a school play. Almost 2 million teenagers will receive SAT scores and face college verdicts thick and thin. At least 40 million people will be sizing up one another for love online, where 71 percent of them believe they can judge love at first sight. And now that we know each other . . . 250,000 weddings will be called off, and 877,000 spouses will file for divorce.[1]

More feedback awaits at work. Twelve million people will lose a job and countless others will worry that they may be next. More than 500,000 entrepreneurs will open their doors for the first time, and almost 600,000 will shut theirs for the last. Thousands of other businesses will struggle to get by as debates proliferate in the boardroom and the back hall about *why* they are struggling. Feedback flies.[2]

Did we mention performance reviews? Estimates suggest that between 50 and 90 percent of employees will receive performance reviews this year, upon which our raises, bonuses, promotions—and often our self-esteem—ride. Across the globe, 825 million work hours—a cumulative 94,000 years—are spent each year preparing for and engaging in annual reviews. Afterward we all certainly feel thousands of years older, but are we any wiser?[3]

Margie receives a "Meets Expectations," which sounds to her like "Really, You Still Work Here?"

Your second grader's art project, "Mommy Yells," was a hot topic at the school's Open House Night.

Your spouse has been complaining about your same character flaws for years. You think of this less as your spouse "giving you feedback," and more as your spouse "being annoying."

Rodrigo reads over his 360-degree feedback report.[4] Repeatedly. He can't make head or tail of it, but one thing has changed: He now feels awkward with his colleagues, all 360 degrees of them.

Thanks for the Feedback is about the profound challenge of being on the receiving end of feedback—good or bad, right or wrong, flippant, caring, or callous. This book is not a paean to improvement or a pep talk on how to make friends with your mistakes. There is encouragement here, but our primary purpose is to take an honest look at *why* receiving feedback is hard, and to provide a framework and some tools that can help you metabolize challenging, even crazy-making information and use it to fuel insight and growth.

• • •

In 1999, along with our friend and colleague Bruce Patton, we published *Difficult Conversations: How to Discuss What Matters Most.* Since then, we've continued to teach at Harvard Law School and to work with clients across continents, cultures, and industries. We've had the privilege of working with an amazing assortment of people: executives, entrepreneurs, oil rig operators, doctors, nurses, teachers, scientists, engineers, religious leaders, police officers, filmmakers, lawyers, journalists, and relief workers. Even dance instructors and astronauts.

Here's something we noticed early on: When we ask people to list their most difficult conversations, feedback *always* comes up. It doesn't matter who they are, where they are, what they do, or why they brought us in. They describe just how tough it is to give honest feedback, even when they know it's sorely needed. They tell us about performance problems that go unaddressed for years and explain that when they finally give the feedback, it rarely goes well. The coworker is upset and defensive, and ends up less motivated, not more. Given how hard it is to muster the courage and energy to give feedback in the first place, and the dispiriting results—well, who needs it?

Eventually, someone in the group will pipe up to observe that *getting* feedback is often no easier. The feedback is unfair or off base. It's poorly timed and even more poorly delivered. And it's not clear why the giver thinks they are qualified to offer an opinion; they may be the boss, but they don't really understand what we do or the constraints we're under. We are left feeling underappreciated, demotivated, and more than a little indignant. Who needs it?

Interesting. When we give feedback, we notice that the receiver isn't good at receiving it. When we receive feedback, we notice that the giver isn't good at giving it.

We wondered: What is it that makes feedback such a conundrum for both givers and receivers? We started listening closely to people as they described their dilemmas, struggles, and triumphs, and noticed those same struggles in ourselves. As we worked to develop ways to approach feedback differently, we soon realized that the key player is not the giver, but the receiver. And we came to see how this could transform not just how we handle performance reviews on the job, but how we learn, lead, and behave in our professional roles and in our personal lives.

WHAT COUNTS AS FEEDBACK?

Feedback includes any information you get about yourself. In the broadest sense, it's how we learn about ourselves from our experiences and from other people—how we learn from life. It's your annual performance review, the firm's climate survey, the local critic's review of your restaurant. But feedback also includes the way your son's eyes light up when he spots you in the audience and the way your friend surreptitiously slips off the sweater you knitted her the minute she thinks you're out of view. It's the steady renewal of services by a longtime client and the lecture you get from the cop on the side of the road. It's what your bum knee is trying to tell you about your diminishing spryness, and the confusing mix of affection and disdain you get from your fifteen-year-old.

So feedback is not just what gets ranked; it's what gets thanked, commented on, and invited back or dropped. Feedback can be formal or informal, direct or implicit; it can be blunt or baroque, totally obvious or so subtle that you're not sure *what* it is.

Like that comment your spouse made a moment ago: "I don't like the way those pants look on you." *What do you mean, you don't like the way these pants look on me?* Is there something wrong with this particular pair of pants, or was that a passive-aggressive reference to the weight I've put on? Another dig about how I'm living in the past or can't dress myself, even as an adult? Are you trying to help me look nice for the party, or is this your way of easing into asking for a divorce? (*What do you mean I'm overreacting?*)

A BRIEF HISTORY OF FEEDBACK

The term "feed-back" was coined in the 1860s during the Industrial Revolution to describe the way that outputs of energy, momentum, or signals are returned to their point of origin in a mechanical system.[5] By 1909 Nobel laureate Karl Braun was using the phrase to describe the coupling and loops between components of an electronic circuit. A decade later the new compound word "feedback" was being used to describe the recirculating sound loop in an amplification system—that piercing squeal we all know from high school auditoriums and Jimi Hendrix recordings.

Sometime after World War II the term began to be used in industrial relations when talking about people and performance management. Feed corrective information back to the point of origin—that would be you, the employee—and voilà! Tighten up here, dial back there, and like some Dr. Seuss contraption, you're all tuned up for optimum, star-bellied performance.

In today's workplace, feedback plays a crucial role in developing talent, improving morale, aligning teams, solving problems, and boosting the bottom line. And yet. Fifty-one percent of respondents in one recent study said their performance review was unfair or inaccurate, and one in four employees dreads their performance review more than anything else in their working lives.[6]

The news is no more encouraging on the manager's side: Only 28 percent of HR professionals believe their managers focus on more than simply completing forms. Sixty-three percent of executives surveyed say that their biggest challenge to effective performance management is that their managers lack the courage and ability to have difficult feedback discussions.[7]

Something isn't working. So organizations are spending billions of dollars each year to train supervisors, managers, and leaders on how to *give* feedback more effectively. When feedback meets resistance or is rejected outright, feedback givers are encouraged to be persistent. They are taught how to *push* harder.

We think we have it backwards.

PULL BEATS PUSH

Training managers how to *give* feedback—how to push more effectively—can be helpful. But if the receiver isn't willing or able to absorb the feedback, then there's only so far persistence or even skillful delivery can go. It doesn't matter how much authority or power a feedback giver has; the receivers are in control of what they do and don't let in, how they make sense of what they're hearing, and whether they choose to change.

Pushing harder rarely opens the door to genuine learning. The focus should not be on teaching feedback givers to give. The focus—at work and at home—should be on feedback *receivers*, helping us all to become more skillful learners.

The real leverage is creating pull.

Creating pull is about mastering the skills required to drive our own learning; it's about how to recognize and manage our resistance, how to engage in feedback conversations with confidence and curiosity, and even when the feedback seems wrong, how to find insight that might help us grow. It's also about how to stand up for who we are and how we see the world, and ask for what we need. It's about how to learn from feedback—yes, even when it is off base, unfair, poorly delivered, and frankly, you're not in the mood.

We like the word "pull" because it highlights a truth often ignored: that the key variable in your growth is not your teacher or your supervisor. It's *you*. It's well and good to hope for that special mentor or coach (and cherish the ones you come across). But don't put off learning until they arrive. Those exceptional teachers and mentors are rare. Mostly, our lives are populated by everyone else—people who are doing their best but may not know better, who are too busy to give us the time we need, who are difficult themselves, or who are just plain lousy at giving feedback or coaching. The majority of our learning is going to have to come from folks like these, so if we're serious about growth and improvement, we have no choice but to get good at learning from just about anyone.

THE TENSION BETWEEN LEARNING AND BEING ACCEPTED

It seems like that shouldn't be so hard. After all, humans are naturally wired for learning. The drive to learn is evident from infancy and rampant by toddlerhood. Even as adults we memorize baseball stats, travel in retirement, and throw ourselves into yoga because discovery and progress are deeply gratifying. Indeed, research on happiness identifies ongoing learning and growth as a core ingredient of satisfaction in life.

We may be wired to learn, but it turns out that learning *about our-*

selves is a whole different ball game. Learning about ourselves can be painful—sometimes brutally so—and the feedback is often delivered with a forehead-slapping lack of awareness for what makes people tick. It can feel less like a "gift of learning" and more like a colonoscopy.

Tom's boss gives him a dressing-down about his "organizational skills." On his drive home, Tom silently catalogues his boss's inadequacies. He pulls over and jots down a list to keep them organized.

Monisha, the head of HR, hoped the grim results from the firm's climate survey would spark candid conversation among senior leadership about the need for change. Instead, she got a terse e-mail from the CFO enumerating the survey's methodological flaws, dismissing the results, and questioning Monisha's motives.

Kendra's sister-in-law lets slip that the family thinks she is hysterically overprotective of her children. Perhaps not precisely those words, but that's the tape running in Kendra's mind as she sets the table for the extended family Sunday dinner.

It's no wonder that when we see tough feedback coming, we are tempted to turn and run.

But we know we can't just tra-la-la down the road of life ignoring what others have to say, safely sealed in our emotional Ziploc. We've heard it since we were young. *Feedback is good for you*—like exercise and broccoli. *It makes you stronger and helps you grow.* Doesn't it?

It does. And our life experiences confirm it. We've all had a coach or family member who nurtured our talent and believed in us when no one else did. We've had a friend who laid bare a hard truth that helped us over an impossible hurdle. We've seen our confidence and capabilities grow, our relationships righted, and our rough edges softened. In fact, looking back, we have to admit that even that horrendous ex-spouse or overbearing supervisor taught us as much about ourselves as those who were on our side. It wasn't easy, but we know ourselves better now, and like ourselves more.

So here we are. Torn. Is it possible that feedback is like a gift *and* like a colonoscopy? Should we hang in there and take it, or turn and run? Is the learning really worth the pain?

We are conflicted.

Here's one reason why. In addition to our desire to learn and improve, we long for something else that is fundamental: to be loved, accepted, and respected just as we are. And the very fact of feedback suggests that how we are is not quite okay. So we bristle: Why can't you accept me for who I am and how I am? Why are there always more adjustments, more upgrades? Why is it *so hard* for you to understand me? Hey boss, hey team. Hey wife, hey Dad. *Here I am. This is me.*

Receiving feedback sits at the intersection of these two needs—our drive to learn and our longing for acceptance. These needs run deep, and the tension between them is not going away. But there's a lot each of us can do to manage the tension—to reduce anxiety in the face of feedback and to learn in spite of the fear. We believe that the ability to receive feedback well is not an inborn trait but a *skill* that can be cultivated. It may be fraught, but it can be taught. Whether you currently think of yourself as someone who receives feedback well or poorly, you can get better. This book shows you how.

THE BENEFITS OF RECEIVING WELL

Receiving feedback well doesn't mean you always have to *take* the feedback. Receiving it well means engaging in the conversation skillfully and making thoughtful choices about whether and how to use the information and what you're learning. It's about managing your emotional triggers so that you can take in what the other person is telling you, and being open to seeing yourself in new ways. And sometimes, as we discuss in chapter 10, it's about setting boundaries and saying no.

The bold-faced benefits of receiving feedback well are clear: Our relationships are richer, our self-esteem more secure, and, of course, we learn—we get better at things and feel good about that. And perhaps most important to some of us, when we get good at receiving feedback even our toughest feedback interactions come to feel a little less threatening.

In the workplace, treating feedback not just as something to be endured, but something to be actively sought, can have a profound impact. Feedback-seeking behavior—as it's called in the research literature—has been linked to higher job satisfaction, greater creativity on the job, faster adaptation in a new organization or role, and lower turnover. And seeking out *negative* feedback is associated with higher performance ratings.[8]

Perhaps this isn't surprising. People who are willing to look at themselves are just easier to work with and to live with. Being with people who are grounded and open is energizing. When you're open to feedback your working relationships have more trust and more humor, you collaborate more productively and solve problems more easily.

In personal relationships, our ability to deal with complaints, requests, and coaching from our friends and loved ones is crucial. Even in the best relationships we get frustrated with each other; we hurt each other accidentally and—on occasion—on purpose. Our ability to sort out how we're feeling, why we're upset, where we are bumping into one another, drives the long-term health and happiness of those relationships. Marriage researcher John Gottman has found that a person's willingness and ability to accept influence and input from their spouse is a key predictor of a healthy, stable marriage.[9]

In contrast, working or living with someone who shuts out feedback or responds with defensiveness and arguments is exhausting. We walk on eggshells and live in fear of pointless conflicts. Frank discussion fades and feedback goes unspoken, depriving the "receiver" of the chance to understand what's gone wrong or to fix it. The transaction costs involved in the simplest problem solving become prohibitive, and important thoughts and feelings have no outlet. Problems fester and the relationship stagnates. Insulation leads to isolation.

That's not just depressing, it's destructive, particularly today. Columnist Thomas Friedman observes, "We're entering a world that increasingly rewards individual aspiration and persistence and can measure precisely who is contributing and who is not. If you are self-motivated, wow, this world is tailored for you. The boundaries are all gone. But if you're not self-motivated, this world will be a challenge because the walls, ceilings and floors that protected people are also disappearing."[10]

The rewards are great, and the stakes have never been higher.

This suggests that it's not just about us; it's also about our kids. Whether or not we realize it, how we talk about an unfair performance evaluation in front of our children teaches them how to react to a bad call that costs them the ball game. Our kids respond to tough challenges the way they see us respond to tough challenges. Will a bully's name-calling eat away at their self-image? They will look to how we respond to our own setbacks; that teaches them more about resilience than all our pep talks and lectures combined.

The transformative impact of modeling is crucial at work as well. If you seek out coaching, your direct reports will seek out coaching. If you take responsibility for your mistakes, your peers will be encouraged to fess up as well; if you try out a suggestion from a coworker, they will be more open to trying out your suggestions. And this modeling effect becomes more important as you move up in an organization. Nothing affects the learning culture of an organization more than the skill with which its executive team receives feedback. And of course, as you move up, candid coaching becomes increasingly scarce, so you have to work harder to get it. But doing so sets the tone and creates an organizational culture of learning, problem solving, and adaptive high performance.

DIGGING FOR PONIES

There is an old joke about a happy young optimist whose parents are trying to teach him to see the world more realistically. To that end, they decide to give him a large sack of horse dung for his birthday.

"What did you get?" asks his grandmother, wrinkling her nose at the smell.

"I don't know," cries the boy with delight as he excitedly digs through the dung. "But I think there's a pony in here somewhere!"

Receiving feedback can be like that. It's not always pleasant. But there just might be a pony in there somewhere.

THE FEEDBACK CHALLENGE

1

THREE TRIGGERS

That Block Feedback

Let's start with some good news. Not all feedback is difficult. Your son's teacher, astonishingly, praises his social skills. Your customer offers a clever suggestion about how to handle his order that expedites the process. You want bangs, but your hairdresser has a better idea, which is, actually, a better idea. We get this sort of feedback all the time. It helps or it doesn't, and either way we're not much bothered by it.

Most of us do just fine with positive feedback, although even praise can sometimes leave us uneasy. Perhaps we're not sure it's genuine or we fear we haven't earned it. But closing the deal, or learning that someone you admire admires you, or getting that perfect bit of coaching that kicks your skill level up a notch can be electrifying. We did it, it worked, someone likes us.

Then there's the tougher stuff—the feedback that leaves us confused or enraged, flustered or flattened. You're attacking *my* child, *my* career, *my* character? You're going to leave me off the team? Is that really what you think of me?

This kind of feedback triggers us: Our heart pounds, our stomach clenches, our thoughts race and scatter. We usually think of that surge of emotion as being "in the way"—a distraction to be brushed aside, an obstacle to overcome. After all, when we're in the grip of a triggered reaction we feel lousy, the world looks darker, and our usual communication skills slip just out of reach. We can't think, we can't learn, and so we defend, attack, or withdraw in defeat.

But pushing our triggered reactions aside or pretending they don't exist is not the answer. Trying to ignore a triggered reaction without first identifying its cause is like dealing with a fire by disconnecting the smoke alarm.

So triggers are obstacles, but they aren't *only* obstacles. Triggers are also information—a kind of map—that can help us locate the source of the trouble. Understanding our triggers and sorting out what set them off are the keys to managing our reactions and engaging in feedback conversations with skill.

Let's take a closer look at that map.

THREE FEEDBACK TRIGGERS

Because feedback givers are abundant and our shortcomings seemingly boundless, we imagine that feedback can trigger us in a googolplex of ways. But here's more good news:

There are only three.

We call them "Truth Triggers," "Relationship Triggers," and "Identity Triggers." Each is set off for different reasons, and each provokes a different set of reactions and responses from us.

Truth Triggers are set off by the substance of the feedback itself—it's somehow off, unhelpful, or simply untrue. In response, we feel indignant, wronged, and exasperated. Miriam experiences a truth trigger when her husband tells her she was "unfriendly and aloof" at his nephew's bar mitzvah. "Unfriendly? Was I supposed to get up on the table and tap dance?" This feedback is ridiculous. It is just plain wrong.

Relationship Triggers are tripped by the particular person who is giving us this gift of feedback. All feedback is colored by the relationship between giver and receiver, and we can have reactions based on what we believe *about* the giver (they've got no credibility on this topic!) or how we feel *treated by* the giver (after all I've done for you, I get this kind of petty criticism?). Our focus shifts from the feedback itself to the audacity of the person delivering it (are they malicious or just stupid?).

By contrast, **Identity Triggers** focus neither on the feedback nor on the person offering it. Identity triggers are all about *us*. Whether the feedback is right or wrong, wise or witless, something about it has caused our identity—our sense of who we are—to come undone. We feel overwhelmed, threatened, ashamed, or off balance. We're suddenly unsure what to think about ourselves, and question what we stand for. When we're in this state, the past can look damning and the future bleak. That's the identity trigger talking, and once it gets tripped, a nuanced discussion of our strengths and weaknesses is not in the cards. We're just trying to survive.

Is there anything wrong with any of the reactions above? If the feedback is genuinely off target or the person giving it has proven untrustworthy, or we feel threatened and off balance, aren't these responses pretty reasonable?

They are.

Our triggered reactions are not obstacles because they are unreasonable. Our triggers are obstacles because they keep us from engaging skillfully in the conversation. Receiving feedback well is a process of sorting and filtering—of learning how the other person sees things; of trying on ideas that at first seem a poor fit; of experimenting. And of shelving or discarding the parts of the feedback that in the end seem off or not what you need right now.

And it's not just the receiver who learns. During an effective conversation, the feedback *giver* may come to see why their advice is unhelpful or their assessment unfair, and both parties may understand their relationship in a clarifying light. They each see how they are reacting to the other, showing a way forward that's more productive than what either imagined before.

But it's nearly impossible to do any of this from inside our triggers. And so we make mistakes that cause us to put potentially valuable feedback into the discard pile, or just as damaging, we take to heart feedback that is better left at the curb.

WHY WE GET TRIGGERED AND WHAT HELPS

Let's look more closely at each of the three triggers and get an overview of what we can do to manage them more effectively.

1. TRUTH TRIGGERS:
THE FEEDBACK IS WRONG, UNFAIR, UNHELPFUL

There are lots of good reasons not to take feedback, and at the front of the line stands this one: it's wrong. The advice is bad, the evaluation is unjust, the perception someone has of us is outdated or incomplete. We reject, defend, or counterattack, sometimes in the conversation but always in our minds.

But understanding the feedback we get well enough to evaluate it fairly turns out to be much harder than it appears. Below are three reasons why and what helps.

Separate Appreciation, Coaching, and Evaluation

The first challenge in understanding feedback is that, surprisingly often, we don't know whether it *is* feedback, and if it is, we're not sure exactly what kind it is or how on earth it's supposed to help us. Yes, we did ask for feedback; no, we did not ask for whatever it is that they've just offered us.

Part of the problem is that the word "feedback" can mean a number of different things. A pat on the back is feedback, and so is a dressing-down. Helpful pointers are feedback, and so is getting voted off the island. These aren't just positive and negative; they're fundamentally different kinds of feedback, with entirely different purposes.

The very first task in assessing feedback is figuring out what kind of feedback we are dealing with. Broadly, feedback comes in three forms: appreciation (thanks), coaching (here's a better way to do it), and evaluation (here's where you stand). Often the receiver wants or hears one kind of feedback, while the giver actually means another. You finally show your professional artist friend the self-portrait you painted. At this stage of your development, what you need is a little encouragement, something along the lines of "Hey, cool. Keep working at it." What you get instead is a list of twelve things you need to fix.

We can flip this story. You showed your work to your professional artist friend because you were hoping for a list of twelve things to fix, and instead get a "Hey, cool. Keep working at it." How is that going to help you get better?

Know what you want, and know what you're getting. The match matters.

First Understand

Sounds obvious, seems easy: Before you figure out what to do with the feedback, make sure you understand it. Like us, you probably think you're doing this already. You listen to the feedback. You accept it or you reject it. But in the context of receiving feedback, "understanding" what the other person means—what they see, what they're worried about, what they're recommending—is not so easy. In fact, it's flat-out hard.

Consider Kip and Nancy. They work for an organization that recruits talent for sought-after jobs overseas. Nancy tells Kip that he seems biased against candidates with nontraditional backgrounds. Nancy says that his bias is "seeping through" during interviews.

At first, Kip dismisses this feedback. His bias does not "seep through" because he does not have a bias. In fact, although Nancy is unaware of it, Kip himself has a nontraditional background, and if anything, he worries that he tends to favor candidates who've had the initiative to chart their own course in life.

So as far as Kip can tell, this feedback is simply wrong. Are we suggesting that he should accept it as right, nonetheless? No. We're saying that Kip doesn't yet know what the feedback actually *means*. The first step is for him to work harder to understand exactly what Nancy sees that is causing concern.

Kip eventually asks Nancy to clarify her feedback, and she explains: "When you interview traditional candidates, you describe common challenges the job presents, and observe how they reason through it. With nontraditional candidates, you don't discuss the job. You just shoot the breeze about the candidate's coffee cart business or travels with the merchant marine. You're not taking them seriously."

Kip is starting to understand and offers Nancy his view in response:

"In my mind, I'm taking them very seriously. I'm listening for their persistence and resourcefulness—critical skills for demanding overseas jobs with unclear boundaries and harsh conditions. That's better than presenting some hypothetical challenge."

Following the guideline to *first understand*, Kip is getting a sense of where Nancy is coming from and Nancy is getting a sense of Kip's perspective. A good start, but as we'll see below, there's still a ways to go.

See Your Blind Spots

Complicating our desire to understand feedback is the matter of blind spots. Of course, *you* don't have blind spots, but you know that your colleagues, family, and friends certainly do. That's the nature of blind spots. We're not only blind to certain things about ourselves; we're also blind to the fact that we're blind. Yet, gallingly, our blind spots are glaringly obvious to everybody else.

This is a key cause for confusion in feedback conversations. Sometimes feedback that we know is wrong really is wrong. And sometimes, it's just feedback in our blind spot.

Let's come back to Kip and Nancy. Nancy sees something important that Kip can't: Kip. She watches and hears Kip when he is conducting interviews. She's noticed that Kip is more animated when he interviews nontraditional candidates; he talks louder and interrupts more often, giving them less space—and sometimes almost no space—to make their case.

Kip is so surprised by this observation that he can barely believe it's true. He simply was not aware he was doing that. And he's dismayed: If what Nancy is saying is right, then despite his good intentions, he might actually be disadvantaging the candidates that he is most excited to talk to. His slight bias in favor of these nontraditional candidates is actually working against them.

So Kip and Nancy have each learned something from their conversation. Nancy understands Kip's intentions in a more generous light, and Kip is starting to get a handle on how his behavior is actually affecting the interviews. The conversation isn't over, but they are in a better place to straighten things out.

Managing truth triggers is not about pretending there's something to learn, or saying you think it's right if you think it's wrong. It's about recognizing that it's always more complicated than it appears and working hard to first understand. And even if you decide that 90 percent of the feedback is off target, that last golden 10 percent might be just the insight you need to grow.

2. RELATIONSHIP TRIGGERS:
I CAN'T HEAR THIS FEEDBACK FROM *YOU*

Our perception of feedback is inevitably influenced (and sometimes tainted) by who is giving it to us. We can be triggered by something about the giver—their (lack of) credibility, (un)trustworthiness, or (questionable) motives. We can likewise be triggered by how we feel treated by that person. Do they appreciate us? Are they delivering the feedback in a respectful manner (by e-mail? Are you kidding?). Are they blaming us when the real problem is them? Our twenty years of simmering history together can intensify our reaction, but interestingly, relationship triggers can get tripped even when we have only twenty seconds of relationship history at this red light.

Don't Switchtrack: Disentangle What from Who

Relationship triggers produce hurt, suspicion, and sometimes anger. The way out is to disentangle the feedback from the relationship issues it triggers, and to discuss both, clearly and separately.

In practice, we almost never do this. Instead, as receivers, we take up the relationship issues and let the original feedback drop. From the point of view of the person giving us the feedback, we have completely changed the topic—from their feedback to us ("be on time") to our feedback to them ("don't talk to me that way"). The topic of "who" defeats the topic of "what" and the original feedback is blocked. We call this dynamic Switchtracking.

Let's come back to Miriam at the bar mitzvah. In addition to experiencing a truth trigger, Miriam also endures a relationship trigger. When her husband, Sam, accuses her of being aloof, she feels unappreciated and hurt, and so she switchtracks: "Do you have any idea what I went through just to get to that bar mitzvah? I rearranged Mom's dialysis and got Matilda bathed and dressed so she'd look presentable at the party for *your* nephew, the one whose name you can't even remember."

Miriam raises important concerns about appreciation and division of chores, but she is effectively changing the topic from Sam's feedback about her unfriendliness to her feelings about Sam's lack of appreciation. If Sam is genuinely troubled that Miriam is not treating his family as warmly as he'd like, that's an important conversation to have—as is the conversation about Miriam's feeling underappreciated. But they are two different topics, and should be two different conversations.

Trying to talk about both topics simultaneously is like mixing your apple pie and your lasagna into one pan and throwing it in the oven. No matter how long you bake it, it's going to come out a mess.

Identify the Relationship System

The first kind of relationship trigger comes from our reaction to the other person: I don't like how I am being treated, or I don't trust your judgment. We can have these reactions even when the feedback itself has nothing to do with the relationship. You might be teaching me how to hit a tennis ball or balance a checkbook.

But often, feedback is not only happening in the context of a relationship; it's created by the relationship itself. Embedded in the hurly-burly of every relationship is a unique pairing of sensitivities, preferences, and personalities. It is the nature of our particular pairing—rather than either of us individually—that creates friction. The giver is telling us that we need to change, and in response we think: "You think the problem is *me*? That's hilarious, because the problem is very obviously *you*." The problem is not that I am *over*sensitive; it's that you are *in*sensitive.

Another example: You set aggressive revenue targets to motivate me. But they don't motivate me; they discourage me. When I come up short, your fix is to set even higher targets to "light a fire under me." Now I feel *more* hopeless. We each point our finger at the other, but neither of us is putting our finger on the problem. Neither of us sees that we are both caught in a reinforcing loop of this two-person system and that we are each doing things that perpetuate it.

So feedback in relationships is rarely the story of you *or* me. It's more often the story of you *and* me. It's the story of our relationship system.

When they blame you, and it feels unfair, blaming them back is not the answer. To them, *that* will seem unfair, and worse, they'll assume you're making excuses. Instead, work to understand it this way: "What's the dynamic between us and what are we each contributing to the problem?"

3. IDENTITY TRIGGERS:
THE FEEDBACK IS THREATENING AND I'M OFF BALANCE

Identity is the story we tell ourselves about who we are and what the future holds for us, and when critical feedback is incoming, that story is under attack. Our security alarm sounds, the brain's defense mechanisms kick in, and before the giver gets out their second sentence we're gearing up to counterattack or pass out. Our response can range from a minor adrenaline jolt to profound destabilization.

Learn How Wiring and Temperament Affect Your Story

Not everyone shuts down in the same way, in response to the same things, or for the same amount of time. This is the first challenge of understanding identity triggers: At a purely biological level, we're all wired differently and we each respond in our own way to stressful information, just as we each respond in our own way to roller-coaster rides. Raissa can't wait to get on the roller coaster for a second and third time; Elaine feels that that one ride may have ruined the entire rest of her life. Understanding the common wiring patterns as well as your own temperament gives you insight into why you react as you do, and helps explain why others don't react the way you expect them to.

Dismantle Distortions

Consider Laila. Whether due to wiring, life experience, or both, she is highly sensitive to feedback. Whatever the feedback is, she distorts and magnifies it. She's not responding to the words of the giver; she's responding to her distorted perception of those words.

When her boss comments that she'll need to be "on her game" at tomorrow's meeting, she wonders whose game her boss thinks she's been on up to now. *Does he think I don't know what I'm doing? Does he think I don't understand the importance of the meeting?* She recalls other interactions she's had with him and starts to question whether he's ever had any confidence in her and, given what a screwup she is, whether he even should. Fifteen years of past mistakes come flooding to the fore. She doesn't sleep that night, and is a mess during the meeting.

Luckily for Laila (and the rest of us), it is possible to learn to keep feedback in perspective, even when doing so doesn't come naturally. Laila needs to become aware of the ways she typically distorts feedback and the patterns her mind follows. Once aware, she can begin systematically to dismantle those distortions. That in turn helps her to regain her balance and allows her to engage with and learn from the feedback.

Cultivate a Growth Identity

In addition to her tendency to distort the feedback, Laila has a mindset challenge: She sees the world as one big test. Every day at work is a test, every meeting is a test, every interaction with a boss or friend is a test. And every instance of feedback is a test result, a verdict. So even when someone offers her coaching or encouragement—"be on your game tomorrow!"—she hears it as a damning assessment that she's not.

Research conducted at Stanford points to two very different ways people tell their identity story and the effect that can have on how we experience criticism, challenge, and failure. One identity story assumes our traits are "fixed": Whether we are capable or bumbling, lovable or difficult, smart or dull, we aren't going to change. Hard work and practice won't help; we are as we are. Feedback reveals "how we are," so there's a lot at stake.

Those who handle feedback more fruitfully have an identity story with a different assumption at its core. These folks see themselves as ever evolving, ever growing. They have what is called a "growth"

Triggered Reaction	Learning Response
TRUTH	
That's wrong. That's not helpful. That's not me.	**Separate Appreciation, Coaching, and Evaluation** We need all three, but mixing them puts us at cross-purposes. **First Understand: Shift from "That's Wrong" to "Tell Me More"** Feedback labels are vague and confusing. The giver has information we don't (and vice versa). We each interpret things differently. **See Your Blind Spots: Discover How You Come Across** We can't see ourselves or hear our tone of voice. We need others to help us see ourselves, and our impact on those around us.
RELATIONSHIP	
After all I've done for you? Who are you to say? You're the problem, not me	**Don't Switchtrack: Separate We from What** Talk about both the feedback and the relationship issues. **Identify the Relationship System: Take Three Steps Back** Step back to see the relationship system between giver and receiver, and the ways you are each contributing to the problems that are prompting you to exchange feedback.
IDENTITY	
I screw up everything. I'm doomed. I'm not a bad person—or am I?	**Learn How Wiring Affects How We Hear Feedback** Individuals vary widely in our reactions to positive and negative feedback; extreme reactions color our sense of ourselves and our future. **Dismantle Distortions: See Feedback at "Actual Size"** Work to correct distorted thinking and regain balance. **Cultivate a Growth Identity: Sort toward Coaching** We are always learning and growing. Challenge is the fastest track to growth, especially if we can sort toward coaching.

identity. How they are now is simply how they are *now*. It's a pencil sketch of a moment in time, not a portrait in oil and gilded frame. Hard work matters; challenge and even failure are the best ways to learn and improve. Inside a growth identity, feedback is valuable information about where one stands now and what to work on next. It is welcome input rather than upsetting verdict.

■ ■ ■

In chapters 2 through 9, we take a closer look at each of our triggers, the way they trip us up, and key strategies for handling them more productively. In chapters 10 and 11 we turn to the question of when it's okay to turn down feedback and how to handle the feedback conversation itself. In chapter 12 we offer a handful of powerful ideas for testing out feedback and getting quick traction on growth.

Finally, in chapter 13, we look at feedback in groups, and present ideas for creating pull in organizations. When it comes to our teams, our families, our firms, and our communities, we really are in it together. We can generate pull within our organizations and our teams by inspiring individuals to drive their own learning and seek out surprises and opportunities for growth. And we can help each other to stay balanced along the way.

While names have been changed, the stories are based on the experiences of real people. We hope you recognize yourself at times, feel reassured always, and come to see that you are not alone in the struggle.

TRUTH TRIGGERS

and the challenge to
SEE

Truth Triggers (and the challenge to SEE)

In the next three chapters we look at truth triggers. Truth triggers are created by our cognitive and emotional reaction to feedback when it seems wrong or off target. When we are triggered, it's hard to *see*—to see what type of feedback we're getting (chapter 2), to see what the giver means (chapter 3), and to see ourselves clearly (chapter 4).

Chapter 2 distinguishes among three types of feedback and helps you see why it matters which kind of feedback you want and which kind of feedback you are getting. It always comes down to purpose.

In chapter 3, we show you how to interpret feedback—where it's coming from, what it's suggesting you do differently, and why you and the giver might disagree. We examine why understanding feedback is so hard in the first place, and give you the tools you need to get it right.

In chapter 4 we look at blind spots, and make the case that you have them even if you're pretty sure you don't. We show you the impact they have, and why it's such a challenge to see yourself as others do. And we'll offer some ideas for how to beat your blind spots and learn despite them.

As you approach these chapters, have this question marinating in the back of your mind: Why is it that when we *give* feedback we so often feel right, yet when we *receive* feedback it so often feels wrong? After finishing chapter 4, you'll have the answer.

2

SEPARATE APPRECIATION, COACHING, AND EVALUATION

It's a beautiful spring Saturday.

Dad takes his twin daughters, Annie and Elsie, to the park to work on their batting. He shows them how to adjust their stance, maintain a level swing, and keep their eye on the ball.

Annie finds the experience exhilarating. She's spending time with her dad on the freshly cut grass, and can feel herself improve with each crack of the bat. Elsie, meanwhile, is glum. She slumps against the fence, and when Dad tries to cajole her into the batter's box to offer tips on timing, she scowls: "You think I'm uncoordinated! You always criticize me!"

"I'm not criticizing," Dad corrects. "Honey, I'm trying to help you improve."

"See!" Elsie wails. "You think I'm not good enough!" The bat clatters to the dirt as she stomps off the field.

ONE DAD, TWO REACTIONS

Dad is puzzled. From his point of view, he's treating both twins the same, yet their responses to his feedback could not be more different. One receives his coaching as intended, using the tips to sharpen her skills and build her confidence. The other retreats in frustration, refusing to try, angry with him for even offering an opinion.

Dad *is*, in fact, treating the girls the same. He's offering the same advice in the same tone of voice. If we were watching the action from the bleachers, we'd see no difference.

But at the plate, the difference is clear. Each girl is hearing something different in Dad's words. To Annie, Dad's advice is like a softball thrown down the middle of the plate; to Elsie, it's like being hit by a pitch.

This is one of the paradoxical aspects of getting feedback. Sometimes we feel like Annie—grateful, eager, energized. At other times we react like Elsie—hurt, defensive, resentful. Our responses don't always hinge on the skill of the giver or even on what is being said. Rather, they're based on how we are hearing what's said and which kind of feedback we think we are getting.

THERE ARE THREE KINDS OF FEEDBACK

The company you work for was recently acquired, your role changed, and your team reshuffled. It's a chaotic and uncertain time, and you and a colleague from the old company meet up regularly after hours at the bar across the street to compare notes on the transition.

One evening you mention to your friend that you're not getting any feedback from your new boss, Rick. Your friend is surprised: "Just yesterday Rick was telling everyone at the meeting how grateful he is to have you on the team. I'd call that feedback. What do you want, a trophy?"

Sure, Rick *appreciates* you, which is nice. But you have something else in mind: "Here's the problem. I used to be the head of marketing for the greater Miami area. Now I'm head of product campaigns for the Pacific Rim. I don't even know what the Pacific Rim *is*." A trophy would be nice, but what you really need is some *coaching*.

A few weeks later your friend asks how it's going. Generally well, you explain: "I told Rick that I needed more direction. So we meet each week to go over what I'm doing and questions I have. He's got a lot of insight into the region." Your friend is envious: "So Rick appreciates you. Rick coaches you. Sounds like you're pretty set on the feedback front."

But you're not. There's one other thing. Since the merger, you're unsure where you stand. Titles and roles now overlap, and there's always talk of cutbacks. "I can't tell whether I'm just filling a hole until Rick can find someone with better background for this," you admit to your friend. "I'm learning as fast as I can, but I don't know if I'm part of his long-term vision or just a stopgap."

Your friend suggests you raise the issue directly with Rick, and you do. Rick tells you that he's done a careful *evaluation* of your work and thinks it's extremely strong. And then he lets on that he's grooming you to be his successor when he moves on to a new role at the parent company.

That evening you share the good news with your friend, and he congratulates you heartily. And then adds: "As long as we're on the topic of feedback, how come you never ask for feedback from me?" You counter: "Because you don't have feedback for me." After an awkward silence, you say, "Okay, what?" And with surprising aggressiveness, your friend says this: "When's the last time you picked up the check? When's the last time you talked about anyone but yourself?" Holy cow.

Your friend calls this feedback, but you're pretty sure it's called picking a fight.

These conversations between you and Rick, and you and your friend, highlight that when we use the word "feedback," we may be referring to any of three different kinds of information: appreciation, coaching, and evaluation. Each serves an important purpose, each satisfies different needs, and each comes with its own set of challenges.[1]

APPRECIATION

When your boss says how grateful he is to have you on the team, that's appreciation.

Appreciation is fundamentally about relationship and human connection. At a literal level it says, "thanks." But appreciation also conveys, "I see you," "I know how hard you've been working," and "You matter to me."

Being seen, feeling understood by others, matters deeply. As children these needs are right on the surface as we call across the playground, "Hey, Mom! Mom! Mom! Watch this!" If, as adults, we learn not to pester quite so obviously, we never outgrow the need to hear someone say, "Wow, look at you!" And we never outgrow the need for those flashes of acknowledgment that say, "Yes, I see you. I 'get' you. You matter."

Appreciation motivates us—it gives us a bounce in our step and the energy to redouble our efforts. When people complain that they don't get enough feedback at work, they often mean that they wonder whether anyone notices or cares how hard they're working. They don't want advice. They want appreciation.

COACHING

When you ask your boss for more direction, you're asking for coaching.

Coaching is aimed at trying to help someone learn, grow, or change. The focus is on helping the person improve, whether it involves a skill, an idea, knowledge, a particular practice, or that person's appearance or personality. In the realm of executive coaching, "coaching" is sometimes used as a term of art to describe a facilitative approach to learning, where the coachee sets the agenda. We include this, but use the word more generally to include mentoring or any other feedback that is intended to help someone grow.

Your ski instructor, the guy at the Apple Genius Bar, the veteran waiter assigned to show you the ropes on your first day, and that empathetic friend who advises you on your mixed-up personal life are all coaches in this sense. So are bosses, clients, grandparents, peers, siblings, even our direct reports and children. And of course, we all have "accidental" coaches. That knucklehead in the Land Rover behind you has a point that you should get off your cell phone and stay in your lane.

Coaching can be sparked by two different kinds of needs. One is the need to improve your knowledge or skills in order to build capability and meet novel challenges. In your new role you're working to learn about the markets, products, channels, culture—and location—of the Pacific Rim.

In the second kind of coaching feedback, the feedback giver is not responding to your need to develop certain skills. Instead, they are identifying a problem in your relationship: Something is missing, something is wrong. This type of coaching is often prompted by emotion: hurt, fear, anxiety, confusion, loneliness, betrayal, or anger. The giver wants this situation to change, and (often) that means they want *you* to change: "You don't make our family a priority," "Why am I always the one who has to apologize?" or "When's the last time you picked up the check?" The "problem" the coaching is aimed at fixing is how the giver is feeling, or a perceived imbalance in the relationship.

EVALUATION

When your boss says your performance is "extremely strong" and that he's grooming you for his job, that's evaluation (in this case, positive). Evaluation tells you where you stand. It's an assessment, ranking, or rating. Your middle school report card, your time in the 5k, the blue ribbon awarded your cherry pie, the acceptance of your marriage proposal—these are all evaluations. Your performance review—"outperforms" or "meets expectations" or "needs improvement"—is an evaluation. And so is that nickname your team has for you when you're not around.

Evaluations are always in some respect comparisons, implicitly or explicitly, against others or against a particular set of standards. "You are not a good husband" is shorthand for "You are not a good husband compared with what I hoped for in a husband" or "compared with my saintly father" or "compared with my last three husbands."

Evaluations align expectations, clarify consequences, and inform decision making. Your rating has implications for your bonus, your time in the backstroke means you did or didn't qualify. Part of what can be hard about evaluation is concern about possible consequences—real or imagined. You didn't qualify (real), and never will (predicted or imagined).

And sometimes, evaluations contain judgments that go beyond the assessment itself: Not only didn't you qualify in the backstroke, but you were naïve to think you would, and so, once again, you've fallen short of your potential. The judgment that you are naïve or falling short is not based on the assessment—the outcome of the race. It's an additional layer of opinion on top of it. And it is the bullwhip of negative judgment—from ourselves or others—that produces much of our anxiety around feedback.

Surprisingly, reassurance—"You can do this" and "I believe in you"—also falls into the category of additional judgments, but on the positive side.

PLAYING TO THE GALLERY

Six years of classical violin lessons instilled in Luke solid technical skills, but no love of the violin. Then someone handed him a ukulele, and he was hooked. He quickly made a name for himself locally, and when *America's Got Talent* came to town, he auditioned successfully for the show.

The seventeen-year-old performed in front of a hometown audience of five thousand. The spotlight obscured the audience but not the three neon red X's that glowed at his feet. Sharon Osbourne shook her head, and Howard Stern said theatrically, "My mother made me play the clarinet. Your mother should *never* have let you play the ukulele." The audience roared with laughter.

Stunned, Luke turned wordlessly and stumbled offstage, where he was accosted by a camera crew: "How do you feel? *What do you make of the judges' feedback?*"

Good question.

In the days and weeks that followed, amid red-X nightmares, one thing finally became clear to Luke: The primary purpose of the show is not a thoughtful evaluation of each contestant's talent, for the contestant's sake. The main purpose is to entertain the TV audience. This was feedback *to him* only in the loosest sense. It was evaluation, certainly, almost a parody of evaluation: The judges told him where he stood vis-à-vis a future on the show, and certainly they conveyed their contempt for the ukulele as an instrument.

It's easy to see the distinction between entertainment and real feedback when it involves someone else. But when it's about us, it's harder.

These days it's more important than ever to learn how to make that distinction. The arenas for vitriolic "feedback" are proliferating: online comments, message boards, blogs, talk radio, reality TV. Harsh commentary, malicious attacks, and anonymous venting in these forums are common, catering to reader cheers or jeers. The commenters are focused on saying something they think is clever or biting or attention-getting, and they may not even be aware of the real people behind the post they are using as a punching bag.

Luke is still performing. "It wasn't easy to get back on stage, in part because I had to step onto the same stage three weeks later," he says. He had previously won the region's teen talent competition with his playful juxtaposition of Bach, Sinatra, and rock and roll and he was invited to do a showcase performance as the winner.

Now Luke says he wouldn't trade his *America's Got Talent* experience for the world. "I learned a huge amount about myself. Nothing scares me now," Luke laughs. "The worst thing that could happen? It already did, and I survived."

WE NEED ALL THREE

Each form of feedback—appreciation, coaching, and evaluation—satisfies a different set of human needs. We need evaluation to know where we stand, to set expectations, to feel reassured or secure. We need coaching to accelerate learning, to focus our time and energy where it really matters, and to keep our relationships healthy and functioning. And we need appreciation if all the sweat and tears we put into our jobs and our relationships are going to feel worthwhile.

Type of Feedback	Giver's Purpose
Appreciation	To see, acknowledge, connect, motivate, thank
Coaching	To help receiver expand knowledge, sharpen skill, improve capability
	Or, to address the giver's feelings or an imbalance in the relationship
Evaluation	To rate or rank against a set of standards, to align expectations, to inform decision making

EVALUATION SHORTFALLS

Because evaluation is so loud and can have such hurtful consequences, it's tempting to consider removing it from the feedback mix. Do we really need it?

It *is* smart to avoid evaluation when your purpose is coaching. Don't say, "You're no good," when what you really mean to say is "Here's how to get better."

But doing away with evaluation altogether leaves a conspicuous silence. Should I put my name in for the new position, or am I wasting my time? Where is this relationship going? Are we moving in because we'll soon be engaged, or because you want to save some money while you wait for someone better?

We are anxious about being assessed and judged, but at the same time, we need an "evaluative floor" on which to stand, reassuring us that we are good enough so far. Before I can take in coaching or appreciation, I need to know that I'm where I need to be, that this relationship is going to last.

When evaluation is absent, we use coaching and appreciation to try to figure out where we stand. Why does the boss give me so much coaching on handling the customer more effectively? And why was I singled out for appreciation in that first group e-mail, but not the second? Should I be concerned? In the absence of clear signals, I'll keep putting my ear to the ground to listen for rumblings in anything that passes by.

APPRECIATION SHORTFALLS

Appreciation can seem the least important of the three kinds of feedback—who needs flowery words or flattery? Aren't you getting a paycheck? We're still married, aren't we?

Yet the absence of appreciation can leave a gaping hole in any relationship—personal or professional. Sure, I want to know how to improve, but I also want to know that you see how hard I'm working, how much I'm trying, what I do that's special. Without that, your coaching isn't going to get through, because I'm listening for something else.

In *First Break All the Rules,* authors Marcus Buckingham and Curt Coffman describe a landmark Gallup survey of eighty thousand workers. The survey found that "Yes" answers on twelve key questions—dubbed the Q12—had strong correlations with employee satisfaction, high retention, and high productivity. Of the twelve questions, three are directly related to appreciation:

Question 4: "In the last seven days, have I received recognition or praise for doing good work?"

Question 5: "Does my supervisor, or someone at work, seem to care about me as a person?"

Question 6: "Is there someone at work who encourages my development?"[2]

When workers answer "No" to these questions, it's not necessarily because supervisors don't care or aren't saying "Thanks." But they're not doing so in a way that matters.

Three qualities are required for appreciation to count. First, it has to be specific. This is tricky; most of us offer both appreciation and positive evaluation in grand strokes like "Good work!" or "You were fabulous!" or "Thanks for everything!"

In contrast to the vagueness of our appreciation, our negative feedback—or "areas for improvement"—often consists of a list of 118 detailed items. We focus on the negative because we are focused on an immediate problem: Yes, you did a good job overall, but our task at this moment is to address the latest supply chain snafu or the product placement. When we're under pressure to get things done, our feelings of anxiety, frustration, and anger about what's wrong trump any feelings of appreciation, even if, upon reflection, we really *are* appreciative.

Over time, appreciation deficits set in. And these often become two-way: I think you don't appreciate all I do and all I put up with, and you think I don't appreciate whatever-it-is you do. Call it Mutual Appreciation Deficit Disorder (MADD), and you have the ingredients for a troubled working relationship.

Second, appreciation has to come in a form the receiver values and hears clearly. Gary Chapman makes a similar point about love in his book *The 5 Love Languages*. Some of us take in love through words ("I love you"), while others hear it more clearly through acts of service, quality time, physical contact, or gifts. If I feel unloved, it could be because you don't love me—or it could be because you're expressing it in a way that I don't take in.[3]

The same is true for appreciation. For some, a monthly paycheck is all the "attaboy" they need. For others, public recognition is meaningful, whether in the form of team e-mail, kudos at a meeting, or organizational awards. For some it's promotion and titles—even if they earn the same or *less* pay. And for many of us, it's the feeling we get from knowing we're a trusted adviser or indispensable player. I know you appreciate me because we laugh a lot, or because you come to me first with tough challenges.

Third, meaningful appreciation has to be authentic. If employees start to sense that everyone receives appreciation for the smallest accomplishments—"thanks for coming to work today"—appreciation inflation sets in, and the currency becomes worthless. Nor can appreciation be issued through gritted teeth: "I can't believe I inherited such a screwup, but I need to check this appreciation box, so, uh, *good work!*" Nobody's fooled, and now they trust you even less.

COACHING SHORTFALLS

Some coaching relationships require extraordinary effort while others feel almost magically uncomplicated. But in either case, when coaching works, it can be deeply gratifying and impactful for both people.

Of course, coaching can also be stressful, confusing, and ineffective. In some organizations, coaching is not formally rewarded—or "counted"—and is thus rarely given. Even when encouraged, mentors need only a few experiences where their efforts to help only make things worse, suck up time, or are met with arguments or ingratitude before they decide it's not worth the trouble.

Even well-intended coaches and coachees can become frustrated. We're *trying* to coach or to be coached, but because our efforts are resisted, unappreciated, or ineffective, we end up with a coaching shortfall. Coaching shortfalls mean that learning, productivity, morale, and relationships all suffer. And that's particularly tragic when people on both sides of the relationship are well meaning and trying hard.

BEWARE CROSS-TRANSACTIONS

One of the key challenges of feedback conversations is that wires often get crossed. There are two ways this happens. First, I might want a different type of feedback from the type you gave me—for example, I was looking for appreciation, but you gave me evaluation. Second, you may have intended to give me one kind of feedback, but I interpreted it incorrectly—for example, you sought to give me coaching, but I heard it as evaluation.

Once crossed, these wires are tough to untangle.

Consider the feedback confusion at the law offices where April,

Cody, and Evelyn work. They all report to a partner named Donald, who has never been particularly good at giving feedback. Encouraged by Human Resources and the annual campaign around performance, they each make an appointment to talk to Donald about getting more feedback.

Donald's assistant, April, goes first. Donald is actually pleased that April took the initiative to ask for feedback. He gives April a number of concrete suggestions for how she could manage her time better, including getting her workspace better organized and being more assertive about saying no. April says thanks, leaves Donald's office, and wonders what the heck just happened.

April just wanted a bit of appreciation. She has been working for Donald for eight years and has become good at anticipating his needs. Others say she works tirelessly, but she often feels stressed and overwhelmed. Donald never comments on a job well done, never says thanks. In fact, he hardly seems to notice her at all. April is in serious need of a pat on the back and a great big "I see all that you do for me."

What she got instead was coaching—ideas on how she could improve.

The conversation hit her hard, leaving her feeling more invisible than ever. She wonders if she should quit. The problem wasn't that Donald's feedback was wrong or poorly delivered. His coaching was thoughtful and actually quite useful. April's distress results from the cross-transaction: She wanted one thing and got another.

First-year lawyer Cody fared no better. He submitted a research memo to Donald last Thursday and was hoping to get specific suggestions for how to approach such assignments more efficiently in the future. He often feels adrift and knows the research takes him more time than it should. He wants coaching. Donald reads the memo carefully, smiles and reassures Cody: "Based on this memo and the other work you've done, I'd say you're right on track for a first-year lawyer." Cody gets evaluation. And like April, he's dismayed: "How is that going to help me figure out what I'm doing?" He faces his next assignment feeling more lost than ever.

Evelyn is a senior associate wondering where she stands in the march toward partnership. As she begins to describe what she's looking for, Donald jumps in: "Evelyn, I know I'm not good with a compliment, but I can tell you that it means a lot to me when I see you staying late and here on weekends. I notice that. I'm sorry if I haven't always said so over the years."

Evelyn gets appreciation—the great big thanks that April craved. But, of course, what Evelyn wanted was evaluation. She wants to know where she ranks in relation to her peers as partnership looms. Evelyn appreciates the appreciation, but she is now more anxious than ever. Her billable hours have always been high, but the last two associates with high billable hours failed to make partner because they weren't bringing in new business. Evelyn wonders whether Donald's thank-you was code for "thank you and goodbye"—an indirect way of saying things aren't going to work out. Evelyn is left reading the tea leaves of appreciation for any traces of the evaluation she seeks.

Donald and his colleagues are 0 for 3 on good feedback conversations. Put another way, they're 3 for 3 on cross-transactions. In this farcical round-robin, April wants appreciation but gets coaching, Cody wants coaching but gets evaluation, and Evelyn wants evaluation but gets appreciation. All the while Donald is so pleased with his newfound feedback-giving abilities that he wonders whether he might be just the guy to lead an in-house training for other partners on how to give feedback well.

A COMPLICATION: THERE IS ALWAYS EVALUATION IN COACHING

Back out on the ball field, Dad is doing his best to be clear with his twin daughters. In his mind, his intention is straightforward: He's coaching. That's how Annie hears it, but as we know, Elsie hears it as evaluation: "You think I'm uncoordinated!" and "You think I'm not good enough!" Elsie worries that in Dad's eyes, she is not stacking up.

So, even though Dad is being thoughtful about his purposes, there's *still* a cross-transaction. Why does Elsie hear the coaching as evaluation? Any number of reasons. Maybe she feels implicit comparisons to her sister, feels insecure about her athletic prowess, or believes her dad isn't always fair. Perhaps she's been looking forward to time with

Dad all week, but had something other than baseball in mind. Or it could just be that she didn't sleep well or didn't eat breakfast.

In addition to whatever else is going on between Elsie and her dad, there's a structural component to their miscommunication as well: there's some amount of evaluation in all coaching. The coaching message "here's how to improve" also implicitly conveys the evaluative message that "so far you aren't doing it as well as you might."

Dad is doing his best to avoid evaluation. He's not saying, "I'm appraising each of you. Annie, you're coordinated. Elsie, you are not." That would be explicit evaluation (not to mention a strange thing for a father to say). And yet, because there's evaluation in all coaching, he can't avoid it completely. To Annie, it's irrelevant; she's hearing the coaching and dismissing the evaluative piece. To Elsie, the evaluation is the loudest part of the message and drowns out everything else.

Elsie's reaction to her dad's feedback reminds us that the giver has only partial control over how the balance between coaching and evaluation is received. I may intend my comment about keeping two hands on the steering wheel as commonsense coaching, but you may hear it as evaluation: You're irresponsible.

On the receiving end, we constantly funnel the advice we're given into either evaluation or coaching slots. How you hear your girlfriend's suggestion to "call your mother" depends on your relationship with your girlfriend (was she reminding or chiding?). And that employee down at Motor Vehicles who tells you you're in the wrong line? Was that comment meant as coaching (this will save you time) or evaluation (you can't even follow the simplest instructions, you dolt)?

This dynamic is rampant in the workplace. Performance management systems are set up to achieve a number of important organizational goals, including both evaluation and coaching. We evaluate employees to ensure that they receive fair promotion and pay, that they are clear about incentives and standing, and that their work is done efficiently and well. We coach to help people grow and improve, preparing them for greater success on that next rung up.

All too often, feedback that is offered as coaching is heard as evaluation. ("You're telling me how to improve, but really, you're saying you're not sure I'm cut out for this.") And efforts to elicit coaching from mentors yield feedback that is laced with evaluation, producing defensiveness and frustration rather than learning.

WHAT HELPS?

Two things keep us on track: getting our purposes aligned, and separating (as much as possible) evaluation from coaching and appreciation.

GET ALIGNED: KNOW THE PURPOSE AND DISCUSS IT

Cross-transactions happen when the giver and receiver are misaligned. The fix? Discuss the purpose of the feedback explicitly. It seems obvious, but even competent, well-meaning people can go their whole lives without ever having this part of the conversation.

Most of this book is advice for feedback receivers. But here, we offer thoughts to both giver and receiver. Ask yourself three questions:

(1) What's my purpose in giving/receiving this feedback?
(2) Is it the right purpose from my point of view?
(3) Is it the right purpose from the other person's point of view?

Is your primary goal coaching, evaluation, or appreciation? Are you trying to improve, to assess, or to say thanks and be supportive? You won't always be able to fit the messiness of real life into these clean categories, but it's worth trying. Reflecting on your purpose before a conversation takes place will help you to be clearer during the conversation itself. And even if you can't straighten out your purposes, there's a benefit to understanding that your purposes are a little confusing, even to you.

During the conversation, check in periodically: "I'm intending to give you coaching. Is that how you're hearing it? From your point of view, is that what you need?" The receiver may respond that it would be nice to know if she's doing *anything* right—a signal that she's craving some appreciation and maybe a bit of positive evaluation.

Be explicit about what you think the conversation is about, and be explicit about what would be most helpful to you. Then discuss and, if you each need something different, negotiate. Remember: Explicit disagreement is better than implicit misunderstanding. Explicit disagreement leads to clarity, and is the first step in each of you getting your differing needs met.

The receiver may need to take the bull by the horns: "You're offering coaching, but it would help to get a quick evaluation: Am I doing all right overall? If so, then I can relax and am eager for your coaching." Or: "You're saying this is coaching, but I'm hearing it as evaluation, too. Am I right that you're saying I'm falling behind?"

This is what eventually helped Elsie and her dad. He stopped pitching and asked, "Elsie, what's up?" and Elsie burst into tears. Dad learned that Elsie was actually yearning for appreciation. She had been practicing all week and expected to wow her dad with her improved skills come Saturday morning. But when the big moment failed to produce big hits, she was crushed. She needed Dad's comforting acknowledgment of her hard work and disappointment more than she needed his batting tips.

SEPARATE EVALUATION FROM COACHING AND APPRECIATION

The bugle blast of evaluation can drown out the quieter melodies of coaching and appreciation.

Even if I walk into my performance review determined to learn how to improve, evaluation can get in the way. If I was expecting an "exceeds expectations" and receive only a "meets expectations," then whatever coaching I receive is likely to go unheard. That's true even if the coaching is designed to help me get what I want—an "exceeds" next year. Instead of hearing the coaching, I'm focused on the thoughts and emotions broadcast by my internal voice: *What about all the times I bailed you out with headquarters? What's wrong with you? What's wrong with me? And what will this mean for my compensation?*

If your organization has formal feedback conversations at yearly or semiyearly intervals (where, for example, supervisor and supervisee develop objectives or a learning plan for the coming year, with specific skills and outcomes targeted), the evaluation conversation and the coaching conversation should be separated by at least days, and probably longer.

The evaluation conversation needs to take place first. When a professor hands back a graded paper, the student will first turn to the last page to check their grade. Only then can they take in the instructor's margin notes. We can't focus on how to improve until we know where we stand.

Ideally, we receive coaching and appreciation year-round, day by day, project by project. It's like when we're driving. If someone ahead of us doesn't go when the light turns green, we don't think to ourselves, *I'm going to collect all the ideas I have for that driver and give them feedback at the end of the year.* We honk *now.* Now is when that driver needs to move, now is when they need the "coaching."

• • •

Understanding whether we are getting appreciation, coaching, or evaluation is a first step. But even when our purposes are all lined up, feedback can be hard to understand, and is all too easily dismissed. That's the topic of the next chapter.

Summary: SOME KEY IDEAS

"Feedback" is really three different things, with different purposes:

- *Appreciation* — motivates and encourages.
- *Coaching* — helps increase knowledge, skill, capability, growth, or raises feelings in the relationship.
- *Evaluation* — tells you where you stand, aligns expectations, and informs decision making.

We need all three, but often talk at cross-purposes.

Evaluation is the loudest and can drown out the other two. (And all coaching includes a bit of evaluation.)

Be thoughtful about what you need and what you're being offered, and get aligned.

3

FIRST UNDERSTAND

Shift from "That's Wrong" to "Tell Me More"

Irwin, a supervising attorney in the public defender's office, tells his recent hire Holly that she gets "too enmeshed" in the personal lives of
clients, and doesn't maintain appropriate professional distance. "You're
not their mother," Irwin warns. Holly leans in: "Look, Irwin, I grew up
on these streets. I know what it means to have someone in your corner
really fighting for you." "Still," says Irwin, "you need to establish boundaries."

Holly says she'll keep that in mind. But she won't. It's hard enough
to take feedback that's right; Holly's not going to waste time on feedback that's wrong.

In this, Holly is like the rest of us. We don't want to take feedback
that's invalid or unhelpful and so, quite reasonably, we screen for that.
We listen to the feedback with this question in mind: "What's wrong
with this feedback?" And as it turns out, we can almost always find
something.

WE'RE GOOD AT WRONG SPOTTING

If you've ever received feedback at work—or had an in-law—you are
familiar with the many shapes and sizes of wrong:

It's 2 + 2 = 5 wrong: It is literally incorrect. I could not have been
rude at that meeting because I was not *at* that meeting. And my
name is not Mike.

It's different-planet wrong: Somewhere in the universe there may
exist a carbon-based life form that would have taken offense at
my e-mail, but here on Earth everyone knows it was a joke.

46

It used to be right: Your critique of my marketing plan is based on how marketing worked when you were coming up. Before the Internet. And electricity.

It's right according to the wrong people: Some see me that way, but next time, talk to at least one person who is not on my Personal Enemies List.

Your context is wrong: I do yell at my assistant. And he yells at me. That's how our relationship works—key word being "works."

It's right for you, but wrong for me: We have different body types. Armani suits flatter you. Hoodies flatter me.

The feedback is right, but not right now: It's true that I could lose a few pounds—which I will do as soon as the quintuplets are out of the house.

Anyway, it's unhelpful: Telling me to be a better mentor isn't helping me to *be* a better mentor. What kind of mentor are you anyway?

Why is wrong spotting so easy? Because there's almost always *something* wrong—something the feedback giver is overlooking, shortchanging, or misunderstanding. About you, about the situation, about the constraints you're under. And givers compound the problem by delivering feedback that is vague, making it easy for us to overlook, shortchange, and misunderstand what they are saying.

But in the end, wrong spotting not only defeats wrong feedback, it defeats learning.

UNDERSTANDING IS JOB ONE

Before we determine whether feedback is right or wrong, we first have to *understand* it. That sounds pretty obvious, but in fact, we usually skip understanding and dive in with instant judgments.

"I don't skip that," you might think. "I understand what the feedback means because they just told me what it means. They were giving me feedback, and I was listening." A good start, but it's not enough.

FEEDBACK ARRIVES WITH GENERIC LABELS

Feedback often arrives packaged like generic items in the supermarket labeled "soup" or "cola." The labels the giver uses seem clear—"Be more proactive," "Don't be so selfish," "Act your age"—but there's actually little content to them. You would never eat the soup can label, and there's no nutritional value to a feedback label either.

Recall Irwin's advice to Holly: "You're too enmeshed," "Maintain appropriate professional distance," "You need boundaries." These are all labels (even "You're not their mother"). If Holly followed Irwin's advice, what exactly would she need to do differently?

Holly thinks the meaning is clear: Put in fewer hours on each case; get less upset when you lose; don't look the defendant in the eye and say you believe in him; don't share your own story of struggle and redemption. In short, care less. Holly isn't interested in caring less, and she doesn't buy the feedback.

These are all reasonable interpretations of Irwin's labels. He could have meant these things. But he didn't. In fact, Irwin thinks making a strong personal connection with defendants is crucial, and letting them know you're on their side even more important. He didn't mean to set limits on caring or effort or trust.

What did he mean? Irwin explains: "In this business, we have to be explicit about boundaries. I've overheard defendants asking Holly for ten or twenty bucks, and I've watched her give it to them. Look, if they need ten dollars, they probably need a lot more than ten dollars. Connect them with institutional resources to get them squared away. There was a client when I was starting out who I was very personally

Got Feedback?

Irish creative team Mark Shanley and Paddy Treacy were tired of vague, incomprehensible client feedback and decided to channel their frustration into creating "ad posters" that captured some of their favorites.

An instant hit, they invited friends from across the graphic design community to showcase their own bewildering client coaching.

See more of Mark and Paddy's collection at www.sharpsuits.net or add your own "worst feedback" stories, videos or graphics at www.stoneandheen.com.

Client feedback posters created by: **Polar Bear:** Mark Shanley + Paddy Treacy at markandpaddy.com; **Hair:** Steve Rogers; **Passport:** Austin Richards; **Chill Factor:** Maxi.

attached to, and I equated that with never saying no to him. Pretty soon, he started taking advantage of me. And worse, he stopped trusting my professional advice because he saw me as just another chump he could hustle."

Would Holly agree with Irwin's feedback if she understood it? Maybe. Or maybe not. But at least she'd be in a better position to decide.

Labels do serve some useful functions in feedback. Like the soup label, they give us a general idea of the topic, and they can act as shorthand when we return to that topic later. But the label is not the meal.

GIVER AND RECEIVER INTERPRET THE LABEL DIFFERENTLY

Labels always mean something specific to the giver. Think of what bugs you about someone close to you—your brother, boss, friend, or coworker. What probably popped into your head is a label:

> "He's so _____ ."
> "She's too _____ ."
> "My spouse never _____s."
> "My coworker is so un-_____ ."

In our minds, we have a high-definition movie that captures all that we mean by those labels—the bad behavior, the angry tone, the irritating habits that we endure. When we use a label, we're seeing that movie, and it's painfully clear. It's easy to forget that when we convey the label to someone else, the movie is not attached. All they're hearing is a few vague words. This means that even when we "take" the feedback, it's easy to misconstrue the meaning.

Nicholas is told by his boss, Adrianna, to be "more assertive" on the sales floor. Adrianna rose to manager in part because of her legendary selling skills, and Nicholas is eager to follow her advice. Later in the day, Adrianna overhears him pushing a customer to agree to the terms of the deal "right now, today—before you walk out that door."

Adrianna is shocked and demands to know why Nicholas was

threatening a customer. Confused, he explains that he was being "more assertive," just as she had suggested. Heavens.

Adrianna's original advice was based on watching Nicholas on the sales floor relate to customers during a potential sale. She worried that his laid-back, low-energy persona communicated a lack of interest in both the customer and the product. By "be more assertive" Adrianna meant something along these lines: Be energetic. Show some excitement, let your personality shine through. Knock them out with how engaged and caring you are. Almost the opposite of how Nicholas understood it.

This "what was heard" versus "what was meant" coaching mismatch is surprisingly common:

Coaching	What Was Heard	What Was Meant
Be more confident.	Give the impression that you know things even if you don't.	Have the confidence to say you don't know when you don't know.
Don't be so picky about whom you date.	You're not a great catch, so you don't deserve a great catch.	Don't make the mistakes I've made. Don't end up like me.
I wish you weren't so darn opinionated.	Don't be interesting to talk to. Be apathetic and bland.	You don't listen to me or anyone else. It's exhausting.

Evaluations can be just as confusing:

Evaluation	What Was Heard	What Was Meant
You've received a 4 out of 5 this year.	Last year I got a 4. I worked much harder this year and got another 4. Hard work isn't noticed.	No one gets a 5. Few get a 4 and you've now done it twice! You are doing outstanding work.
I'd like to see you again.	You are my soul mate.	That was fun.

Given how often we talk in labels, it's somewhat astonishing that any feedback changes hands successfully.

Play "Spot the Label"

In the course of your life, you'll encounter people who are unusually skilled at giving you feedback. They'll say things like, "Let me describe what I mean and you can ask me questions to see if I'm making sense." But most givers aren't this skilled, and so it falls to you as receiver to work to understand what's under the label. The surest way of doing that is to spot the label in the first place.

Actually, once you're looking for them, spotting labels is easy; what's hard is remembering to look. It's like counting the number of times someone says the word "and." It's impossible to do if you aren't consciously trying to, but once you decide to listen for it, it's simple. Same with labels: if you're listening for them, you'll hear them everywhere.

After you spot a label, there's a second step: You have to fight the temptation to fill in your own meaning. If you already "know" what was meant, there's nothing to learn and no reason to be curious. "'Be more affectionate'? Excellent, she wants me to initiate sex more often." But does the label "be more affectionate" actually mean "initiate sex more often"? Here are some other choices:

(a) hold hands in public;
(b) pitch in more around the house;
(c) be more playful and cuddly;
(d) tell me you love me at least once a decade.

The correct answer? You won't know until you talk about it, and you won't talk about it if you assume you already know.

WHAT'S UNDER THE LABEL?

The most common advice about feedback is this: Be specific. It's good advice—but it's not specific enough. What does it mean to be specific, and specific about *what*?

To answer that question, we start with an observation: If we strip back the label, we find that feedback has both a past and a future. There's a *looking-back* component ("here's what I noticed"), and a *looking-forward* component ("here's what you need to do"). The usual feedback labels don't tell us much in either direction.

So to clarify the feedback under the label we need to "be specific" about two things:

(1) where the feedback is coming from, and
(2) where the feedback is going.

Coming From and Going To

Let's take an example. You say I'm a reckless driver. That's the label. Where is it *coming from*? A specific time we drove together, the fact that I call you from my cell when I'm driving, or your fears about that fender bender I had last year? I'll be able to more easily decipher the feedback if I know the answer.

And where is the feedback *going*? What's the advice? Do you want me to stop tailgating or wear my glasses at night or drive more slowly on neighborhood streets or get more sleep the night before a long trip?

Below, we look in more depth at how to discuss and understand both where the feedback is coming from and where it's going. On the "coming from" side, we'll examine a key distinction: the difference between the giver's "data" (what they observe) and their interpretation (the meaning they make from what they observe). And on the "going to" side, we'll consider the difference between feedback that is coaching, which aims at advice, and feedback that is evaluation, which clarifies consequences. These distinctions are captured in this diagram,[1] which will make more sense once you've read through the next few pages.

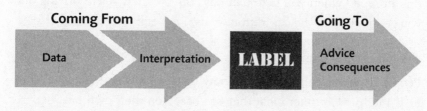

Digging into where the feedback is coming from and going to takes a bit of practice, but once you do it a few times in real life, it becomes second nature.

ASK WHERE THE FEEDBACK IS COMING FROM

Feedback givers arrive at their labels in two steps: (1) they observe data, and (2) they interpret that data—they tell a story about what it means.

They Observe Data

The feedback you get is rooted in the observations of your giver— whatever they've seen, felt, heard, smelled, touched, tasted, remembered, or read that is relevant. In the academic literature this is called their "data," although data in this context goes beyond mere facts and figures. Data can include anything directly observed: someone's behavior, statements, tone, clothes, work product, year-to-date revenue, socks on the floor, rumors around the office. Here are examples of data that might eventually find their way into feedback.

Your boss hears you tell a coworker that you're too busy to help.

Your tennis partner notices that you are no longer able to remember the score.

Your report did not distinguish between online and brick-and-mortar sales.

You were quiet at dinner, until you barked at the kids.

Data can also include the giver's emotional reactions. "When you didn't e-mail me back, I was frustrated." "I'm anxious about what's getting dropped when you take half days off." "When you're driving and you get so close to the car in front of us, I am cold-sweat terrified."

They Interpret the Data

People don't typically offer their raw observations as feedback. They first "interpret" or filter what they see based on their own past experiences, values, assumptions, and implicit rules about the world. So instead of saying, "I heard you tell Gus that you're too busy to help," your boss says, "You're not a team player."

Adrianna has data about Nicholas—his sales pitch, his responses to customer questions, his tone of voice, his body language. She has lots of non-Nicholas data as well. She's seen dozens of salespeople interacting with customers, and has a whole warehouse of data about her own experiences with selling over the years.

Without being aware of it, Adrianna *interprets* what she sees and turns her direct data into judgments: Nicholas is *too* laid back. He shows no apparent interest in his customers—essential for engaging *their* interest—and he's losing sales that he could close.

These are all interpretations of the data. You can't observe "too laid back"; *laid back* is itself a judgment about observed behaviors, and *too* laid back is a judgment about the optimal level of laid back. And Adrianna might observe him failing to make sales, but whether he could close them if he behaved differently is a guess. It involves assumptions about the consequences of his approach and a prediction about the future if he were to change. But until the future arrives, it's conjecture—it's Adrianna's interpretation of what she sees.

It is said that all advice is autobiographical, and this, in part, is what is meant. We interpret what we see based on our own life experiences, assumptions, preferences, priorities, and implicit rules about how things work and how one should be. I understand your life through the lens of my life; my advice for you is based on me.

They Confuse Data and Interpretation (We All Do)

You might be thinking, *Conversations would be much easier if the giver just shared the data. Givers shouldn't say, "Your report was confusing and lacked depth." They should share the data: "I noticed that you didn't distinguish between online and brick-and-mortar sales. Let's discuss that. . . ."*

It would be nice if they did, but usually they don't—not because they're trying to be cagey or unclear. The process of moving from data to interpretation happens in the blink of an eye and is largely unconscious. Artificial intelligence expert Roger Schank has an observation about this: He notes that while computers are organized around managing and accessing *data*, human intelligence is organized around *stories*.[2] We take in selective data and make immediate interpretations, resulting in instant judgment-laced labels: *That meeting was a waste of time. Your skirt's too short. Those people at the next table can't parent properly.*

If we were asked what we had witnessed, we'd say: "I saw people parenting badly." We think that's the actual data because that's how we've stored it in memory. But the actual data was the particular way the woman looked at the baby or the way the man did (or didn't) respond when the baby wailed. *Bad parenting* is not the data; it's our auto-story about the encounter.

Now that you're getting the hang of this, notice that a couple of pages ago we cited as data the fact that you "barked" at the kids. In fact, "barking" is itself an interpretation of what you did. Someone else might say you were curt, sharp, or perhaps even clear. It's easy to confuse our interpretation (barking) for the data (what was actually heard).

So feedback givers rarely share the raw observations behind their labels because they simply aren't aware of them. It's up to you to help them sort it out. Your goal here is not to ignore or dismiss the interpretation. Data is crucial, but so is the interpretation. At the very least, it's one person's view of things. So you want to get a clear picture of both data and interpretation.

When Nicholas is told by Adrianna that he needs to be more assertive, he can break it down this way in his mind: "'More assertive' is a label. I don't know where it's going or where it comes from. In terms of where it comes from, I want to understand the data it's based on—what Adrianna saw or heard—and how Adrianna is interpreting that information."

When Nicholas asks for the data, it will take some back and forth. Adrianna might respond by saying, "What I saw on the sales floor is that you were too laid back." That's moving in the right direction, but as we said above, "laid back" is not data, it's an interpretation. Nicholas needs to understand the observations behind that interpretation in order to understand precisely what "laid back" looks and sounds like to

Adrianna. This will take some discussion: "It's my tone? What about my tone? My body language? Show me. . . ."

ASK WHERE THE FEEDBACK IS GOING

So far, we've been talking about your feedback's sordid past. Now we turn to the feedback's future.

Not all feedback has a forward-looking component. You notice that your tennis partner has trouble remembering the score. If you share that observation with their spouse, you may not have any advice that goes along with that. You *might*—"here are three behavioral changes to watch for that may signal dementia"—but it also could be that your purpose is achieved just by sharing the observation with the spouse.

Often, though, feedback will have a forward-looking component. As we'll see below, with coaching, that piece is about advice; with evaluation, it's about consequences and expectations.

When Receiving Coaching: Clarify Advice

In any given case, you might or might not choose to follow someone's advice. But we can test whether advice is clear by asking this: If you *do* want to follow the advice, would you know how to do so?

Too often the answer is no, because the advice is simply too vague. "If you win a Tony award, be sure your speech sparkles." "Children need love, but they also need predictability and limits." "If you want to shine at work, make yourself indispensable."

There are two problems with these: (1) We don't know what they actually mean, and (2) even if we did, we wouldn't know what to

Coaching

Looking Back		Looking Forward
What did you observe about me, about the world, about whatever matters to this topic? What can you see that I can't?		What's your advice? What would I do or say to implement it? Show me, model it, give me an example.

do to follow the advice. What does "sparkles" mean, and how would our speech acquire this magical glow?

So on the receiving end we have to help the giver be clearer. "Sparkles? Describe what you mean. Show me some examples of speeches that sparkle. And show me some examples of speeches you think fell flat." The contrast is often illuminating and together you'll home in on what makes an acceptance speech effective.

Here's another illustration. Tom is swamped at work, and his friend Liz suggests he "needs to learn to say no." This advice as given is both unhelpful and annoying. All Tom has learned so far is that Liz doesn't understand how things work where he works.

But before dismissing the advice, Tom should get curious about what "saying no" looks and sounds like to Liz. He asks her how he would implement the advice if he decides to take it. This prompts Liz to describe her own struggles to say no: "Here's what I found helpful. I sat down with my team and shared the dilemma. I explained that I didn't want to turn away work, but was coming to realize that I'd become a bottleneck, and couldn't do the kind of job I want to on each task." Sharing the dilemma let her coworkers in on the challenge, which was beneficial in its own right, but also gave her team the chance to find creative solutions that she might not have come up with on her own.

Liz also tells Tom about a new policy she has adopted: "I don't say yes or no to a request in the moment. Instead, I ask some sorting questions." The questions she finds most helpful are these: "Is this more or less urgent than what you needed yesterday?" and "Are there pieces of this that are more important than other pieces, and why?" She then tells the requester: "I want to take a careful look at what's on my plate before I get back to you." This helps her override her impulse to say yes automatically, and helps make the workload and priorities a shared problem.

When you discuss advice in this kind of detail you can start to visualize it, and once it's visualized, you can see why something that seemed useless when presented as a "say no" label just might be useful after all.

When Receiving Evaluation:
Clarify Consequences and Expectations

It's not easy to clarify advice, and it can be even tougher to clarify the consequences and expectations that follow from an evaluation. Why? Because we're still vibrating from the impact of the evaluation itself. Whether we are delighted or devastated, we're not in a curious state of mind.

Yet it's particularly important to understand the forward-looking part of feedback when it's evaluation. *What does this mean for me? What will happen next, what is expected of me? Given where I stand, what should I do now?*

Here's what typically happens:

The evaluation: After a series of tests, Max is told that his ability to hear certain higher frequencies has diminished by about 80 percent.

What Max says: *Really? I'm surprised by that.*

What Max later wishes he had asked: *What caused the loss, and what can I do to prevent further loss? What exactly are "higher frequencies"? How do they matter in hearing? What does "diminished by about 80 percent" mean? How is my hearing compared with that of other people my age? Does the context matter for what I'll be able to hear? Will this get worse, and if so, how fast?*

The evaluation: Margie is not tapped as the new department head.

What Margie says: *That's disappointing. Who got it?*

What Margie later wishes she had asked: *Can you say more about what you felt I was missing as you looked at my fit for the job? What concerns did people have? Do you have suggestions for how I might fill in some gaps in my experience or skill set? How will this decision affect my project mix? How about my compensation, now and in the coming year?*

The evaluation: The holidays come and go, and your live-in girlfriend of three years still refuses to marry you.

What you say: [Nothing].

What you wish you had asked (and maybe still can): *What are you assuming about the future? Are you unsure about marriage, or about me? Are there things about our relationship that we should talk about? Do you think you'll be ready tomorrow? Next year? Never? What do you need in order to be ready? How about a breakup? Is a breakup good for you?*

You already have the skills for asking forward-looking questions; the trick is using them. It's like pulling the rip cord on your parachute. It's not hard to do; the key is remembering to do it when it matters. Toward this end, it's useful to have a short list of good questions in your back pocket before you walk into any evaluation conversation.

And, unlike forgetting to pull the rip cord, if you don't ask the questions that matter, you can usually come back to have a follow-up conversation later.

Evaluation

Looking Back		Looking Forward
What were the criteria you used? What did you consider to be the most important? Are there concerns I should know about? Are there skills or experience that I am missing?		What are the consequences? How will this affect me in the coming year? What should I be thinking about or working on? When might we reassess?

SHIFT FROM WRONG SPOTTING TO DIFFERENCE SPOTTING

So far, we've been talking about what's under the feedback giver's labels, and how the receiver can ask good questions to figure out where the feedback comes from and where it's going. The feedback giver has ideas in their head and we've been talking about how to get those ideas from that person's head into your head.

But we've been leaving something out. You aren't trying to get the giver's ideas into your *empty* head, you're trying to get the giver's ideas into your *full* head. You have your own views and opinions regarding this feedback, your own data and interpretations, your own life experiences, assumptions, and values. All the sorts of things that form the giver's feedback in the first place are also going on in your head.

This, in fact, is a big reason we wrong spot: We know that the feedback is wrong or off target because we have our own experiences and views, and our views are not the same as theirs. Therefore, theirs are wrong. The only other choice would seem to be that their views are right and ours are wrong, but that seems even less likely.

There's another way to think about it. As receivers, we shouldn't use our views to dismiss the giver's views, but neither should we discard our own. Working to *first understand* their views doesn't mean we pretend we don't have life experiences or opinions. Instead, we need to understand their views even as we're aware of our own. And that's almost impossible to do unless we make a key shift—away from *that's wrong* and toward *tell me more: Let's figure out why we see this differently.*

If the reason we see a particular piece of feedback differently isn't simply that one of us is wrong, then what *is* the reason? There are two: We have different data, and we interpret that data differently. Above, we explored their data and interpretations in order to understand the feedback. Below, we're putting their point of view next to ours and exploring each of our data and interpretations in order to understand why there is sometimes a gap between how they see things and how we see them.

DIFFERENT DATA

We each observe different data because we're different people. We have different roles, live in different places, inhabit different bodies. We have different educations and training, different sensitivities, and care about different things.

Sometimes different data is a matter of access: Your boss knows what your peers are paid but you don't; workers in the Cairo office know the local culture in a way that headquarters in London can't; when lovers peer into each other's eyes, they each see a person the other cannot.

Where you sit in an organization affects what you see. The CEO and the receptionist have different data because of how and where they spend their time, whom they talk to, and what they are responsible for. The CEO knows what's causing conflicts with the board, frustrating key customers, and worrying market analysts. The receptionist observes every single person who comes into the building—board members, vendors, new hires, janitors, and journalists—and overhears what they talk about in the waiting area. The receptionist hears the gossip and complaints, and what people do and don't like about the CEO's approach to handling conflicts with the board, key customers, and market analysts.

Even when we have access to the same data, we tend to notice different things. We are all moving along the same sidewalk, but the historian may notice the brickwork, the jogger the impact on her knees, and the fellow in the wheelchair the areas that are less accessible.

We're engulfed by information—far too much to take in—and so we select small samples to pay attention to and ignore the rest. Right now, as you're reading this book, pause and notice something you didn't before. Maybe there's background noise, a breeze, or the "fashion sense" of the person across the way. Until a moment ago you were filtering all that out, and you probably didn't realize you were doing so. We don't notice what we don't notice, so we don't notice *that* we don't notice.

Having access to or taking in different data helps explain the trouble Mavis is having. She's an attorney on a cross-functional product team that includes sales, production, and legal, as well as an account manager. Each team serves a client from start to finish, pitch to performance.

At her annual review Mavis receives blunt feedback from Davis, the account manager: "You don't understand the 'business side' of the business. Your laborious legal reviews slow the sales process and we lose out to fleeter competition."

Mavis is frustrated by this. These salespeople—and Davis—are just wrong. As a lawyer, Mavis is aware of certain things that other team members are not. She knows what the legal issues are, but more than that, she knows exactly how many deals get litigated and what the settlements cost the firm in dollars and reputation. And front of mind is her mandate from the general counsel: "Regulators are cracking down; we must execute with impeccable integrity. Our sales folks are top-notch, but it's Legal's job to rein them in." Mavis assumes, unconsciously, that Davis and others see what she sees. But they don't. In some cases, they have access to the information but no interest. In most cases, they don't even have access: They aren't in the legal department meetings with the general counsel and don't get the litigation reports.

In contrast, here is what Davis sees. He talks with customers about what they need and why. He sees the weekly sales reports, including stats on the pitch-to-close ratio. He hears what other firms are promising customers, and has learned that often, the terms Mavis rejects on legal grounds are approved at other firms. Davis also knows the shifting sales landscape. These days it's all about price point and efficiency: Beat the market or lose the deal. No deal, no firm, no Davis, no Mavis. No joke.

Mavis won't make progress in deciphering the feedback until she asks this: "Why do we see this differently? What data do you have that I don't?" Davis and Mavis each have pieces of the puzzle the other doesn't and they can't put the puzzle together until all the pieces are laid out on the table.

Life would be a lot easier if we routinely asked that question about different data. But we don't. Why? Because *wrong spotting* is so much more compelling than *difference spotting*. Being aware of what they see that we don't is just not as delicious as listening for how they're wrong. And once we spot an error, we can't contain ourselves; we have to jump in and set things straight. But we have to fight that instinct. We have to consciously and persistently choose to ask about their data and share our own.

Biases Drive Data Collection

There's another factor that makes difference spotting tough. What we do and don't notice isn't random. If your giver likes you and thinks you're terrifically competent, they're going to notice all the fantastic things you do. They'll go out of their way to find them. Your radiance also influences how they interpret what they see. That mistake you made is simply the exception that proves just how competent you usually are, and maybe it wasn't really a mistake at all.

But if friction develops in the relationship—when the infatuation of new love fades, the stakes rise, or humidity sets in—biases shift. Now your giver begins to focus on the things you messed up while ignoring those you got right. Your "willingness to take risks" is now seen as "risky," your "firm hand on the tiller" is now regarded as an unwillingness to let go. Others seek data that confirm their preexisting view of us, whether that view is good or bad. It's human nature.[3]

Meanwhile, we have biases of our own. All things being equal, we'll find a sympathetic story that explains and justifies our own behavior. We remember what we got right, and as we'll explore in the next chapter, we ascribe generally good intentions to ourselves. Ninety-three percent of American motorists believe they are better-than-average drivers. In a 2007 *BusinessWeek* poll, 90 percent of the managers surveyed believed their performance in the workplace to be in the top 10 percent.[4]

These biases can make difference spotting tougher still since we each feel it's the other who is biased. In fact, we're both biased, and we each need the other in order to see the whole picture more clearly.

DIFFERENCES IN INTERPRETATION

The second reason why feedback that makes sense to the giver might not make sense to you is this: Even when you are both looking at the same data, each of you can *interpret* them differently.

Janie complains to Ripley that he's not doing his part to keep the house clean. After listening attentively, Ripley assures Janie that he will change. And in his mind he does. But Janie continues to feel the house is a disaster. The situation is incredibly stressful to her, and she doesn't understand why Ripley says he's helping when he's clearly not. And Ripley doesn't understand why Janie continues to complain now that the problem has been addressed.

Ripley and Janie have access to the same data but interpret them differently. When Janie looks around the house, she sees clutter and chaos, and despairs that her life is out of control. She feels stretched too thin between work and home and is ashamed when she imagines what her mother would say if she saw how they live. Ripley looks at the same clutter and sees a rich family life bursting with the energy and joy of kids being kids. For him, that chaos is comforting.

Janie and Ripley assume they understand each other because they are each plainly looking at the same chaotic/comforting house. But here it's the interpretation that matters. Ripley won't understand Janie's feedback until he sees the meaning of the mess from her point of view.

Differences in how we interpret what we see are so fundamental to understanding the feedback we get that it's worth taking a closer look at a couple of key factors that are often embedded in our interpretations.

Implicit Rules

One of the primary reasons we interpret data differently is that we have different rules in our heads about how things *should* be. But we don't think of them as *our* rules. We think of them as *the* rules.

Everyone at your old job loved you. Everyone at your new job doesn't. They say you're difficult, but you know you haven't changed, and the people you work with seem normal enough. What's different? The implicit rules that govern interaction. At your old job, being direct was appreciated: Knock heads, sort things out. At the new place, you're supposed to be "nice." You're not a big fan of nice; in your experience, nice equals indirect, which equals passive-aggressive, which equals frustrating and inefficient. Which makes you difficult. Now that you understand the implicit rules, you at least understand why you are seen the way you are.

Organizational culture, regional culture, and even family culture are all collections of implicit rules for "how we do things around here." But everyone has their own individual set as well. Implicit rules can be about specific matters—like whether being "on time" means seated and ready to go or just wandering in. And implicit rules can be about more general issues—like the way life "is" or what it means to be a friend. Such rules often come in contrasting pairs:

"It's a dog-eat-dog world" versus *"Smile and the world smiles with you."*

"Conflict is bad" versus *"Conflict is healthy."*

"It's important to be liked" versus *"It's important to be respected."*

Feedback that isn't making sense can suddenly fall into place when we understand the implicit rule underlying the interpretations. I assumed that asking questions at the company meeting showed engagement; I learn that it's read as rude and contrarian.

Heroes and Villains

One principle for how we organize our experiences is this: We are (usually) the sympathetic hero of the story. In his speech to a graduating class at Kenyon, writer David Foster Wallace observed that there is "no experience you've had that you were not at the absolute center of." We are each "lords of our own tiny skull-sized kingdoms." [5] In our story we are Dorothy, the Princess, or Rudolph, not the Wicked Witch, the Pea, or any of the other reindeer.

This complicates feedback.

A son visits his father who is recovering from surgery. Upon arrival he is horrified to find his father in enormous pain, and the surgeon refusing to authorize more medication to alleviate it. He marches down the corridor to report the surgeon's heartless treatment to the department head. The surgeon follows, rolling her eyes at her department head to communicate *her* assessment: *Another difficult family member wasting valuable time better used to treat patients.*

Part of the challenge here is data: Surgeon and son each see the father's suffering in light of information the other doesn't have. The son *knows* his father—war hero, football star, stoic. If he's writhing in pain, that pain must be intolerable. The surgeon *knows* the effects of this surgery and the length of recovery from it—the intense postoperative pain quickly dissipates. She's also seen patients become addicted to pain medication, and has witnessed the toll it takes on them and their families.

What further complicates the situation is that both surgeon and son see themselves as the hero in the story. Each believes they are protecting the father from suffering and each sees the other as misguided at best—and in the heat of the moment, even as something of a villain. Now we've got two heroes fighting over who is wearing the white hat. The feedback they have for each other isn't just about medication. It's a morality play.

ASK: WHAT'S RIGHT?

Difference spotting—understanding as specifically as you can exactly why you and they see things differently—is a crucial lens through which to take in feedback. You begin to better understand where the feedback comes from, what the advice is, how to implement it, and why you and the feedback giver see certain things differently.

At this point in the process, it can also be useful to make a list of the ways their feedback might be "right." We need to be careful here, because right spotting can inadvertently lead to wrong spotting. If you're looking for what's right, you can fall back into the right-wrong frame and, at least as often, you'll find what's wrong.

So we're not using the word "right" to mean some final determination about objective truth. We mean it more as a mindset: What makes sense about what they're saying, what seems worth trying, how you can shift around the meaning in some way that gives them the benefit of the doubt in terms of how the feedback might be helpful. It's like walking through a forest and identifying birds instead of trees. Noticing the birds doesn't make the trees "wrong."

Let's come back to Mavis and Davis. Mavis can ask why she and Davis see things differently, but she also might ask what's right about Davis's feedback. What's right is that speed matters. What's right is that members of the sales team are frustrated. What's right is that some competitors are (apparently) making different legal judgments about terms. What's right is that closing deals matters to Mavis, to Davis, and to the firm. Looking for what's right about the feedback is a place where the conversation between them has traction to explore joint solutions, and one where Davis's feedback isn't so easily dismissed.

Feedback	What's Different?	What's Right?
Davis to Mavis: You're making us lose new business.	Different data, including real litigation risks, general counsel admonition, pitch-to-close ratio, and what other firms are doing.	Speed matters. If others are making different legal judgments we should learn why and see if we agree or disagree. Closing deals matters to both of us.
Margie doesn't get the promotion as new department head.	Decision makers know what skills are needed at the next level, and also what others say about Margie's ability to lead. Margie knows the long hours and extra work she has been putting in. Also, different implicit rules: Margie assumes seniority matters—promotions are a reward for hard work, and you learn the new job on the job. Her boss believes you don't promote until the skills needed in the new job are evident.	What's right is that I have less experience with the budgeting process than other candidates. What's right is that if I understand the criteria for promotion, whether I agree with it or not, I can make an informed decision about my own goals and next steps.
She still won't marry me.	She may have different assumptions and feelings about the relationship, or about marriage. She may have different implicit rules about when you know enough to make a commitment, or have past experiences that increase her anxiety. She may focus on her greatest fears, while I focus on my best hopes.	What's right is that she's not ready. What's right is that understanding why may help me see whether we have the same goals and feelings. What's right is that I have a responsibility to myself to make a good choice going forward, given always-imperfect information.

WHEN YOU STILL DISAGREE

Sometimes you will get to the point of fully understanding where a giver's feedback comes from and what it is they're suggesting, and you will simply disagree with it. In fact, now that you really do understand it, their feedback might seem even further off target or more unfair than before.

That might be a frustrating and difficult place for the two of you to be, but from a communication standpoint, you've succeeded. Your goal is to understand the feedback giver, and for them to understand you. If you end up thinking the feedback is helpful, then you'll take it. If you don't, at least you'll understand where the feedback comes from, what they were suggesting, and why you're rejecting it. The same is true of evaluation. The better you understand the origins and consequences of the evaluation, the better able you are to explain why you disagree with it.

Being transparent and honest about your reactions is not inconsistent with being open and curious, by the way. You can say what's going on in your head:

Wow. That's upsetting to hear.

I never would have imagined that.

That is so far from how I see myself—or hope to be seen—that I'm almost speechless. I want to explain why, but I also want to make sure that I really understand what you're saying.

You're not cutting off the conversation with comments like this, but sharing your reactions and continuing to try to understand. Having said this, we should admit that we have a theory here: We figure that the better you understand the feedback, the more likely you are to find *some*thing in it that is useful, or at the very least to understand the ways in which you are being misunderstood, and why.

"WHY CAN'T FEEDBACK JUST BE OBJECTIVE?"

It's reasonable to wonder: If subjectivity and interpretation make feedback so hard, why not just be objective and stick with the facts? Many organizations are trying to do just that by developing competency models and behavioral guides and using formulas and metrics for measuring performance. These can be helpful to align expectations and clarify criteria. But they don't take the subjectivity out of feedback. Nothing does.

Whatever metric you come up with, there will always be subjective judgments *behind* that metric: Why is *x* most important, and why isn't *y* included? There are subjective judgments driving how that metric is applied: You "meet expectations" based on what I expect. Are those expectations fair? Yes? No? How do we know? Eventually we arrive at someone's judgment.

What about bottom-line profits—aren't those objective? In one sense, yes. The number is a number and it's independent of anyone's subjective hopes or beliefs about it. But what does that number *mean*? Is half a percent above the market average good or bad? Is double the expected profits good, or were the expected profits totally off to begin with? And what's the relationship between the CEO's performance and the profits? We can argue about that, can't we?

No matter how clearly you define the criteria and the metrics, somebody has to apply the criteria to a person's performance, and that involves making judgments. If advice is autobiographical, so is evaluation. The evaluation we give people is a reflection of our own (or our organization's) preferences, assumptions, values, and goals. They might be broadly shared or idiosyncratic, but either way, they are ours.

And that's as it should be. People who are skilled coaches or evaluators are valuable precisely because their gifts of judgment are strong. An iPhone app can tell a singer if she's hitting each note precisely; she hires a voice coach for his judgment, his experienced point of view. He can help her sing in a way that *moves* people. An app can't tell you whether you are leading effectively, creating cohesion, persistence, or energy. The people you lead can.

The goal shouldn't be to remove interpretation or judgment. It should be to make judgments thoughtfully, and once made, to have them be transparent and discussable.

A CONVERSATION WITH COMMENTARY

Let's look at a conversation in which the receiver has some truth-trigger reactions, but even so, works hard to understand the feedback. The background is this: Monisha, the head of HR, has been asked by the CEO, Paul, to design and conduct an employee climate survey to determine where the senior executive team could improve. Monisha and her team spend months collecting data from employees around the globe, and the results are disquieting.

As Monisha presents the findings to the senior executive team, she and Johann, the CFO, have a tense exchange:

Johann: Monisha, how many different ways are you going to tell us that our employees think the executive team is incompetent? We get it. But I'll be honest, I don't put much stock in any of this.

Monisha: Johann, I understand this is surprising, but I think it's important that we—

Johann: Garbage in, garbage out. You recall what that means?

Monisha: Do you have a specific question about what I'm presenting? I can walk you through the methodology.

Johann: I'm sure you have lots of wonderful things to say about your methodology, but unfortunately, some of us have a business to run.

And with that, Johann walks out.

Paul is chagrined at Johann's handling of the exchange, but truth be told, he feels similar frustration and skepticism. The meeting adjourns, and Paul has the wherewithal to tell Monisha that he knows how hard her team has worked on the project, and that while he's unhappy about the results, he'd like to better understand them. He asks Monisha to stop by the next day to talk.

PAUL'S PREPARATION: MINDSET AND GOALS

Paul's initial reaction is that the feedback doesn't square with his sense of the organization. But his purpose in the conversation is not to accept or reject, but first to understand. He'll seek to remain curious, spot labels, and clarify Monisha's data and interpretations. He'll also share his own thoughts and views.

THE CONVERSATION

Paul: Monisha, there's a lot here for us to dig into and discuss. I have two initial reactions. One is, "Wow, if this is how people are feeling, then this is a real wake-up call, and I've got to understand this better." At the same time, I admit that some parts of it don't fit with my sense of the climate here. So it's confusing, which is why I'm glad you're here to talk it through with me.

Comment: Nice. Paul's statement reflects a mindset that is open to learning, and at the same time, he's being honest about how he's currently thinking and feeling.

Monisha: Paul, you can dismiss this feedback, and I can understand the inclination to do that, but I don't think hiding from reality is going to get us anywhere.

Comment: Not the response he hoped for, but Paul shouldn't take the bait. He shouldn't protest: "I'm not hiding from reality!" He should stick with the topic: what the results mean and how they can be helpful.

Paul: The feedback doesn't match up with what I thought was going on, but that doesn't mean that what I thought was going on is accurate. So this is what I want to investigate and understand.

Monisha: I think the primary finding is that our mid-level managers are feeling disempowered and out of the loop.

Paul: Let's get specific. What does it mean that they're feeling "disempowered and out of the loop"?

Comment: Well done. Paul doesn't defend with a comment like, "Well, we can't include them in every decision." Instead, he inquires, trying to dig under the label.

Monisha: We surveyed everyone from associates to VPs. There was a pervasive sense that the executive team doesn't communicate well, input is not sought, and contributions are not appropriately valued.

Paul proceeds to ask about numbers—how many employees thought this, how the survey was structured, etc., and Monisha presents that information.

Paul: So, let's look at a concrete example.

Monisha: A number of people mentioned the ethics initiative. People were very unhappy that they had to attend a series of ethics workshops over the course of a year, while the senior leadership attended a session that was just two hours.

Paul: Well, we don't call them "ethics workshops" or "ethics meetings," but ethics are embedded in our jobs, day in and day out. I'm constantly meeting with lawyers, compliance people, risk management people. Ethics and values are at the heart of everything I do.

Comment: It seems reasonable for Paul to think these things, and reasonable for him to share them. But in this context, he would be better served to share them in a way that invites further conversation. Like this:

Paul: If people are feeling that this is a cynical program, or that senior leadership doesn't buy in, I can imagine why they'd feel frustrated. From my point of view, much of my job is about ethics. I meet with lawyers, compliance people, risk managers. But the mid-level people are obviously seeing it differently, and that's a concern.

Monisha: Yes, they are seeing it differently. Part of it is a matter of perception, of messaging. But I think there's something deeper going on here. A genuine attitude problem.

Paul: I'm not clear what you mean. What do you mean by messaging versus attitude?

Comment: That's good. If you don't fully understand something, slow things down and ask.

Monisha: Here's the difference between a messaging problem and an attitude problem: What was the primary motive behind senior management's doing only two hours of ethics work?

Paul: For one, we wanted to send the message that this really matters.

Monisha: But I think the message they heard was that "the senior team doesn't really need it." It's not the message you intended to send, but that message is actually an *accurate* reflection of the senior team's attitude.

Paul: Hmm, that's interesting. So you're saying we sent a message we didn't intend, but which is actually the truth.

Monisha: I think so.

Paul: Just to clarify, do you think that's the perception that some people have of me personally? That I think the senior team doesn't need ethics training?

Comment: This is a useful question. If it's not discussed, Paul could leave the conversation with the impression that Monisha was talking about others but not him.

Monisha: I don't have specific information about how people see you in this, but let me ask you: What is your attitude about senior management and ethics training?

Paul: It's as you said. I really do think I spend a lot more time on ethics and I don't feel the need to personally participate in the workshops. But that sends a bad message.

Monisha: So you could do one of two things. You could either be clearer in explaining why you don't think senior management needs this but others do, or you could cultivate a mindset where you genuinely believe you do need it, and then participate fully. I imagine even as you hear that, you're thinking, "I'm just too busy for that."

Paul: I am thinking that. Ideally, I could participate, but I'm just too busy.

Monisha: Which leaves those at lower levels thinking, if senior management is too busy for this, how important is it? Or alternatively, maybe they think it is important, which means it's important for senior leadership, too.

Paul: Okay, I'm beginning to see how someone might be resentful or feel that we're being hypocritical. This is a little shocking. In any event, this is a lot to think about, and we haven't even covered most of the survey. But what we have covered has helped me get a better sense of how others might see the leadership of the organization and why.

This conversation between Paul and Monisha is not easy, but it's important. The key is purpose and mindset. Paul is not looking to agree or disagree, defend or accept. He's trying to understand. It's not a problem-solving session, it's an understanding session. If Paul had followed his instincts, he would have disagreed with Monisha at the outset, and the conversation might have ended there. Instead, he listens for labels and works hard to look under them, and when he's unsure about what Monisha means, he doesn't let it slip by. He asks.

■ ■ ■

Giving up wrong spotting isn't easy, and you don't have to give it up altogether. You can still indulge in recreational wrong spotting on the weekends, with friends over a beer. Argue, accuse, vent, deny—give each other a hard time. If it's fun, it's fun.

But when it matters, when you're getting feedback that is important to the giver or potentially helpful to you as receiver, put the wrong spotting aside. You need to get good at difference spotting, and on occasion, break out your right-spotting skills. Real learning requires you to take up this harder but more rewarding sport.

Summary: SOME KEY IDEAS

Feedback is delivered in vague labels, and we are prone to wrong spotting.

To understand your feedback, discuss where it is:

- *Coming from:* their data and interpretations
- *Going to:* advice, consequences, expectations

Ask: What's *different* about

- The data we are looking at
- Our interpretations and implicit rules

Ask: What's *right* about the feedback to seek out what's legit and what concerns you have in common.

Working together to get a more complete picture maximizes the chances you will (both) learn something.

4

SEE YOUR BLIND SPOTS

Discover How You Come Across

Annabelle is a superstar. She's fast, creative, tireless, and careful. She remembers birthdays. But what makes her irreplaceable is her impossible combination of analytic smarts and beguiling, quirky charm.

And everyone on her team is sick of her.

It's not a crisis. Annabelle is not a bully or a backstabber. Just the opposite: She cares about her team members and believes they are most productive when they're happy.

But they are not happy. Annabelle knows this because her second 360 in three years tells her this. She's "difficult," "impatient," "doesn't treat us with respect." That's tough to take. Conveying respect is precisely the thing Annabelle has been working on since her prior review. And after three years, here it is again, with no acknowledgment of how hard she's been trying.

Annabelle wonders whether something else is going on. Maybe her subordinates are playing politics or enjoy taking anonymous shots at the boss. Or maybe it's projection. Sometimes people fall into a parent-child relationship with an authority figure to work through unrelated developmental issues.

Annabelle is right: Something else *is* going on. But team members are not playing politics, out to get her, or shadowboxing with absent parents.

Although Annabelle is *trying* to treat her team members with respect, she's sending unconscious signals that undermine her efforts. Tony explains: "When Annabelle is under pressure, she is difficult to work with. She says please and thank you, but underneath she's full of impatience and contempt. If I go to her office with a question, she rolls her eyes and answers sharply. Then she'll show me the door, which, she cheerfully reminds me, is always open."

Annabelle knows how she *intends* to come across. But she is blind to her actual impact on others.

Annabelle is not alone.

Zoe thinks she's supportive of new ideas, but is always the first to shoot down a creative suggestion.

Mehmet takes neutral questions ("Did you have a good weekend?") as criticism ("Do you assume I didn't?") and is confused about why others see him as prickly.

Jules keeps talking long after you've signaled you need to go. Even, sometimes, after you've already gone.

How can these folks be so oblivious? Is it possible we are this oblivious, too?

It is.

In fact, there is always a gap between the self we think we present and the way others see us. We may not recognize ourselves in others' feedback, even when everyone else would agree that it's the conventional wisdom about who we are and how we are.

Why is it that there is such a gap between our self-perception and others' stories about us? The good news is that the ways we are understood and misunderstood by others are amazingly systematic and predictable.

THE GAP MAP

The Gap Map highlights the key elements that factor into the way I mean to be seen versus the way I am actually seen. Read from left to right, the Gap Map makes the cause of our blind spots visible.

Let's start on the far left with our own thoughts and feelings. From these, we formulate intentions—what we're trying to do, what we want

The Gap Map

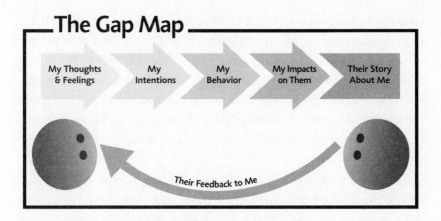

| My Thoughts & Feelings | My Intentions | My Behavior | My Impacts on Them | Their Story About Me |

Their Feedback to Me

to have happen. To achieve our intentions, we do and say things, we put behavior out into the world. These behaviors have an impact on others, and based on this impact, others develop a story about our intentions and character. They then offer some version of these perceptions to us as feedback. By the time others are describing you—to you—the figure they're describing may bear only vague resemblance to the "you" you know. We flinch, we squint, we shake our heads. We don't recognize ourselves.

Somewhere in this game of telephone, messages get garbled. By looking more closely at how information moves across the map, we can pinpoint where and why.

Let's use the Gap Map to explain what is going on with Annabelle.

Recall the background: Three years ago, in her first 360, Annabelle learned that her subordinates felt she wasn't treating them respectfully. She was dismayed to discover that they were unhappy and genuinely wants them to be happier, so she has been working on being "respectful" ever since.

Now let's jump onto the map to see what happens. Annabelle's focus is on changing her behavior (arrow 3); but her thoughts and feelings (arrow 1) remain unchanged. And this is a problem.

What *are* Annabelle's actual thoughts and feelings about her team? They are embedded in expectations and assumptions that have accrued over many years. Annabelle has high standards for herself and high standards for those around her. This comes from a combination of her temperament and her early family life, as well as her school and work experiences, where she got positive feedback for being quietly resourceful. Like a town that slowly takes shape on the curve of a river, these experiences accumulated into a village of values, assumptions, and expectations about what it means to be "good" or "competent."

Thus we arrive at the cross-currents swirling around her situation: Annabelle is often dismayed when team members come to her with the kinds of questions that she would have felt eager to figure out on her own. She believes they aren't trying or don't care enough. As a result she often feels impatient, annoyed, and disappointed in her team.

This creates a misalignment between her internal thoughts and feelings on the one hand (arrow 1), and her intentions (arrow 2) on the other. She believes that she keeps this misalignment hidden, but in fact those internal thoughts and feelings are leaking into her behavior (arrow 3) through her facial expressions, tone of voice, and body language.

Her colleagues "read" these leaking thoughts and feelings and then wonder about Annabelle's intentions. She sees her intentions as positive: "I want my colleagues to feel respected and I'm trying so hard to act respectful." But her team members tell a different story. They see her as deceptive and even manipulative: "You want us to *think* you respect us when you don't. Now you're not just disrespectful, you're disingenuous."

Annabelle's team is now even more unhappy and frustrated, and they make this clear in her current 360. Annabelle receives the evaluation and feels shocked, unappreciated, and misunderstood. She and her colleagues are in a challenging downward cycle.

Below, we'll explore some of the things that others observe about us that we can't—our blind spots—and then examine three "amplifiers," systematic differences between how others tell the story of who we are versus how we tell that same story, which exacerbate the gaps on the map.

BEHAVIORAL BLIND SPOTS

A blind spot is something we don't see about ourselves that others *do* see. We each have our own particular items in our blind spot basket, but there are some blind spots that we all share.

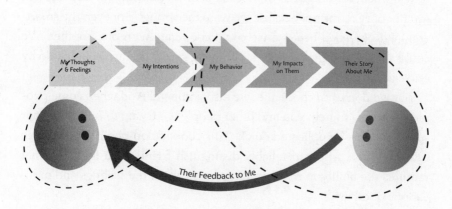

If we circle on our map the things I am aware of and the things you are aware of, it turns out that my behavior is in *your* awareness and mostly *not* in my awareness. We all know this about human interactions, and yet somehow it comes as a surprise that our own behavior is largely invisible to us.

YOUR LEAKY FACE

Who can see your face? Everyone. Who can't see your face? You.

We convey a tremendous amount of information through facial expressions. But our own face is a blind spot. The culprit is human anatomy: We're trapped inside ourselves looking out. We know what we look like in the bathroom mirror, but we don't know what we look like out in the world, in motion, interacting with real people, reacting to real events in our lives.

A decent pair of eyestalks would help—the kind that swivel, like the ones aliens sport in B movies from the 1950s. With eyestalks we'd get a lot of insight into why people react to us the way they do: "Oh, *now* I see why you think I'm being defensive. I *do* look defensive."

Why is so much communicated through facial expression? It's not because our faces are so wonderfully clear or expressive; we don't have a feelings newsfeed on our foreheads. It's because most humans are so wonderfully good at reading *other people's* faces. This ability has been in development for hundreds of thousands of years. Humans succeeded in evolutionary terms not because we were the strongest or even the smartest. We succeeded because we could cooperate with one another. We could do things together (like hunting big game) that we couldn't do by ourselves.

But we don't *only* cooperate; we also compete. And when some people are trying to help you and other people are trying to hurt you, your social life gets complicated quick. This cooperation-competition dance rewards those who can reliably distinguish friend from foe. And that requires the ability to make smart guesses about the feelings and motivations of others.[1]

How do we make those guesses? We listen to what others say about their feelings and motivations, certainly, but that alone isn't enough. What if others are trying to deceive us? We needed a way to assess feelings and motivations that didn't rely solely on intentional communication. So we developed the ability to read nuances in faces and tone, and through this we formulate a "theory of mind"[2] about those we interact with.

The human deftness at reading people is most visible in its absence. Those who fall on the autism spectrum often struggle with exactly this. They often don't look others in the eye and can't read the social cues transmitted by faces or tone.[3] This language that seems so natural to most people can be a struggle for them to learn.

The rest of us read those cues constantly and largely unconsciously. Science writer Steven Johnson notes that we can measure "other people's moods just by scanning their eyes or the corners of their mouth," adding that it's a "background process that feeds into our foreground processes; we're aware of the insights it gives us but usually not aware of how we're actually getting that information, and how good we are at extracting it."[4]

YOUR LEAKY TONE

Tone of voice also conveys a surprising amount of information about our feelings. Others get meaning not just from what we say but *how we say it*. The precise percentage is impossible to determine (one study suggests 38 percent),[5] but the point remains: Tone says a lot.

An actor can say "I love you" a hundred different ways to convey a hundred different meanings. It can be an expression of passion or resignation, confidence or doubt. It can be a proclamation or a question. Do you *know* I love you? *Do* I love you? Do you love *me*? Tone, pitch, and cadence—what linguists call intonation contours—enhance or subvert meaning, and transmit rich information about the speaker's emotions.

Infants sort what they hear through the superior temporal sulcus (STS), located just above the ear. At four months all auditory information—whether their mother's voice or a car horn—is attended to by the STS. But by seven months, babies start singling out human voices as the *only* sounds that trigger attention from the STS,[6] and the STS shows especially heightened activity when that voice carries emotion. This little piece of our brain is dedicated to taking in language and reading tone and meaning.

But get this: When we ourselves speak, the STS *turns off*. We don't hear our own voice, at least not the same way we hear everyone else. This explains why we are so often surprised when we get feedback based on *how* we said something. ("Tone? I'm not using some kind of tone!") It also helps explain why our voice sounds so unfamiliar when we hear ourselves on an audio recording. When transmitted from a speaker, our own voice gets routed through our STS, and we suddenly hear ourselves the way others do. ("I sound like *that*?!") We've been hearing ourselves every day of our lives, and yet we haven't.

Interestingly, this may be part of the reason top opera singers so often have voice coaches. "We refer to them as our 'outside ears,'" says soprano Renée Fleming. "What we hear as we are singing is not what the audience hears."[7]

University College London researcher Sophie Scott speculates that our "listening" STS brain doesn't attend to the sound of our own voice in part because we are so absorbed in listening to our thoughts. Our attention can focus on only one thing at a time, so we focus on our intentions—figuring out how to say what we're trying to say. Annabelle's focus is on her thoughts and intentions, not on her behavior and tone.[8]

So, like our facial expressions, our tone often betrays our thoughts and feelings in ways we don't realize. We try to sound relaxed, but come across as uncomfortable; we mean to sound confident, but come across as bombastic and insecure; we want to communicate love but instead plant a seed of doubt.

YOUR LEAKY PATTERNS

It's easy to understand how the subtle things we do can fall into a blind spot—a furrowed brow here, an edgy tone there. What's astonishing is that we can be unaware of even big, seemingly obvious patterns of behavior.

This becomes apparent to Bennett one evening during a game of charades with his family. When his five-year-old son mimes a person pacing while barking into a cell phone, his daughter lights up: "It's Daddy!" Bennett winces: "How is that *me*?" "Because," she says, "you're *always* on your cell phone!"

He is? Bennett works hard to minimize time on his cell when his kids are around. But that's not how they see it: In their minds he is constantly interrupting family time to make or take a call. One reason for the difference in their views is the perception of time. When we are on the phone, we're immersed in the conversation taking place, and time moves along. Those around us overhear the dreaded *half-a-logue*; there's no story, just an unintelligible half conversation, and time creeps.

Even the big patterns in our lives that are almost comically obvious to others may be blind spots to us. Over the last four years you've been in six different relationships. At the beginning of each one, you proclaim to all your friends: "This is *the one*." The relationship moves through a manic phase, with extravagant trips and adventures, and then settles down for a few months, and then seemingly out of nowhere, you end it. The only thing remarkable about any of this is that while your friends could chart the course of your new relationship on a graph from the get-go, you are 100 percent oblivious to the fact that the relationships share any pattern. In fact, it's not until your closest friend does draw you a graph that you start to see it.

E-MAIL BODY LANGUAGE

Surprisingly, even on e-mail, people try to read emotions and tone. Or more precisely, despite lacking access to the sender's face and voice, we retain the desire to know their mood and intentions, so we gather what clues we can.

E-mail can provide obvious clues, like ALL CAPS, lots of !!??!s, and who is suddenly (strategically?) cc'ed, as well as more subtle ones, like word choice or timing. We wonder why they responded instantly, or why they waited so long. Was their three-word response pointed or merely to the point? Was their outpouring of words just thorough, or a sign of exasperation? We know what they *said*; we want to know what they *meant*.

THEY MAY SEE EXACTLY WHAT WE ARE TRYING TO HIDE

The fact that others are always reading our faces, tone, and behavior doesn't mean they are always reading us right. They can often tell when what we say doesn't match the way we feel, but they can't always tell quite how.

Sometimes people simply read us wrong. You are feeling shy at cocktail hour, wishing someone would approach you. But as you linger by the door, others see you as "aloof" or "too good for the rest of us." They are picking up something in your demeanor, but their interpretation is off.

Other times people pick up on exactly the thing we are hoping to hide. Annabelle's colleagues are getting it right. The eye rolling, the sighs, the smile through gritted teeth—she's trying to hide her true feelings, but alas, she's sprung a leak. She doesn't have to say "I'm disgusted." Her face says it for her.[9]

THREE BLIND-SPOT AMPLIFIERS

Others observe things about us that we literally can't observe about ourselves. Our blind spots are their hot spots. But differing observations are only part of the blind-spot disconnect. There are three dynamics that amplify the gap between how we see ourselves and how others see us. The three amplifiers are interrelated, but each is worth examining on its own.

AMPLIFIER 1: EMOTIONAL MATH

Emotions play a huge role in the gap between how others see us and how we assume we are seen. We subtract certain emotions from the equation: "That emotion is not really who I am." But others count it double: "That emotion is *exactly* who you are."

Sasha's daughter recently left for college, and Sasha feels unexpectedly bereft. Her friend Olga has been her lifeline, supportive in every way. So Sasha is stunned to hear from a mutual friend that Olga described Sasha as "self-obsessed and victim-y."

Sasha doesn't recognize herself in that description. Sure, she talks about feeling lonely, but that's normal when your only kid goes off to college, isn't it? What Sasha isn't fully aware of is the relentless nature of her complaints to Olga. For hours on end, days in a row, she talks about her pain, without noticing the effect on Olga and without ever asking Olga about her life. (Olga is confronting a difficult time of her own.)

We can empathize with both Sasha and Olga. Sasha is in pain, and Olga is overwhelmed with being leaned on for support. We understand why Sasha complains to Olga and why Olga vents about it to a friend. Our point is not to judge either, but to note the way that Sasha discounts her emotions from her story of who she is. This emotional math explains Sasha's reaction upon hearing the feedback. She's not just hurt that Olga talked to a mutual friend, she's also baffled by the content. *It's just not true*, she thinks. *Why would Olga say that?*

Anger, too, is often invisible to its owner in the moment. You and your colleague are under intense pressure to finalize tomorrow's presentation to the board. Late in the evening your colleague is struck by a game-changing idea and excitedly shares it with you. You cut him off: "You want to start over? At this hour? No #@%& chance!" You exit the conference room quickly to prevent yourself from saying more.

The next day when your colleague mentions your outburst and the way you "stormed" out of the room, you are in disbelief: "I've never once raised my voice at you," you assert. "And I don't 'storm.'" And in your mind, you never have. When we are angry, we are focused on the provocation, the threat. And it's the threat that we remember later. For our colleague, our anger *is* the threat. It's not just part of the story, it's the heart of the story. Your anger is integral to how your colleague sees you and interacts with you.

As the example above reveals, strong emotions can seem as if they are part of the environment rather than part of us. *It's not that I was angry*, we think, *it's that the situation was tense*. But situations are not tense. People are tense.

AMPLIFIER 2: SITUATION VERSUS CHARACTER

Emotional math is really a subset of a larger dynamic. When something goes wrong and I am part of it, I will tend to attribute my actions to the situation; you will tend to attribute my actions to my character.[10]

When I take the last piece of cake at the party, you say it's because I'm selfish (character). I say it's because no one else wanted it (situation). When I hop on a conference call five minutes late, you say I'm scatterbrained (character). I say I was juggling five things at once (situation). When I take another personal day, you say I'm unreliable (character). I explain that I had to arrange transportation for my ailing aunt Adelaide (situation).

The difference here is not just a matter of cutting ourselves a break. It's really an alternate way of telling the story. In extreme cases this helps explain why a person who is convicted of business fraud, who bankrupted scores of investors, for instance, can think of himself as an upstanding member of society: "I've always been community-minded and generous. I never meant to hurt anyone. But I got caught up in something that spun out of control." It was the situation, not me.

AMPLIFIER 3: IMPACT VERSUS INTENT

The third amplifier has already been hinted at on the Gap Map: We judge ourselves by our intentions (arrow 2), while others judge us by our impacts (arrow 4). Given that even good intentions can result in negative impacts, this contributes to the gap in the story you tell about me versus the story I know is "true."

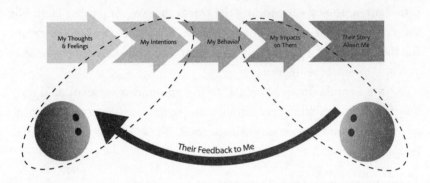

We see this happening with Annabelle. She is often frustrated by and contemptuous of her colleagues. But she wants them to feel appreciated and happy, so she formulates an intention to come across as respectful. She is trying to do something positive. What could be wrong with that?

What's wrong is that the impact on her colleagues is negative. Her colleagues don't think, *Well, the impact was negative, but the important thing is that you had good intentions.* Instead, they notice the negative impact and conclude that Annabelle is both difficult and insincere. Annabelle judges herself by her intentions; her colleagues judge her by her impacts.

This is a common pattern. My story about my interactions with others is driven by my intentions. I have good intentions—I'm trying to help, to guide, even to coach. I assume my good intentions lead to good impacts—they feel helped, guided, and appreciate my efforts to help them grow. Hence, people must know I'm a good person.

But for those around us, our impact drives their story. Despite my best intentions, I may have a negative impact on you; you feel bossed around and micromanaged. You then assume that I'm acting purposefully, or at least that I know I'm being bossy and don't care enough not to be. And if I have negative or negligent intentions I must be a bad person. Now you give me feedback that I'm bossy and controlling, and I'm shocked and bewildered. I discard it because it doesn't match who I am. It's wrong. And you conclude that I'm either oblivious to who I am or so defensive that I refuse to acknowledge what everyone knows is true.

The "fix" is to separate intentions from impacts when feedback is discussed. When Annabelle gets the feedback that she's difficult, she insists that she's not difficult, saying in essence, "I have positive intentions and therefore positive impacts." But she doesn't actually realize what impacts she's having. Instead, she should talk about intentions and impacts separately: "I've been working hard to be more patient [arrow 2, my intentions]. And yet it sounds like that's not the impact I'm having [arrow 4]. That's upsetting. Let's figure out why."

Feedback givers also confuse impacts and intentions. Their feedback is packed with assumed intentions. Instead of saying, "You try to steal credit for other people's ideas" (which includes a description of intentions), they should share the impact the behavior had on them: "I was upset and confused when you said it was your idea. I felt I deserved the credit for that idea." But few feedback givers are this skilled or careful (because they're obviously terrible people).

THE RESULT: OUR (GENERALLY POSITIVE) SELF

All of these amplifiers—our tendency to subtract certain emotions from our self-description, to see missteps as situational rather than personality-driven, and to focus on our good intentions rather than our impact on others—add up. And so we get statistics like this: 37 percent of Americans report being victims of workplace bullies, but fewer than 1 percent report being bullies. It's true that one bully can have many victims, but it's unlikely that each averages thirty-seven.[11]

What's more likely is that at least some percentage of those feeling bullied are receiving ill treatment from people who are unaware of their impact. They judge themselves by their intentions ("I was just trying to get the job done right!") and attribute others' reactions to their hypersensitivity (character) or the context ("Look, it was a tense situation. Anyone would have reacted that way"). Telling this latter group not to bully others is no solution, because they don't realize that they're doing so. Instead, discussing the impact of specific behaviors (and prohibiting them when appropriate) helps the offending party see themselves in the moment and begins to illuminate their blind spot. And teaching people how to invite and understand feedback—even if it feels upsetting or wrong—might help parties on both sides sort things out more successfully.

WE COLLUDE TO KEEP EACH OTHER IN THE DARK

This begs the question: Why don't people *tell* us? Why does it take a mutual friend's indiscretion for Sasha to hear that she is exhausting Olga's sympathies? Why does it take three years and another 360 for Annabelle to find out that her contempt is still coming through loud and clear?

When we're on the giving side, we often withhold critical feedback because we don't want to hurt others' feelings or start a fight. We figure they must already know, or that it's someone else's job to tell them, or that if they really wanted to hear about it, they'd ask.

The result of this withholding is that it's easy for the receiver to take misplaced comfort in the absence of corroborating views: If what you're saying were true, other people would have told me. Since they haven't, it must not be true. It's just one more reason that seeing ourselves clearly is such a challenge.

WHAT HELPS US SEE OUR BLIND SPOTS?

Let's start with what *doesn't* help. You can't see yourself more clearly just by looking harder. Here's why: When you do take a good hard look, what you'll see is that you don't have any blind spots and that the feedback is wrong. You will wonder about the cause of this wrong feedback, and your mind will slide into an explanation about the ulterior motives or personality disorders of those who gave you the feedback. We have the same Gap Map reaction to them as they do to us, just in reverse. We know that we are upset by wrong feedback and assume that others are giving it to us intentionally. Which means they must have an agenda or that something is seriously wrong with them.

USE YOUR REACTION AS A BLIND-SPOT ALERT

Thoughts like the above are so systematic that you can actually put them to good use. Instead of dismissing the feedback or the person giving it to you, use these thoughts as a blind-spot alert. When you notice yourself wondering *What was their agenda?* and *What's wrong with them?*, make sure your next thought is *I wonder if this feedback is sitting in my blind spot.*

ASK: HOW DO I GET IN MY OWN WAY?

To find out, we have to get specific. The feedback we ask for is usually too general, or others assume that what we are really inviting is appreciation (and sometimes they're right). We say something as noncommittal as "So how am I doing?" or "Do you have any feedback for me?," which leaves our giver guessing about what we really want— How are you doing with *what*? This project? Our relationship? Your leadership? Your life?—and how honest they should be. It's not unlike asking your nine-year-old, "How was your day?" We shouldn't be surprised by their less-than-stimulating response: "Fine."

Instead, ask (the feedback giver, not your nine-year-old): "What do you see me doing, or failing to do, that is getting in my own way?" This question is more specific about the honesty you desire as well as your interest in the impact you have on others. It's also a narrower and easier question for others to answer. They may start timidly ("Well, on occasion I suppose that you sometimes . . ."), but if you respond with genuine curiosity and appreciation, they'll be able to paint you a picture that is clear, detailed, and useful.

LOOK FOR PATTERNS

Our usual response to upsetting feedback is to reach for other feed-back that contradicts it, in order to protect ourselves. You say I'm self-absorbed? Then how come I won the community service award last year? You think I interrupt? Let me stop you right there . . . because I practically had to sit on my hands last week during your inane presentation.

How I See Me	How You See Me
Shy	Aloof
Upbeat	Phony
Spontaneous	Flaky
Truth Teller	Nasty
Passionate	Emotional
Smart	Arrogant
High Standards	Hypercritical
Outgoing	Overbearing
Quirky	Annoying

Instead of whipping out contradictory feedback, take a breath and look for consistent feedback—consistent in two ways. First, consider to what extent you are each describing the same behavior but interpreting it differently (as the table to the left illustrates). Others may be misunderstanding you (shy versus aloof), or you may be unaware of your impacts (outgoing versus overbearing). The feedback is not initially what you expect, but once it's reinterpreted, you can at least identify the behavior being discussed.

Here's a second way to look for consistencies: Ask yourself, *Where have I heard this before?* Is this the first time you've gotten such feedback, or have you heard similar things from other people (or the same exact person) over the years? Patterns offer useful clues about blind spots. If your first-grade teacher and your first wife both complained about your hygiene, it might be time to listen.

GET A SECOND OPINION

If important feedback doesn't resonate, take the whole set of questions to a friend. Don't say, "This can't be true, can it?" Instead, lay out the problem explicitly: "Here's feedback I just got. It seems wrong. My first reaction is to reject it. But I wonder if this is feedback in a blind spot?

Do you see me doing this sometimes, and if so, when? What impact do you see it having?" You have to let your friend know that you want honesty, and here's why.

Honest Mirrors Versus Supportive Mirrors

Offering feedback is often called "holding up a mirror" to help someone see themselves. But not all such mirrors are identical in what they reflect. When it comes to feedback, there are two kinds of mirrors— Supportive Mirrors and Honest Mirrors.

A supportive mirror shows us our best self, well rested and under flattering light. We go to a supportive mirror for reassurance. Yes, how we acted in that moment was not a pretty picture, but it's not how we *really* look. It's not a big deal. It's a bad picture of you. Throw it away. You're a good person.

An honest mirror shows us what we look like right now, when we're not at our best and our bedhead is bad. It's a true reflection of what others saw today, when we were stressed and distracted and leaking our frustration. "Yes, you really did come across that way. It's not a good thing."

Consciously or unconsciously, we often ask the people closest to us to be supportive mirrors. We share a piece of feedback from the guy in Purchasing, implicitly inviting our friend to be on our side: "He's overreacting, right? He just doesn't understand I've got bigger things to worry about, right?" Like the Wicked Queen in *Snow White*, we aren't asking the mirror for an honest assessment. We're asking for reassurance and support.

Reassurance and support are vital, and our friends and loved ones are uniquely able to offer it. But this role can put them in a bind: People we rely on for support are often hesitant to share critical, honest feedback with us. And that feedback might be helpful: "You know what? I don't think everything Purchasing Guy said is right, and I don't think he said it in the best way, but I can see what he's getting at. There are some things you could work on."

They are hesitant not out of cowardice, but out of confusion and concern. They want to do what's best for us, but aren't sure whether *just* being supportive is the right thing. And yet they also aren't sure whether and how to break out of the pattern that has been set. They are right to be concerned. When someone has been a supportive mirror, we can feel betrayed and blindsided if they suddenly become an honest one.

You can use the idea of honest mirrors and supportive mirrors to clarify what you're asking of your friends. When you hand over your freshly finished screenplay or show them around your recent renovation, give them some guidance. In what measure are you looking for honesty or needing support? Being clear will help avoid crossed wires.

RECORD YOURSELF

For many of us, watching ourselves on video or hearing ourselves on audio is unpleasant at best. But it can be enormously illuminating, enabling us to hear our own tone and see our own behavior in ways that are normally invisible to us.

Audiotaping her weekly brainstorming meeting is what helped Zoe identify one of her blind spots. She prides herself on nurturing creativity and was shocked to hear through the grapevine that her nickname among coworkers is Annie Oakley, as in "she shoots down every idea." So she asked if one of her team members could use a smartphone to record a few of their meetings. Asking a team member to take on the task not only gave the team some control, it also alleviated worries that she might be collecting data on *them* rather than on herself.

Zoe was stunned when she listened to the recording. "The first words out of my mouth are *always* negative. Whenever someone offered an idea, my first move was to challenge it. 'Here's what I'm worried about,' or 'Here's why I doubt that can work.' It's so obvious on the recording, but I had no idea I was doing it."

Zoe immediately understood what was going on. She genuinely believes that fresh ideas are the lifeblood of the company, but she also fears wasting time. Her anxiety about that possibility undermined the conversation, as she invited ideas but then immediately invoked concerns about going down unfruitful paths. Armed with this awareness, she and her team are now working to manage the tension together.

Technology for collecting information about your blind spots is ever evolving. At the MIT Human Dynamics lab, Sandy Pentland and colleagues have developed electronic badges and smartphone apps that gather data as people interact throughout the day. Designed to track tone, pitch, pace, gestures, and other nonverbal cues, these devices help the researchers examine how such social signals influence productivity and decision making.[12] Some of their initial findings are startling: Across contexts as different as business teams, speed-dating, and political opinion polling, approximately 40 percent of variation in outcomes can be attributed to social signaling, behavior mostly occurring in our own blind spots. In other words, the content of the conversation— the business pitch, the five-minute date, or the polling question— wasn't all that different. But the successful pitches, prospects, and pollsters showed aligned social signals with their counterparts. Talkers and listeners smiled, were more animated, vocal pitch rose, and gestures got in sync.

By looking only at these signals the MIT researchers can predict successful or unsuccessful outcomes. Their technology has been used to help those with autism see and understand social cues; soon they may be helping us all understand the impact we have as leaders, colleagues, and family members on those around us, and on the outcomes we get.

FOCUS ON CHANGE FROM THE INSIDE OUT

When Annabelle was given feedback that colleagues found her contemptuous, she heard the problem as being about her behavior: "They don't like it when I act disrespectful, so I'll work on acting respectful."

But her colleagues didn't want her to *seem* respectful; they wanted her to *feel* respectful. Annabelle should assume that people will ultimately read her true attitude and feelings, whatever they are. So she has two choices. She can either (1) discuss her true feelings—explain why she is frustrated with her colleagues, where her expectations come from, and what would help; or (2) work hard to change her feelings— not how she comes across, but her genuine underlying feelings.

Option (1), perhaps surprisingly, can take a lot of the pressure off.

Annabelle can make her expectations explicit and then problem solve with the team: Are the expectations realistic? If so, how do we get team members to meet them? And what is Annabelle doing that might be hindering them from stepping up? If she's second-guessing their efforts, it won't take long for them to stop first-guessing.

Option (2) requires Annabelle to negotiate with her own feelings and attitudes. It's not about pretending or concealing, it's about developing authentic empathy and appreciation for her colleagues. She may need to see her colleagues' efforts in a new way, get to know them better as people, or work harder to see what they are doing well.

As she negotiates with herself, she can enlist the support of her team: "I get frustrated easily when I'm under pressure. I'm learning that I show it in ways I didn't realize. I'm working on reacting better under pressure, and you can help me by pointing out my reaction in the moment."

Just acknowledge the pattern that everyone already sees, and be clear that you're trying hard to change.

HAVE A PURPOSE

This chapter is subtitled "Discover How You Come Across." We should be clear that we mean that in the context of someone having feedback for you. We aren't urging you to make sure you know everything about how everyone sees you, whether you want to or not, and whether they want you to or not.[13] People have all sorts of complex thoughts about us; some of their negative thoughts would surprise us, and some of their positive thoughts might surprise us even more.

In most circumstances, knowing that someone has a generally favorable view of us is all we need to know. If not the whole story, it's true enough, and it serves us well to feel that other people think well of us. It helps us feel comfortable, confident, and happy.

That reasoning breaks down, though, when someone is trying to give us feedback. That's when it's important to work to learn more about how they see you on this front, either because it will help them or because it will help you. That's when illuminating your blind spots makes a difference.

Summary: SOME KEY IDEAS

We all have blind spots because we:

- can't see our own leaky faces
- can't hear our tone of voice
- are unaware of even big patterns of behavior

Blind spots are amplified by:

- Emotional Math: We discount our emotions, while others count them double.
- Attribution: We attribute our failure to the situation, while others attribute it to our character.
- Impact-Intent Gap: We judge ourselves by our intentions, while others judge us by our impact on them.

To see ourselves and our blind spots we need help from others.

Invite others to be an honest mirror to help you see yourself in the moment.

Ask: How am I getting in my own way?

RELATIONSHIP TRIGGERS

and the challenge of
WE

Relationship Triggers (and the challenge of WE)

In the prior section, we looked at truth triggers and the challenge to *see* the feedback clearly. In this section we examine relationship triggers. Here, our reactions are caused not by the feedback itself, but by our relationship with the person giving us the feedback. This is the challenge of *we*. The question of who is offering us feedback doesn't seem like it should matter. Regardless of the source, the advice is either wise or foolish, the ideas worthwhile or worthless. But it *does* matter. We are often more triggered by the person giving us feedback than by the feedback itself. In fact, relationship triggers may be the most common derailers of feedback conversations.

In chapters 2, 3, and 4, we looked at truth triggers—ways we get thrown off by the content of the feedback. In chapters 5 and 6, we explore the common reasons we get thrown off based not on the *what* of feedback, but on the who, where, when, why, and how. Each of which really just comes back to the who. "You're telling me this *now*, at my best friend's wedding? Seriously?" We disqualify that feedback because how, when, where, and why it arrives says something damning about the who. *Therefore, I don't have to listen.*

In chapter 5, we observe that we can dismiss feedback because of how we feel *treated by* the giver—for example, they are being unfair or disrespectful. And we can also dismiss feedback based on what we think *about* the giver—perhaps we believe they have no credibility, or we suspect they have bad intentions. We'll show you how you can learn and benefit from feedback even when it's delivered poorly or comes from someone you don't like or trust. And we'll take a look at why in the world you'd want to.

The feedback we talk about in chapter 5 could be about anything—how to eat healthier, or your revenue numbers this year. In chapter 6, we look at feedback that is actually created by the relationship itself. Feedback is often prompted by differences, incompatibilities, or friction between you and the giver. The giver is suggesting that if you would change ("Be on time!" or "Quit being so controlling!"), the problem would be solved. We often react by asserting that *we* are not the real problem, *they* are. The problem is not that we are five minutes late; it's that they are so uptight. And we wouldn't need to be so controlling if they would get off their backside and take some initiative.

So they think we are the problem and we think they are the problem. We'll show you why feedback in relationships is rarely about you *or* me. It's usually about you *and* me and our relationship system. Understanding relationship systems helps you move past blame and into joint accountability, and talk productively about these challenging topics, even when the other person thinks this feedback party is all about you.

As you read the next two chapters, have a couple of feedback givers in mind from your own life. What makes hearing feedback from them so hard, and what might you learn from them, even so?

5

DON'T SWITCHTRACK

Disentangle What from Who

In an episode of the HBO sitcom *Lucky Louie*, Louie comes home after a hard day's work at the auto body shop for a long-anticipated romantic weekend with his wife, Kim. He has a gift for her—red roses—which he presents with a flourish. Kim looks disappointed, and after a moment she gives Louie some advice.

Kim: Listen. Try not to take this the wrong way, okay? But if we're going to be married for the next 30 years, I need you to know that red roses are not my thing. I really don't like red roses.

Louie: Okay, well, can I critique how you just told me that? It's not that big a deal. I just think that you should have thanked me for the flowers first, and *then* said the thing about the roses.

Kim: I've told you before that I don't like red roses. Remember that?

Louie: But still, I was thinking of you, so I bought you flowers.

Kim: If you were thinking of me, you wouldn't have gotten me red roses.

Louie: Oh, come on, Kim, I brought you flowers. That's a nice thing! You say thank you. It's called being polite.

Kim: You know what would be polite? If when I told you things, you actually listened!

Louie: Hang on, all I'm asking for here is a tiny bit of gratitude. So maybe they're not your favorite kind of flowers—

Kim: No, I didn't say *not my favorite*, I said, *Don't bring me red roses.*

Louie: What is wrong with you? Are you allergic to saying thank you to people?!

Kim: How do you expect someone to thank you for giving them something they specifically told you they don't want?

Louie: You know what's a better question? How you get given red
roses and turn around and act like this?![1]

Argument: 1. Romantic Weekend: 0.

What happened? The surface story is clear enough: Louie gives Kim
roses, Kim gives Louie feedback, and then they have a fight. Of course,
their reactions suggest that this conversation is about something
deeper: It's not about the roses, it's about the relationship.

RELATIONSHIP TRIGGERS
CREATE SWITCHTRACK CONVERSATIONS

Kim's feedback trips a relationship trigger for Louie.

Her feedback is simple: I don't like or want red roses. More important,
she's frustrated because Louie should *know* she doesn't like red roses—
not because she expects him to read her mind but because she's told
him so, many times. The roses are Exhibit A for her long-standing feeling that Louie doesn't listen to her. Later in the episode Kim explains:

*When I tell you things and you don't listen, it's a huge insult to me. It
makes me feel like I don't matter.*

How does Louie respond to Kim's feedback? He changes the subject,
entirely and completely. But wait—Kim is talking about red roses, and
Louie is talking about red roses. Same topic, right?

But it's not. Kim is using the red roses to raise how she feels unseen
and unheard. Louie walks right past the topic of how Kim feels and
talks instead about his own topic: how *he* feels unappreciated. There's
nothing wrong with that reaction or that topic, but it has zero overlap
with Kim's topic. Now we have two people giving feedback and no one
receiving it.

The dynamic that Louie and Kim have fallen into is so common that
we've given it a name: a switchtrack conversation. Their conversation
gets smoothly shifted, as if by railroad switch, from one topic to two.
Soon they are each heading in their own direction, moving farther and
farther apart.

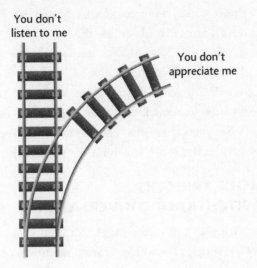

A key part of the dynamic here is that the person receiving the original feedback is unaware that they are changing the subject. Louie does not switch topics to avoid Kim's feedback. He switches topics because he feels triggered. When Kim says she doesn't like red roses, Louie feels hurt and frustrated. For him, Kim's lack of appreciation *is* the topic of the exchange. His emotions shunt the conversation sideways, and Louie heads off down his own track.

SWITCHTRACKING DEFEATS FEEDBACK

Switchtracking has two potential impacts, one good and one bad. The potentially positive impact is that the second topic being put on the table may be important—sometimes more important than the feedback that triggered it. We may have hesitated to raise it earlier, but here it is, finally out in the open. And now that it's out in the open, we can deal with it.

The negative impact is that because we now have two topics, the conversation gets tangled. Dealing with two topics is not a problem in itself—we can address two, twelve, or twenty in a single sitting. But with switchtrack conversations, we don't *realize* there are two separate topics, and so both get lost as we each hear the other person through the filter of our own topic.

When Kim says: "How do you expect someone to thank you for

something they specifically said they don't want?" her topic is "Louie not listening," and this statement says so. But if the comment is heard through Louie's "Kim is ungrateful" topic filter, then the statement itself is further evidence of Kim's ingratitude. What do Kim and Louie learn in this feedback conversation? They each "learn" what they already know: that Louie won't listen even when being told he doesn't listen. And that Kim is selfish and rude, and Louie just can't win.

SILENT SWITCHTRACKING CAN BE WORSE

Sometimes the second track in a switchtrack isn't out in the open, but runs underground. Our reactions remain locked in our heads, silently shouting objections while we resentfully endure the criticism from our stepdaughter or department head. We've long since switched to our own topic: *Wow, you're telling me to calm down? You're the most tightly wound person I've ever met in my life. And I guess I now have to add un–self-aware.* We then walk away and vent our frustrations to others. ("Is Jenna the most neurotic person on the planet, or just this hemisphere? I can't decide.") We triangulate the conflict and short-circuit learning in all directions.

TWO RELATIONSHIP TRIGGERS

So the switchtrack dynamic has four steps: we get feedback; we experience a relationship trigger; we change the topic to how *we* feel; and, step four, we talk past each other. To get better at managing our impulse to switchtrack, we have to get better at understanding the relationship triggers that create these impulses. Below, we look at two key kinds of relationship triggers: (1) what we think about the giver, and (2) how we feel treated by the giver.

WHAT WE THINK *ABOUT* THEM

There are people we admire so much that their actions and advice take on a golden glow. Our default assumption is that their input is wise, thoughtful, deep—just the thing we need to hear. We hang on their every word and strive to emulate them. Their feedback comes preapproved.

What We Think *About* Them

Skill or Judgment: How, when, or where they gave the feedback.

Credibility: They don't know what they're talking about.

Trust: Their motives are suspect.

Then there's everybody else. Feedback from these others may not be pre*dis*qualified, but we are on higher alert. We can disqualify the giver on any number of grounds—the most common involving trust, credibility, and the (lack of) skill or judgment with which they deliver their feedback. And once we disqualify the giver, we reject the substance of the feedback without a second thought. Based on the *who*, we discard the *what*.

Skill or Judgment:
How, When, or Where They Gave the Feedback

The first and easiest target is *how, when,* and *where* the feedback is offered (all of which reflect directly on the *who*). The giver fails to handle the giving with appropriate care; how they give it shows a lack of skill; when and where they give it shows a lack of judgment.

"Why would you say that in front of my fiancé?"

"You waited until now to bring this up?"

"You should have thanked me for the flowers first, and then said the thing about the roses."

We are (often justifiably) outraged by where, when, and how, and a classic switchtrack ensues. We engage in a heated exchange about how inappropriate it was that our anger management problem was raised in front of a client, but never circle back to discuss the actual anger management problem. I'm on my track, you're on yours, and we soon lose sight of each other.

Credibility: They Don't Know What They're Talking About

We can also react to the giver's lack of expertise, background, and experience. He's never started a business; she's never coached organized soccer. He has lived his whole life in Dodge City, Kansas, and is offering his "wisdom" about the immigrant experience. They are full of parenting pointers because they aren't parents. Why should we listen to them?

These are all reasonable reactions. Yet the fact remains that we can often benefit from the insight of newcomers or outsiders unencumbered by knowledge of "the way things are done." They might ask just the right "naïve" question, or offer a unique perspective. It's not entirely surprising that the MP3 technology that revolutionized the music industry, and the smartphone technology that changed telecommunications, came from outside those worlds. New ideas often come from those without traditional credibility, who are freer to think outside the box precisely because they don't know there is a box. History abounds with examples of battles won thanks to the insight of a junior corporal with a deft suggestion.

Even in personal relationships, a fresh perspective can cut through a complicated history and the elaborate rationales we construct over time. A new friend can see ways in which an old friend isn't being fair, or make a suggestion that could ease a dynamic between you and your half brother that is entrenched in habit and history. When someone asks, "Why do you let your business partner put you down so much?," pause before you explain what she's like and how you have to know her to understand. And consider whether their ideas for changing the situation just might help.

The other kind of credibility issue that triggers reactions has to do with values and identity. We don't want to be the kind of leaders— or the kind of people—that they are. So why would we take their coaching?

Fair enough. If they're coaching you on how to deceive your spouse or how to embezzle from the pension fund, by all means, proceed with caution. Yet more often other people's coaching is aimed at helping you navigate the complex environment you share, or dealing with road-blocks in the distance that they have already seen up close. There are often aspects of their counsel that are helpful or even wise, even as you choose to implement them in a way that is more consistent with your own values.

It's not that credibility and background knowledge are irrelevant. Their experience is a factor in weighing the feedback's usefulness, but don't use it to automatically reject their counsel.

Trust: Their Motives Are Suspect

"Trust" in this context refers to the giver's motivations, and is fundamental to our willingness to consider other people's coaching, accept their evaluation, or believe their appreciation genuine.

> **The Rabbit Hole of Intentions**
>
> You want to hurt me.
> You're projecting your own issues onto me.
> You want to show me who's boss.
> You're playing favorites.
> You're threatened by me.
> You have no filter and can't stop blurting out stupid things.
> You're just jealous.
> You're building a case against me.
> You're being nice, but not honest.
> You're trying to control me.
> You're more than a little nuts.

Mistrust can get triggered in several ways. Sometimes we fear that the giver's intentions are nefarious. We don't trust the feedback because the person giving it seems out to undermine or control us. Or we may simply doubt that they have our best interests at heart. Or they might not care about us one way or the other—they're giving us feedback so they can check that obligatory box.

That's fine, we'll check "feedback received" and be on our way.

Other times you wonder if they're telling the truth. Are they saying nice things about your work because they think it's good or because they're too wishy-washy to tell you how they really feel? And what are they saying behind your back?

Intentions are rarely explicitly stated, and even when they are, we may or may not believe them. You say you are "just trying to help," but it sure seems as if you are "just trying to get me fired." The challenge here, as we've seen, is that intentions are invisible. They are locked up in the giver's head, where even the giver may not be fully aware of them. And this makes intentions tricky. We care deeply about others' intentions but we simply can't know them.[2] And so we go down the rabbit hole of trying to guess, and burrow around in the dark. When we finally emerge, we're still uncertain, or worse, we think we know their intentions when we don't. It's not that we should therefore assume good intentions. We should just be aware that we *don't know*, which makes arguing about intentions a conversational dead end.

And besides, the question of intentions is a separate topic from the accuracy or helpfulness of feedback. The giver might be jealous or mean-spirited or totally nuts, and yet their feedback might be dead right, the most useful thing we've heard in months. Or maybe they really and truly do have our best interests at heart. But their suggestion that you wear those yellow leather leggings to the office? Still a bad idea.

So treat trust and content as separate topics, because they *are* separate topics. Explore what might make sense about the feedback itself. And you can share with the giver the impact that their feedback has had on you, without insisting that you're sure of their intentions. Don't use the relationship trigger of trust to automatically disqualify the feedback.

SURPRISE PLAYERS IN THE FEEDBACK GAME

Relationship triggers based on what we think about a giver help explain why our best friends can tell us things that others cannot. If we trust them and think they have credibility on a particular topic (on career advice but not love life advice, or vice versa), we will be inclined to be more receptive to their feedback.

Relationship triggers also explain why sometimes those closest to us *can't* give us feedback, no matter how well intentioned or accurate.

Strangers

Fred was leaning on his crutch, studying the café menu, when a woman tapped him on the shoulder. "I don't mean to intrude," she said, "but I notice that you're using those crutches the same way I used mine last year. Apparently it's not the best way to handle them, and I ended up injuring my hip. I spent six weeks recovering from the original injury and six months recovering from the misuse of the crutches."

The woman showed Fred how to adjust his grip and stride, and he arrived home excited to show his girlfriend Eva what he'd learned. Eva was indignant: "I've been telling you that for weeks. You ignore *me* but the minute some stranger says the same thing, you're sold?"

Indeed. The advice was identical, but the person giving it changed. And that removed the relationship trigger that blocked the feedback when it came from his girlfriend. In Fred's view, Eva rather enjoys bossing him around, something he enjoys rather less. And she has never been on crutches, so what does she know? The café stranger? A whole different story. Why would the stranger say anything unless she was trying to help? And she established right up front that she had walked in Fred's (orthotic) shoes. Credibility. No ulterior motives. Feedback taken.

Those You Least Like and Who Are Least Like You

The other surprisingly valuable players in the feedback game are the people you find *most difficult*. That woman down in Procurement who constantly pesters you for paperwork? The client overseas who seems to think you're an idiot? That relative who makes every family gathering all about her, including funerals? That's who we're talking about.

You don't trust them. You don't like them. They say all the wrong things at all the wrong times. Why in the world would you listen to feedback from *them*?

Because they have a unique perspective on you. We tend to like people who like us and who are *like* us.[3] So if you live mostly without friction with your mate or work well with a colleague, chances are you have similar styles, assumptions, and habits. Your preferences and expectations may not be identical, but the two of you fall into an easy complementariness. Because of this ease, you are often at your best and most productive with them.

They can't help you with your sharpest edges because they don't see those edges. The woman in Procurement does. She thinks you're arrogant, flip, irresponsible. Unpleasant, curt, avoidant. You know the problem is her—she brings out your worst. But it is *your* worst. It's you under pressure, you in conflict.

It's here that we often have the most room to grow. When we are under stress or in conflict we lose skills we normally have, impact others in ways we don't see, are at a loss for positive strategies. We *need* honest mirrors in these moments, and often that role is played best by those with whom we have the hardest time.

If that overseas client thinks you're an idiot, then there's something going on that you're not "getting," and without her help, you're not going to get it. It may be a cultural difference that you need to understand if you're going to be effective in her market. It may be that your tone and word choice are upsetting her in ways you don't realize. That's worth figuring out. And you'll need her help to do it.

Want to fast-track your growth? Go directly to the people you have the hardest time with. Ask them what you're doing that's exacerbating the situation. They will surely tell you.

HOW WE FEEL TREATED *BY* THEM

The first type of relationship trigger derives from what we think about the feedback giver. The second type comes from how we feel treated *by* them.

Whether professional or personal, casual or intimate, we expect many things from our relationships. Among these there are three key relationship interests that commonly get snagged on the brambles of feedback: our needs for appreciation, autonomy, and acceptance.

> **How We Feel Treated *By* Them**
>
> **Appreciation:** Do they see our efforts and successes?
>
> **Autonomy:** Are we given appropriate space and control?
>
> **Acceptance:** Do they respect or accept who we are (now)?

Appreciation

Since her stroke three years ago, you have been your sister's primary caretaker. It has been a challenge. As your exhaustion grows, your patience is stretched thin. This morning you snapped at your sister, and her son happened to be nearby. And he snapped, too: "Don't *ever* talk to Mom that way!"

Fine. He is right. But where's the appreciation for years of caretaking? Where's the acknowledgment for showering and changing her every day; where's the appreciation for how you've fed her and held her and carried her? You understand why your nephew was upset, but in the bigger picture, his feedback is deeply, maybe even hatefully, unfair and out of balance. At least, this is how it feels to you in the moment.

We can be triggered even when a relationship is good and the matter at hand is minor. Ernie gladly covered for Samantha when she took a few days off to visit colleges with her son. When Samantha returned, the first thing she did was question why Ernie hadn't managed to call a client back. There's no simmering history between them, but Ernie is triggered. He doesn't say, "This feedback is great because it's helping me learn how to deal with your clients in a more timely fashion." He says, "What is wrong with you?!" Not because Samantha's feedback is wrong, but because to Ernie it feels unbalanced. And because his expectations of a warm thank-you were so sharply overturned.

This kind of swift reversal is also part of what triggers Louie: I am doing something nice for you, and your reaction is not just neutral, it's negative. In a flash Louie goes from happy to hurt. Whether Kim's feedback is valid or not, he can't hear it. He's still smarting from the unexpected sting.

Autonomy

Autonomy is about control, and in telling us what to do or how to do it, givers can trip this wire in an instant. Often our boundaries are invisible—to others and even to us—until they have been violated. That's when the contours suddenly crystallize.

As kids we're constantly negotiating these boundaries with our parents—"*I'm* in charge of the Cheerios on my highchair tray and I'll sweep them onto the floor if I damn well please." We continue to negotiate these boundaries as adults. Your boss does not get to give you feedback on your e-mail to your team before you send it out. It's *your* e-mail to *your* team about *your* Cheerios marketing campaign. At least, that's how you see it.

We are particularly sensitive to encroachments that seek to control who we are. "Back off," we want to say. "I control my attitudes; I control my behaviors; I control my personality; I control how I dress and walk and talk. When you give me this sort of feedback you are not only violating boundaries, you are misunderstanding your role in my life."

My autonomy map and your autonomy map will occasionally clash, raising questions about who gets to decide. That's a negotiation, and an important set of conversations to have, clearly and explicitly. We can imagine situations where we would empathize with the feedback receiver ("If I have to clear every e-mail to my team with headquarters, we'll never get anything done") and others in which we'd side with the feedback giver ("You're new here, and it's my responsibility to make sure your e-mails comport with our organization's norms"). Whichever way we decide, simply realizing that we're triggered not by the advice itself but by being told what to do will help us address the correct topic. We can have an explicit conversation about the appropriate boundaries of autonomy instead of a pointless argument about whether your suggested grammatical changes to my e-mail make sense.[4]

Acceptance

It's the paradox at the heart of many feedback conversations: We find it hard to take feedback from someone who doesn't accept us the way we are now.

My dad is full of advice. I might be able to hear it if, for once, he'd just say, "You know, kid, you turned out okay."

Nothing I do is ever good enough for my boss. My very presence on her team seems to agitate her, but she knows she needs what I do.

My ex, at the end of the day, simply wanted me to be a different person.

This is complex terrain. The givers want us to change in some way. We want to know that it's okay if we don't. You say you love me in spite of my flaws; I want you to love me *because* of them.

One dynamic that contributes to the challenge is that the giver and receiver may define acceptance differently. What to the giver seems like a recommendation for a small behavioral tweak may feel to the receiver like a rejection of Who I Am.

That's what's going on with David and Cheng. David often gives Cheng advice on climbing the ladder of success: "There's no one more talented than you, but in this industry, image is as important as substance. If you want to get plucked from the chorus line, you've got to kick high."

Cheng finds David's coaching inane and insulting. He explains to David that that's not who he is. If he advances it will be on merit, and if he doesn't advance, at least he lived his life his way. It's not worth sacrificing the humility and authenticity at the core of his identity to become a phony, self-promoting windbag.

David finds Cheng's reaction puzzling. In his mind, he is suggesting a small adjustment to Cheng's behavior that would pay big dividends. It has nothing to do with "who Cheng really is." What he's recommending is superficial—that's the point. David wonders whether Cheng's "this is who I am" mantra is really just a way to insulate himself from criticism.

That raises the second sticky issue around acceptance and change. When we say, "accept me as I am," are we really just asking for immunity from critique? Forgot to pick up the kids after school? That's just who I am! Lost my temper in front of our new funders? Just me being me! Crashed the car after too many drinks at the party? C'est moi!

While we all need to feel accepted as we are, we also need to hear feedback—particularly when our behavior is affecting others. Being accepted isn't an escape hatch from responsibility for consequences, as we discuss in more detail in chapter 10. So, seek acceptance. *And* work to make amends with the kids and with the funders (and with the car).

RELATIONSHIP TRIGGERS: WHAT HELPS?

The goal here isn't to dismiss the relationship issues that trigger reactions. As we've said, sometimes the second topic is at least as important as the first. The goal is to get better at realizing when we've got two topics on the table, and to address each on the merits rather than letting one get tangled up in, or cancel out, the other.

There are three moves that can help us manage relationship triggers and avoid switchtracking. First, we need to be able to spot the two topics on the table (the original feedback and the relationship concern). Next, we need to give each topic its own conversation track (and get both people on the same track at the same time). Third, we need to help givers be clearer about their original feedback, especially when the feedback itself relates to the relationship.

SPOT THE TWO TOPICS

The first skill is awareness. We can't give each topic its own track unless we are aware that there are two topics. Let's take spotting practice. Find the switchtrack in the following examples:

> **Daughter:** Mom, you never let me go out. You treat me like a child. Don't you trust me?
>
> **Mom:** You should be grateful you have a mother who cares.

Topic one is the daughter's view that her mother treats her like an untrustworthy child. The mother responds by switchtracking to topic two: her feeling that her daughter is ungrateful (an appreciation trigger). Better for Mom to stay on topic one. She could ask about the daughter's views: "Let's talk about how you'd like to be treated." Or she could clarify her own thinking about trust: "I want to trust you, and that needs to be earned. . . ." Once they have this conversation, Mom could circle back and raise the question of whether her daughter is grateful and what that means to each of them.

> **Boss:** You didn't meet your sales numbers.

Salesperson: Why are you telling me this right before I head out on vacation?

Topic one is the sales numbers. Topic two is the appropriate time to raise the sales numbers (skill/judgment of the giver).

Wife: This place is a mess! You were supposed to have the kids fed and bathed by the time I got home. Now we'll be late for the recital!

Husband: Don't use that tone with me. I'm not the dog!

Wife: That's where you want to go with this? You did precisely none of the things you promised, and you're making this about me?

Husband: That! That tone right there is exactly what I'm talking about.

Topic one is how the wife feels about her husband not doing what he'd promised. Topic two is the wife's tone and the husband's reaction to it (skill/how, autonomy).

A pedestrian pounds on our car as we sit at a red light. He shouts: "You're in the crosswalk!" We honk and shout: "Don't you dare pound on my car!"

Topic one is the pedestrian's feedback to us that we shouldn't be in the crosswalk. Topic two is our feedback to the pedestrian that he shouldn't pound on our car (autonomy/skill). We will be tempted to focus only on the pounding and not on the original feedback, but the feedback may be legitimate. If we have a tendency to encroach on crosswalks, we may not realize that we make it harder for people in wheelchairs or with kids to make it comfortably across the street.

GIVE EACH TOPIC ITS OWN TRACK

Okay, you've spotted the two topics. Now what?

Signposting

At the point at which you realize there are two topics running simultaneously, say that out loud and propose a way forward. Just like the signal that directs train traffic at the switch, you're offering a directional sign to mark the junction where two tracks—the two topics—are splitting.

Ella is a teacher's assistant who works with children with disabilities. She spends extra time with the children before and after school, and uses her evenings to design activities and collect art supplies. The teacher Ella assists offers very little in the way of coaching or appreciation, and Ella, not wishing to make waves, hasn't requested any.

Eight months into the school year, the teacher speaks up: "You're spending too much time focused on Howard. There are nine other children in this class." Ella is shocked and thinks: *After eight months, the first piece of feedback I get is that I'm caring about a child* too much? *Have you noticed what I mean to these kids? Have you noticed what I put into this job?* Her switchtracking is silent—her objections aren't spoken aloud—but her upset is likely leaking out as she quickly escapes into the hallway.

As Ella calms down, she gains some awareness and thinks: *Oh, there are two topics here. One is whether I'm spending too much time with Howard, and the other is the one that's triggering me right now—feeling totally unappreciated, especially since I haven't gotten any appreciation or coaching all year long.*

The next step is signposting. Ella goes back to the classroom and says to the teacher: "Let's talk about Howard and how I'm spending my time. That's important. This is also the first time I've gotten feedback. So after we talk about Howard, I want us to come back to the question of how I get feedback and what you notice in my work with the kids that is positive."

The template for signposting is this: "I see two related but separate topics for us to discuss. They are both important. Let's discuss each topic fully but separately, giving each topic its own track. After we've finished discussing the first topic, we'll swing back around and discuss the second one."

Of course normal people don't talk this way, and signposting isn't a natural move for most of us. It requires us to step outside the conversation and look in on it. In fact, it's that absence of flow that is one of the reasons it's so helpful. It breaks the normal reactive conversation pattern by being hyper-explicit about what's going on. Use your own words, but be clear.

Which topic should you discuss first? There are two factors to consider. First, an edge should be given to the original feedback. That's what the other person wanted to discuss, and all things being equal, you're better off starting with their topic. But the second factor to take into account is emotion. If your relationship trigger reaction is so strong that it gets in the way of your being able to take in what they are saying, then you should say so and propose that your topic be discussed first. This will help you hear their topic, and at the end of the day, that's what they care about most.

LISTEN FOR THE RELATIONSHIP ISSUES LURKING BENEATH THEIR "ADVICE"

Even when we are alert enough to resist switchtracking, we can fall into another common trap: We stay on the giver's topic (their track), but we misunderstand what that topic is. This happens in part because of the often-clumsy way givers raise their concerns. Our giver says he is giving us "friendly advice" to help us improve, when really he is raising a deeper relationship issue between us. We take the comment at face value and assume we understand. But we don't.

Remember Louie and Kim. Notice that what Kim says when she first offers Louie coaching is essentially: "If you want to give me a gift, I don't like roses." One could be forgiven for thinking the topic is gift giving. But as things play out, it becomes clear that Kim's topic is actually her feelings of being unheard.

This is common. Often when we feel hurt, frustrated, ignored, offended, or anxious, we try to keep feelings out of the picture. We use the guise of well-intended coaching to instead offer a selection of "tips." But we're not really offering coaching for the other person's benefit. We're hoping they will change for *our* benefit.

So when you receive coaching, a question to ask yourself is this: Is this about helping me grow and improve, or is this the giver's way of raising an important relationship issue that has been upsetting them?

"You might want to be more responsive"

might mean: "I'm frustrated that you don't return my calls."

"I think you'd be happier if you didn't think about work night and day"

might mean: "You're so preoccupied with work that it's lonely for me."

"If you delegate some of your workload to me you'll have more time for the important things"

might mean: "I want you to trust me with more responsibility."

"You're drinking too much. It's not good for you"

might mean: "I'm worried about your drinking, and it's getting in the way of our relationship."

Why does it matter if I misunderstand their topic? Sometimes it doesn't. If I drink less, it will be good for me, as well as a relief for them. But if I take their coaching simply as a suggestion for me, I may reasonably disagree about what makes me happy. I may say, "Actually, when I work less, I get restless." Case closed, let's move on. But if their concern is that they feel lonely, I've missed the real topic altogether.

This is not to say that every piece of coaching you get is really hurt feelings in a coaching disguise. Don't simply assume there is always something deeper going on. Instead, check: Are we on the same track? What is the real topic here?

In fact, sometimes even the giver doesn't realize that their coaching comes primarily from their own anxiety or frustration. Your mother asks, "Why aren't you married yet? I don't think you're really making an effort to meet people." Your mother is giving you (unwanted) coaching, yes. And the temptation will be to:

(a) Argue with her assessment ("That's not true, I *am* making an effort"); or
(b) Switchtrack in reaction to not feeling accepted ("I'm perfectly happy being single. Why are you always trying to change me?"); or
(c) Switchtrack to protect your autonomy ("Mom, I'm thirty-eight years old. I can run my own life!" To which she will respond: "Apparently not").

Listen to your own autonomy and acceptance triggers. But also listen for the fears and concerns underlying your mother's advice, which may be at the heart of what's going on for her. Instead of arguing with her dating advice, ask: "What are you worried about?" You might learn any of the following:

I'm worried you don't understand that it will get harder as you get older.

I'm worried you'll end up with someone you don't like (like I did).

I'm worried you'll end up with someone I don't like.

I'm worried you won't be able to support yourself.

I wonder whether you ever take my advice (you don't seem to).

I wonder whether I did something "wrong" to make it turn out this way for you.

I can't relax until you're married.

Notice that none of these worries is really about dating strategies, the initial subject of her "coaching." Understanding her concerns will also help ease your own relationship triggers—this is less about accepting who you are, and more about her worries about who she is, and her worries for you. After understanding this, you can make a good decision about whether your initial triggers around autonomy and acceptance still feel important to discuss.

LOUIE AND KIM: TAKE TWO

Once you are aware of relationship triggers and switchtrack conversations, you will see them everywhere. Like a mouse in a maze, you'll start noticing just how many places feedback conversations can split into two and sometimes three topics at once.

Let's consider how the conversation would go if instead of switchtracking, Louie responded more effectively. He might say something like, "I was hoping the flowers would make you happy, but I can tell that you're upset. Help me understand why." This would be an example of Louie's staying on Kim's track (her feedback to him) to better understand it first. Or he might signpost by saying: "Okay, I forgot you don't like roses. You should remind me again why. And then I have to say that I'm feeling a little underappreciated for my effort. We should talk about both." This would be an example of Louie's being explicit that there are two important topics on the table, each needing its own track.

Of course, if Louie (or Kim) had approached the conversation with more skill, there would be no drama, yelling, or tears. That's a problem for a TV sitcom seeking ratings. But a good thing for you and your real relationships.

Summary: SOME KEY IDEAS

We can be triggered by who is giving us the feedback.

- What we think *about* the giver: Are they credible? Do we trust them? Did they deliver our feedback with good judgment and skill?
- How we feel treated *by* the giver: Do we feel accepted? Appreciated? Like our autonomy is respected?

Relationship triggers create switchtrack conversations, where we have two topics on the table and talk past each other.

Spot the two topics and give each its own track.

Surprise players in the feedback game:

- Strangers
- People we find difficult

People we find difficult see us at our worst and may be especially well placed to be honest mirrors about areas where we have the most room to grow.

Listen for relationship issues lurking beneath coaching.

6

IDENTIFY THE RELATIONSHIP SYSTEM

Take Three Steps Back

You're sitting at breakfast with your wife, who is sleep-deprived and agitated. She's got some feedback for you: *Do something about the snoring.* Don't try to pin this on the dog. It's not the TV or the neighbors. "It's very simple," she says. "You snore. I can't sleep. You've got a problem. Fix it."

You wouldn't dream of blaming the dog. That's ridiculous. The real problem here is your wife. She tells the story this way: *"You snore. The End."* But you know better. Yes, you do snore. But very quietly—so quietly that it should really have its own word. Normal people are not bothered by your snoring. Your first wife never noticed it. The problem is that your current wife is hypersensitive to noise, and particularly when she is feeling stressed and anxious. With teenagers in the house, who isn't stressed and anxious? Yet she refuses to listen to your ideas for how to relax, and she won't use the white noise machine you bought her.

The problem is that your wife is too sensitive and stubborn. *The End.*

WHO IS THE PROBLEM AND WHO NEEDS TO CHANGE?

Feedback is often prompted by a problem: Something isn't working. Something isn't right. Your wife isn't getting enough sleep. Your boss claims you're not pulling your weight on the team. Your relationship with the customer is strained. The new guy is turning out to be a more irritating coworker than you'd planned on. Not surprisingly, feedback follows, in one direction or another.

Nothing wrong with that. When something goes wrong, we need to be able to talk about it so that we can figure it out and fix it.

But here's where things get strange. When we are the ones *giving* the feedback, we know we are offering "constructive criticism" and helpful coaching. We're confident that we've correctly identified the cause of the problem, and we're stepping up to address it.

Yet when we're on the *receiving* end of this kind of feedback, we don't hear it as "constructive" anything. We hear it as blame: *This is your fault. You are the problem. You need to change.* And that feels incredibly unfair, because we are not the problem, it is *not* our fault, at least not *only* our fault: *If you'd stop being so stubborn and use that white noise machine there wouldn't be a problem.*

Even for the most thoughtful among us, it's not easy to put our finger on exactly why these perspectives feel so different. It has to be more than just a matter of which side of the feedback conversation we're on, doesn't it?

It does. But to see why, we need to understand relationship systems.

SEE THE RELATIONSHIP SYSTEM

A "system" is a set of interacting or interdependent components that forms a complex whole. Each part in the system influences other parts in the system; changing one thing has a ripple effect elsewhere. A relationship is a system, a team is a system, and an organization is a system. The food chain is an example of part of the ecosystem; the way you and your daughter communicate almost exclusively via text messaging is part of your current parent-teenager system.

When something goes wrong in a system, we each see some things the other doesn't, and these observations are not randomly distributed between us. When something goes wrong, I tend to see the things that *you* did that led to it, and you tend to see the things *I* did. You know that I'm snoring, and I know that you're sensitive. You know that I missed the deadline, and I know that you always give me false deadlines (apparently until now).

So you're blaming me in good faith, and I'm indignant and turn around and blame you in good faith. We each see, genuinely, what the other is contributing to the trouble, and we each believe we shouldn't be taking *all* the heat for the problem.

That's Systems Insight Number Two: Each of us sees only part of the problem (the part the other person is contributing). Systems Insight Number One is this: Each of us is part of the problem. Maybe not to the same extent, but we're both involved, each affecting the other. If you didn't snore—or whatever you want to call it—your wife might be able to sleep. If your wife were less stressed—or less stubborn—she might be able to sleep. It takes the two of you *being the way you are* to create the problem. That's how systems work.

A systems view helps us understand what's producing the frustration or difficulties or mistakes (and hence prompting the feedback) in the first place. It helps us identify root causes and the ways everyone in the system is contributing to the problem. And it explains the contradictory reactions we have as givers and receivers. Receivers react defensively because they see clearly the giver's contribution to the problem, and givers are surprised by the receiver's defensiveness because the receiver's contribution is obvious to them. And it often appears to each of us that the problem could be best and most easily solved if the *other* person changed.

If we're going to have better conversations about feedback, we need a better handle on the ways that giver and receiver (and often others) are contributing to the problem under discussion. This helps us move beyond blame and defensiveness and toward understanding, and it also produces more durable solutions. Often when we look at a relationship system, we discover simple things each of us can change that will have a big impact on the whole. And that might help everyone get some sleep.

TAKE THREE STEPS BACK

Let's look at systems from three different vantage points—from close in, medium range, and wide angle. Each view enables us to see different patterns and dynamics in our relationship systems.

One Step Back: You + Me Intersections. From here we see the interaction of you and me as a pair. What is the particular you + me combination that is creating a problem, and what is each of us contributing to that?

Two Steps Back: Role Clashes. This view expands our perspective to look at the roles each of us plays on the team, in the organization, or in the family. Roles are often a crucial but largely invisible reason we bump into each other.

Three Steps Back: The Big Picture. From this frame of reference we can view the entire landscape—including other players, structures, and processes that guide and constrain the choices we each make and the outcomes we get.

ONE STEP BACK: YOU + ME INTERSECTIONS

Feedback is often expressed as "This is how you are, and that's the problem." But in relationships, "This is how you are" really means "This is how you are *in relationship to* how I am." It's the combination—the intersection of our differences—that is often causing the problem.

Your need for downtime on weekends is only a problem in relationship to my need for your attention and engagement. Your desire to empty Mom's house right after the funeral is only a problem in relationship to my desire to have time to mourn. It is not a problem that you speak only Swedish and it is not a problem that I speak only English. But together we're in trouble.

These differences often become dynamic systems, creating downward spirals of action and reaction. Sandy and Gil have a flash point around money. Sandy thinks Gil is a cheapskate; Gil thinks Sandy is a spendthrift. When Sandy and Gil were first married, their differences caused only minor squabbles. The situation darkened when Gil was laid off, and they discovered that their ways of coping with money and stress form a perfect mismatched set. When Sandy is worried, she finds comfort in habit and small luxuries. She doesn't indulge a lot these days, but that three-dollar cappuccino feels to her like a vacation from worry. Gil soothes his anxiety by keeping track of how much money they have down to the penny, and finding even symbolic ways to cut back. It helps him feel in control.

Not surprisingly, the two exchange feedback. Gil berates Sandy: "I can't understand how you can be so wasteful at exactly the time we're cutting back." And Sandy scolds Gil: "Did you really need to march back to the supermarket to exchange my Grape-Nuts for the store-brand cereal? *You're* nuts. Is saving thirty-five cents really worth all this tension?"

Each points the finger of blame at the other, and neither sees their own contribution to the dynamic. At any given moment, the feedback looks like this:

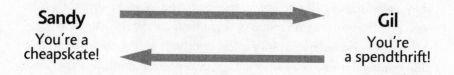

Sandy
You're a
cheapskate!

Gil
You're
a spendthrift!

But over time, there's a downward spiral. As stress increases, Gil's urge to monitor increases, which causes Sandy to crave her small pleasures even more. So she keeps her Grape-Nuts hidden in the corner cupboard, and when Gil finds the box he confronts her. Incredulous that she has gone behind his back, he feels even more out of control, and tries to clamp down harder. "You're a spendthrift" turns into "You're selfish, untrustworthy, and out of control." "You're a cheapskate" turns into "You're controlling, irrational, and overreacting." And each, on the receiving end, dismisses the other's feedback—as just more evidence of the *other's* craziness.

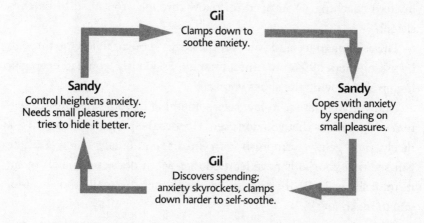

Gil
Clamps down to
soothe anxiety.

Sandy
Control heightens anxiety.
Needs small pleasures more;
tries to hide it better.

Sandy
Copes with anxiety
by spending on
small pleasures.

Gil
Discovers spending;
anxiety skyrockets, clamps
down harder to self-soothe.

Neither Sandy nor Gil sees the system. From the inside, what we see is the *other* person's behavior and its impact on us. We see ourselves as merely responding to the problem that the other person is creating.

Intersections—differences in preferences, tendencies, and traits that cause us to bump into each other—account for a significant proportion of the friction and feedback in both personal and professional relationships. Marriage researcher John Gottman reports that 69 percent of the fights married couples currently have are about the same subjects they were arguing about five years ago.[1] And chances are, they'll be selecting from that same menu of arguments five years from now.

Our own preferences, tendencies, and traits can sometimes be outside our awareness: how we manage uncertainty; how we experience novelty; what makes us feel safe; what recharges or drains our energy; how we experience conflict; whether we are detail- or big-picture-oriented, linear or random, volatile or stable, optimistic or pessimistic. In fact, we may not even realize that our own tendencies *are* tendencies until we are in the company of someone who is different. An American boy laughs when told by a British girl that he has an "American accent." Obviously, it's the Brit who has the accent.

We also don't see our own system patterns, although people outside of them can often spot their contours easily. You are exasperated with your kids: *Why do I have to ask you seven hundred times to get your shoes out of the middle of the kitchen?* Your father-in-law is visiting and offers some (uninvited) coaching: "You need to follow through. You need to be consistent."

This is enough to send you over the edge—you *are* following through by asking them 699 more times, after all. Previously, you had been giving up and moving the shoes yourself.

And yet your father-in-law sees something in your relationship system with the kids that you don't see. He sees the progression as you ask nicely, prod gently, admonish with threats, and finally lose it. And he can see that your kids have learned that Mom doesn't actually "mean it" until she yells. So they ignore you and watch TV while they wait for you to mean it.

Taking one step back means stepping outside your own perspective to observe the system as your father-in-law does. Instead of focusing on what the other person is doing wrong, notice what you are *each* doing in reaction to the other. As you do, you'll begin to spot the larger patterns. Continual pestering, which you thought was the "following through" solution, is actually reinforcing the problem.[2]

TWO STEPS BACK: ROLE CLASHES AND ACCIDENTAL ADVERSARIES

The first step back looks at you and the other person, and the way your tendencies interact and intersect. The second step back adds another layer: This is not just about you and me, this is also about the roles we play.

Roles are defined by their relationship to other roles. You're not an older sibling until you have a younger sibling; you aren't a mentor until you've got someone to "ment." Although there are personality-driven aspects to roles—I'm the funny one, you're the responsible one—roles have an effect on behavior that is independent of character. A role is like an ice cube tray into which you pour your personality. What you pour in matters, but so does the shape of the tray. Whether I'm musical or tone-deaf, humble or a braggart, if I am the cop and you are the speeder, things are likely to play out between us in reasonably predictable ways.

One important role pattern is called "accidental adversaries."[3] If two people bump into each other enough and cause each other enough frustration, each will begin considering the other an "adversary." Each attributes the problem to the personality and questionable intentions of the other. But often the true culprit is the structure of the roles they are in, which are (accidentally) creating chronic conflict. If we are each at one end of a rope and our job is to pull, then merely doing our jobs creates a tug-of-war.

The cop and the speeder might have everything in common—they could be identical twins—but in their interaction at the side of the road, their roles may create conflict. The same is true of disgruntled customers and customer reps, stressed teachers and anxious parents, ex-husbands and the new guy.

Accidental adversaries are created by two things: role confusion and role clarity.

As organizations change and responsibilities shift, roles get messy quickly. It's no longer clear where my position ends and yours begins. Ted asked me for new pricing information, and you jumped in and sent it to him before I had the chance to respond. Ted asked *me* because I'm the pricing guru; Ted didn't ask you because you are *not* the pricing guru. Except that when you tell the story, you *are* the pricing guru, and I'm the guy Ted asked by mistake. Could we really be this confused? We could.

It's impossible to overstate the extent to which role confusion exists, even in the most well-run organizations. Three of us think we're in charge of task A, and none of us thinks we're in charge of tasks B, C, and D. Globalization and virtual relationships heighten the challenges, as do reorgs, mergers, matrixed reporting lines, and every kind of employee mobility. Yesterday we were peers; today you're my boss's boss. Yesterday we shared a cubicle; today you're Skyping me from your office in Lisbon.

The permeable boundaries among departments, functions, and business units contribute to the muddle as well. If I oversee data mining for print media, why do I keep getting memos from Marketing that Barry is in charge of data mining across all media platforms, including print, and that any other reports are considered "unauthorized"?

Sometimes role clashes arise not from confusion but from clarity. The tension is embedded in the organizational structure itself. Compliance officers and traders at a bank will often be in conflict, not just because of rogue traders or overly cautious compliance officers, but because the very nature of their roles puts them at odds. Other common examples are Sales and Legal, surgeons and anesthesiologists, architects and engineers, and HR and everyone. As one HR executive joked, "In HR, we're not happy until you're not happy."

Of course, everyone knows that the HR function is crucial, but busy people can still find it intrusive. We're quick to attribute character as the cause: Those in HR are compulsive, uptight, and excessively rule-bound. On the flip side, HR is frustrated by the deadbeats across all functions who are behind on their time sheets, submit perfunctory performance reviews, and skip out on mandatory training. Why do so many of our people behave like flaky, petulant teenagers?

At the organizational level, these role tensions serve important purposes, but at the interpersonal level they can be destructive, especially if people are misidentifying the source of the conflict. It's essential to disentangle the individual from their role by taking two steps back and asking: *How are our roles contributing to how we see each other, and to the feedback we give each other?* How much is role, and how much is personality or performance? Even if you don't have an answer, just asking yourself the question, or discussing it between you, can shift awareness.

THREE STEPS BACK: THE BIG PICTURE
(OTHER PLAYERS, PROCESSES, POLICIES, AND STRUCTURES)

The third step back enables us to take in the big picture, which includes not only other players but also the physical environment, timing and decision making, policies, processes, and workaround coping strategies. All of these influence behavior and decisions, and the feedback we give one another. They are part of the system we're in.

Imagine that a worker is seriously injured working at a refinery, and you are the safety rep. It's your job to ensure that such accidents never happen again. In searching for the cause, a common tendency is to focus only on the behavior of the injured worker: Was he following protocol? How long has he been in the job? Was he fatigued or drinking? What did he do wrong?

Important questions, but you know it's about more than just this worker. So you take three steps back to consider the big picture, the whole safety landscape. If the worker was fatigued, who knew that he had worked a double shift, and how often do workers operate equipment when overtired? Who last repaired this piece of machinery, and were there notes on the repair? Was the supervisor aware that nonstandard parts were used? What has been the impact of cutbacks in safety training? How does the performance evaluation system incent, or fail to incent, safe behavior? How have changes to the work-rest rules influenced fatigue or information exchange at shift changes?

OTHER PLAYERS

Two senior leaders clash, and team members beneath them are buffeted by conflicting instructions. Innovation and risk taking are inhibited, an us-them attitude takes hold, and an inordinate amount of time is spent trying to manage and "work around" the conflict.

Conflicts between two people can profoundly affect the work patterns and relationships of others around them. Understanding what's going on often necessitates looking at the broader team, department, or cross-functional dynamics.

PHYSICAL ENVIRONMENT

The new elevator system is state-of-the-art, but the dedication to small clusters of floors means you only see people you already work with. You haven't done more than exchange e-mail with the folks downstairs in months.

The physical environment can affect how we work together. Open office space can encourage collaboration or chill candid discussion. Functions that need to work well together can end up in different buildings or different hemispheres.

TIMING AND DECISION MAKING

Francie has to put in for vacation time six months ahead; her brother Finn receives his work schedule only two weeks in advance. Francie doesn't understand why her kid brother can't get his act together to commit to the family vacation schedule, even as an adult.

Differences in structure and timing of decision making can create problems between individuals or groups. Some may need to consult widely and get buy-in from others, while others can make decisions independently.

POLICIES AND PROCESSES

Centralizing marketing in London has created a unified product marketing approach, yet Cambodia says the new campaign won't work on the ground.

Centralizing processes creates efficiencies but makes it more difficult to respond to local needs.

COPING STRATEGIES

Research is consistently late reporting their department numbers to Accounting. Accounting begins to give false deadlines. Research soon catches on, and now they take Accounting's deadlines even less seriously.

Players develop coping strategies for working with others that they find challenging. The effects will show up in the second and third rounds—so-called lag effects.

There's a balance to be struck. We don't want to waste time on a fishing expedition, and it's tempting to quit looking once we have one compelling explanation in hand. But we shouldn't overlook significant inputs and root causes simply because they are not proximate to the injury in time or place.[4]

The chart offers some big-picture factors worth watching for.

FEEDBACK THROUGH A SYSTEMS LENS

Let's step into a second-grade classroom and look at how a systems lens can help us with feedback and communication.

The second-grade teacher speaks carefully: "Your daughter Kenzie is a strong personality. She says things that upset other children." The teacher sees Kenzie as a good kid, but a bit of a bully. He is hoping that Kenzie's mom is able to take the feedback to heart.

Alas, Kenzie is eavesdropping outside the door and bursts in to protest: "Mom! Those kids are so annoying! They're the ones who start it! And I can't help it if they're crybabies!" From Kenzie's point of view, she is not the problem. She is the victim.

The feedback conversation grinds to a halt. Kenzie feels unfairly accused, the teacher is exasperated at Kenzie's unwillingness to take responsibility, and Kenzie's mom is unsure whom to believe. Let's see how we might be able to better understand the teacher's feedback about Kenzie by looking at what's going on from each of our three vantage points.

The first step back looks at individual intersections, and we see this: One difference between Kenzie and some of her classmates is simply inborn. Kenzie is a bit of a drama queen. Everything is either "amazingly fabulous" or "horribly catastrophic." She's a big personality, and among the eight-year-old set, a flair for the dramatic wins Kenzie attention.

The second step back looks at roles. Kenzie was the new kid in school last year, increasing the urgency she felt to find her niche, and also adding a touch of mystery to her persona. Her "way in" was to entertain, and kids gravitated to her, eager to hear her rendition of the teacher's "oops" moment in math or her reenactment of the "humiliation" aboard the morning bus. This encouraged Kenzie to tell even bigger and more exaggerated stories, and it was soon clear to everyone that she had taken on the role of class entertainer. Now we're starting to see the system in motion—Kenzie's behavior influences her classmates' behavior, which in turn influences her.

In contrast to Kenzie, some kids don't like being the center of attention. When one accidentally spills paint on Kenzie's poster in art class, Kenzie yells, "You are the most horrible person *ever!*" It's hard for Kenzie to understand how upsetting her oversized reaction is to a sensitive child, because it wouldn't be so upsetting for her. Other kids are more sympathetic to the accidental paint spiller. They talk among themselves about Kenzie being "mean," and begin to steer clear of her.

So far we have looked at intersections and roles. Let's take a third step back for a broader look at what happens next. The friends who stick with Kenzie are quick to tell her what so-and-so said, or who says they will never play with Kenzie again. They don't exactly mean to wind Kenzie up, but her reaction is so swift and dramatic that it only makes the friendship that much more exciting. *We are on the inside, where the cool people are; the others are losers and crybabies.* Meanwhile, those who empathize with the quieter kids are thinking this: *We have our own group, where the nice kids are; the others are the bad kids and bullies.* From an initial focus on Kenzie, we can pull back and see that there are cliques forming, and that the cliques themselves interact and contribute to the system.

Another factor in the broader system is the physical layout of the playground, which inadvertently reinforces the us-them dynamic. With part of the school under construction, the playground is left with only two four-square courts, where the girls often divide into opposing camps. School policies contribute as well: Whenever there is trouble, the offending student is sent to the principal's office, but there is no process for a reconciliation conversation among students to help them understand and repair relationships. Discipline is based on identifying and removing a single actor, and the larger system is left unaddressed.

From the teacher's perspective at the front of the classroom, the commotion centers on Kenzie. And so Kenzie's parents are called in for some feedback on how their daughter needs to change. If they take the feedback at face value and sit Kenzie down to explain that she needs to be "nicer and less harsh," Kenzie will no doubt bristle in protest. Not because she's trying to get away with something, but because the real problem, from where she sits, isn't only her. Her classmates are crybabies, and also, apparently, tattletales (tune in tomorrow morning for Kenzie's lively reporting on the injustice perpetrated at the mom-teacher meeting).

Certainly, Kenzie needs to understand the impact of her behavior on other kids, and there are things she *does* need to change. But she's not wrong that there are other people and fac-

> **Seeing Feedback in the System**
>
> **One Step Back:** In what ways does the feedback reflect differences in preferences, assumptions, styles, or implicit rules between us?
>
> **Two Steps Back:** Do our roles make it more or less likely that we might bump into each other?
>
> **Three Steps Back:** What other players influence our behavior and choices? Are physical setups, processes, or structures also contributing to the problem?
>
> **Circling Back to Me:** What am I doing (or failing to do) that is contributing to the dynamic between us?

tors contributing to the problem. If the teacher and Kenzie's mom (and even Kenzie herself) are able to discuss the larger system, Kenzie will feel more fairly treated and may become more receptive to coaching. And just as important, they may uncover new strategies for addressing the dynamic. For example, it might be useful for a number of students from the different cliques to sit down and talk about the situation. The us-them dynamic could be broken up by pairing kids across these divides to work on projects together. Or roles might be shuffled. Kenzie could be assigned the role of making sure the quieter kids are included in certain activities. And Kenzie's parents might notice that some of what she's been saying are things she's heard at home, where they often jokingly take things to an extreme: "You're the worst!" or "You're the best!" Hmm.

THE BENEFITS OF A SYSTEMS LENS

There are a number of advantages to understanding feedback through a systems lens.

IT'S MORE ACCURATE

The first benefit is simple: It's reality. Systems thinking corrects for the skew of any single perspective. If I tend to see what you are contributing to the problem, and you tend to see what I'm contributing, we can add our two perspectives together to get a better sense of the whole. As we start to see how each of us is affecting the other, opposing arrows of causality are revealed to be circles and cycles.

IT MOVES US AWAY FROM NEEDLESS JUDGMENT

A second benefit is that systems thinking eases the temptation to treat other people's contributions to the problem as *automatically* "bad" or "wrong" or "blameworthy." We are the exact normal amount of neurotic or detail oriented or risk taking. Others are overly neurotic or careless or too conservative. If we're not careful, "that thing the guys at Corporate do" morphs into "those selfish #$%s over in Corporate." The first is a description of an action; the second is a blanket judgment of the people. We are less likely to make that leap from description to damnation if we see the conflict as a simple intersection, perhaps compounded by clashing roles, inside a larger system. We are more risk tolerant than they are, and that makes investment decisions between us tough. It's harder to demonize the "other" when we are clear-eyed about our part of the problem and the ways our interlocking actions and preferences form a cycle. That's you and your wife, the snoring and the sensitivity. Neither is "bad." Together they are problematic for both of you.

IT ENHANCES ACCOUNTABILITY

Fine, you say, *but what about the times the other person's behavior really is blameworthy?* Your uncle should not have hocked Grandma's silver, your neighbor's son should not have blown up your mailbox, and the woman in the next cubicle should not have fabricated those time sheets. Is a so-called systems approach just a way to dilute or avoid responsibility by shifting the focus from the individual to the system?

We think it's the opposite. You can't take meaningful responsibility for causing a problem until you understand the combination of factors that actually caused the problem. A systems approach helps you clarify your choices and actions, and how they created the outcomes you got. Then when you say you are accountable, it actually means something.

Of course, a systems approach doesn't automatically increase accountability. When a manager says, "One of my new recruits fabricated time sheets, and we should really have more training and oversight," it is a "systems" statement. But it's only a start. It's not clear yet whether the manager is taking any responsibility for what happened, or what he thinks he—or anyone else—is accountable for.

Meaningful accountability requires the manager to take a more detailed look at why the employee made the choices she did, and at the role the manager might have played in that, as well as at the other players, tracking systems, and training that might have contributed to the time sheet transgression. For instance, who explained to the recruit how to think about time spent on various projects, how to account for breaks or travel time? And is there anything the manager did to put pressure on the recruit to log extra hours, or did he informally or even unwittingly encourage a culture of "hard work macho" that set a norm of inflating hours spent?

Understanding that a problem has multiple causes doesn't limit our options for how we move forward to solve that problem. Discipline or punishment may be appropriate, as in cases where actions are illegal, unethical, inappropriate, or otherwise violate policy. Sometimes managers will say, "How can I discipline the employee when I myself contributed to the problem?" That's like saying, "How can we punish a bank robber when we at the bank contributed to the problem by having a faulty security system in place?" Well, it's not good to have a faulty security system in place, and if you have one, it's good to know about it. But the fact that your security system is faulty has nothing to do with whether the robber should go to jail.

Of course, understanding the system may change how you see the problem, and therefore what you think is the best way to address it. If the employee wasn't aware of a policy because you didn't tell them about it, perhaps you correct the ignorance and issue a warning. That's different from an employee who knowingly flouts the policy. A systems approach helps you get a sense of *appropriate* action going forward.

IT HELPS CORRECT OUR TENDENCY TO SHIFT OR ABSORB

There are two common feedback profiles that are particularly challenging to deal with on the topic of accountability: shifters and absorbers. A systems perspective helps us fight these tendencies in ourselves and understand them in others as we talk about feedback.

Blame Absorbers: It's All Me

The first common feedback profile is the blame absorber. When things go wrong, you point the finger at yourself, now and forever. You cheated on me? I must not be attractive enough. Our product didn't sell to expectations? I screwed up the launch. It's raining out? Must be something I said.

In addition to the emotional swamp created by believing everything is your fault, there are learning drawbacks as well. Carrying all the weight of fixing relationships and projects by yourself may feel noble, but it obstructs learning just as surely as rejecting responsibility altogether. Absorbers will tend to see their own contribution to the problem and stop there. They quickly accept feedback and cut the conversation short, failing to explore the intersections, roles, choices, and reactions that created the problem under discussion.

That launch you screwed up? You flatter yourself when you think you could have sunk the effort single-handedly. Chances are there were multiple reasons for the disappointing performance, from concept to time lines to production to marketing to distribution. If you want the next product rollout to go better, you can't expect to fix all these things alone. If you soak up all the responsibility, you let others off the hook.

Responsibility for learning and fixing the problem is hoarded and the best solutions less likely to emerge.

Another challenge for absorbers is that resentment can build over time. Deeper down we know realistically that it's not *all* us, yet others don't seem to be taking their fair share of responsibility. Absorbers also start to bump up against what they can change on their own—when others aren't willing to look at their part of the problem, there's only so much one person can do to affect the system.

It's also worth noting here that absorbers can be prone to remaining in situations of abuse. In an emotionally or physically abusive relationship, the person doing the yelling, denigrating, or lashing out is able to distract attention from their own hurtful behavior by pointing to what the victim did to provoke it. The person giving the feedback ("You shouldn't provoke me") might be accurately describing the victim's part in the system. What they leave out, of course, is their own behavior, which is hurtful, harmful, and unfair. This is one reason that such relationships are so lonely, and why it is so tough to navigate your way out of an abusive relationship system. The feedback givers claim that the things you see and feel aren't even there.

Blame Shifters: It's Not Me

The other feedback profile includes people who are chronically immune to acknowledging their role in problems. When they get feedback or suffer failure, they are quick to point to everyone who hindered their efforts or must be biased against them: It was the finance folks, the new IT system, the neighbors, that squirrel over there.

You might think this stance would be relaxing; after all, feedback simply bounces off you and nothing is ever your fault. But the experience is ultimately exhausting. Shifters find themselves constantly assaulted by everyone else's incompetence or treacherousness. They are victims, powerless to protect themselves. Life happens to them. In fact, life happens *at* them.

If my investor pitch didn't get funded, it must be because the venture capitalists are fools, the markets are impossible right now, or I'm a genius ahead of my time. Because I can't control any of these factors, I feel victimized, angry, helpless, or depressed. In this frame of mind, there is nothing I could have done to change the outcome, because the causes are all external to me. Or so things seem.

A victim stance makes it impossible for feedback to penetrate; I can't learn anything that might help my next pitch. Was my market analysis incomplete? Was I unprepared for questions about competitive products? Did I ignore early feedback from focus groups that perhaps I should have heeded? Seeing my own contribution to my circumstances makes me stronger, not weaker. If I contribute to my own problems, there are things I have the power to change.

IT HELPS US AVOID "FIXES THAT FAIL"

When we don't understand the system that produces the feedback, we often make the mistake of trying to adjust just one component of the system, and expect that to solve the whole problem. But firing the CEO is on its own unlikely to change the entire corporate culture, so the problem persists. Even worse is the fix that actually creates new and unexpected additional issues.

Alice is frustrated. Her direct report, Benny, is consistently late and over budget on project delivery, and it's causing friction with their boss, Vince. So Alice gives Benny some feedback: "You've got to find a way to bring these projects in on time and on budget." Alice is clear: Benny needs to change. Benny gets the message.

What's not explored is *why* Benny is late, and what Alice, Vince, and the board may be doing to contribute to that. Instead the feedback assumes that this is a Benny Problem; it also (implicitly) assumes that Benny has the ability to fix it on his own. But Benny can't remedy it by himself, because part of the difficulty is that the board keeps changing its mind about what it wants, Vince fails to convey that message in a timely fashion, and Alice rarely passes on a clear or complete description of the new parameters. Also, when Benny warns Alice that these changes will cause delays and cost more money, Alice doesn't always get that message back to Vince and the board.

Because no one is asking the systems question, Benny does what Benny can do under the circumstances: He starts giving the board budgets that are twice as high and timelines that are twice as long as he did previously. Now he comes in under (new) budget and on (new) time.

Is this a fix? In fact, if Benny's new budgets and new timelines are more realistic, and if the concern is predictability rather than cost and timeliness, then the fix succeeds, at least in the short term.

But the story doesn't stop here, because the longer timelines and bigger budgets start to have a lag effect on the players in the system. The board now has twice as much time to change its mind, request added functionality, and look over Benny's shoulder at the results. And the larger budgets raise expectations about what Benny can provide. Soon he is working twice as hard, juggling more complex requests, and under even more pressure from Alice and Vince.

When feedback is aimed at just one piece of the larger system, and doesn't look at the other contributing factors, we get the Benny Bad Outcome. How do we get ourselves caught up in fixes that fail? By focusing on only one player in the system and papering over the real problem with a solution that is fundamentally unsound. Solutions like Benny's may seem like good ideas at the time. We're often tempted to solve a short-term problem without taking account of the long-term cost.[5]

TALKING ABOUT SYSTEMS

Exploring systems skillfully starts with the awareness that what you're facing may indeed be a systems problem.

BE ON THE LOOKOUT

Pay attention to your own silent switchtracking reaction to others' feedback: *I'm not the problem!* or *I could get you better numbers if you didn't wait until the last minute to ask for them* or *I'm only crabby because you're always late.* These knee-jerk "not my fault!" thoughts are clues that stepping back to understand the interaction behind the feedback will be helpful.

TAKE RESPONSIBILITY FOR YOUR PART

The next step is to be accountable: Figure out your contribution to the problem and take responsibility for it. Otherwise the giver will hear your suggestion to look at "our relationship system" as making excuses. They'll assume you're attempting to deflect the feedback and point a finger back at them. They won't be interested in your fancy ideas about "systems." In fact, avoid phrases like "relationship system" altogether.

In these conversations, there are two big messages you are trying to send: First, I take responsibility for my part, and second, we are both contributing to this. It is sometimes hard to send both of those messages in the same conversation. They are consistent and logical, but to the person giving you feedback, they can sound contradictory. So think about whether the giver will be able to hear both messages in one conversation, and if not, start by taking responsibility, and once that's settled in, circle back and talk about your observations about the system and your requests of them.

"HERE'S WHAT WOULD HELP ME CHANGE"

A feedback giver may not be ready or able to acknowledge their contribution to the problem. They may still be stuck in thinking this feedback party is all about you.

If that's the case, there's still something you can do. Rather than trying to force them to admit to and take responsibility for their part in the problem, describe how they could get a better reaction from you. You're asking them to change, but you're casting it (legitimately) in service of helping *you* change.

Gil can tell Sandy: "I have the strongest reaction to being surprised, because it makes me panic about where else you might be spending and not telling me. I know I'm overreacting sometimes and I'm working on that. It would help me if you would be willing to be upfront with me about the Grape-Nuts and the mochaccino 'mini-vacations,' and we can budget for them together."

LOOK FOR THEMES:
IS THIS A ME + EVERYBODY INTERSECTION?

Sometimes the feedback you get is the very direct product of your particular intersection with this particular person. You sort of mumble *and* they are hard of hearing.

But at other times a disturbing consistency surfaces—no matter who you are in a relationship with, they have the *same* feedback for you. Your temper is trying. You rarely call anyone back. You are disorganized, forgetful, or scattered. Richard's first girlfriend complained that he was emotionally distant. Richard chalked it up to his girlfriend's idiosyncratic brand of neediness. But when Richard's next two girlfriends said the same thing, he started paying attention (a little).

When you first realize that this Me + You intersection is in fact a Me + Everybody intersection, you might feel a bit disheartened. But there's good news here, too. Me + Everybody systems can actually be fairly simple to change, because when one of you changes (i.e., you), the whole system improves. And in this case, multiple systems will improve. It's a rare life circumstance where so much is within your control.

USE THE SYSTEM TO SUPPORT CHANGE
(NOT THWART IT)

Sometimes feedback is simple: Shine your shoes before inspection. Don't interrupt. Call your mother more often. These are all behaviors you can change reasonably easily and to predictably good effect.

At other times change is more complicated. We may both agree that things would be easier if you were less moody, but another lecture isn't going to help.

What's interesting is that, once we identify the contours of a system, we can often make useful changes that don't require that people change their personalities. We can shift their roles, change the processes we use, or even change the environment. Would putting Sandy in charge of the budget change her emotional experience of spending even three dollars? Would including me in the meeting with the client to discuss my analysis guarantee I would have it done on time? Would swapping household chores so that yours are finished in the morning mean that you are more relaxed and less moody over dinner at night? It's possible. And that's what seeing systems does: It creates possibilities.

Summary: SOME KEY IDEAS

To understand the feedback you get, take three steps back:

- One Step Back: You + Me intersections. Are differences between us creating the friction?
- Two Steps Back: Role clashes. Is this partly a result of the roles we play in the organization or the family?
- Three Steps Back: Big picture. Are processes, policies, physical environment, or other players reinforcing the problem?

Looking at systems:

- Reduces judgment
- Enhances accountability
- Uncovers root causes

Look for patterns in your feedback. Is this a You + Everybody intersection?

Take responsibility for your part.

IDENTITY TRIGGERS

and the challenge of
ME

Identity Triggers (and the challenge of being ME)

At some level we are always scanning for danger. In the next three chapters we find it.

Feedback can be threatening because it prompts questions about the most challenging relationship you have: your relationship with yourself. Are you a good person? Do you deserve your own respect? Can you live with yourself? Forgive yourself?

Interestingly, not everyone reacts to feedback and identity threats in the same way and to the same degree, or takes the same amount of time to recover. In chapter 7, we take a quick peek inside the brain to explore why that is. Your particular wiring—how sensitive or insensitive you are, how quickly you bounce back—influences how you experience both positive and negative feedback. Understanding your wiring will help you to understand your own emotional reactions when receiving feedback.

That's critical, because our feelings influence our thoughts, and the story we tell ourselves about what the feedback means can become distorted. Chapter 8 looks at five ways to dismantle these distortions so that you can see the feedback more clearly, at "actual size."

Once you see the feedback clearly, the next task is to figure out how to square the feedback with your identity—your self-story about who you are in the world. Where chapter 8 examines how we make sense of, and distort, the feedback, chapter 9 examines how we make sense of, and distort, our self-image. Our identity can be more and less sturdy, more and less conducive to learning. In chapter 9, we'll give you three practices to help you move from a vulnerable fixed identity to a robust growth identity, which will make it easier for you to learn from feedback and experience.

7

LEARN HOW WIRING AND
TEMPERAMENT AFFECT YOUR STORY

Krista doesn't lack self-confidence. She laughs as she recounts this story:

My husband and I spent the first six months of our marriage traveling the States by car, with "Honk if you support our marriage!" scribbled in shoe polish on the rear window. People honked and waved like crazy, and it was exhilarating to be supported by friendly strangers. When we returned to regular life, my husband cleaned off the window, but I didn't notice. So, I'd be doing some dumb move in traffic, pulling a U-turn. Someone would be honking furiously, and I'd be waving back with this big grin, saying, "Hey, thanks so much. Thank you! I love you, too!"

"That's typical for me," Krista adds. "I can be oblivious to negative feedback. When I hear that someone doesn't like something I did, I immediately think, *Really? But do you know how amazing I am?* Honestly, I've got so much self-confidence it's practically inappropriate."

Of course Krista's life has seen its share of rain, and she wasn't smiling through it all. But even at her lowest, her upbeat disposition helped to pull her through: "My first husband and I divorced, and a divorce is a giant oozing spitball of negative feedback. I questioned everything about myself—whether anyone could love me, whether I was capable of real love at all. I went to some dark places, like everyone does.

"But," she adds, "I didn't stay very long. I can get from 'no one will ever love me' to 'that's ridiculous, lots of people love me' pretty quickly. Within a year I was in an awesome relationship with my current husband, driving around the country getting honks of loving support."

Alita finds herself at the opposite end of the spectrum. A popular obstetrician, Alita received feedback from last year's patient survey. Her reviews were glowing, and many patients made special mention of her attentive approach to their pregnancy questions. But several patients commented that Alita's schedule often ran late, and that they resented having to wait. The comments came down like a sledgehammer. "I was so disheartened," Alita says. "I give each patient so much time and care, and then they turn around and complain. Until I read my feedback I loved my job. I haven't felt the same about my practice since." The envelope with the most recent patient survey results has been sitting on Alita's desk for the past two months—unopened.

For Krista, feedback is like water off a duck's back, while for Alita, it penetrates deep into her soul. We each metabolize feedback in our own way.

THE LIBERATION OF HARD WIRING

One reason why Krista and Alita respond so differently to feedback is their wiring—their built-in neural structures and connections. Our wiring affects who we are, tilting us toward being anxious or upbeat, shy or outgoing, sensitive or resilient, and it contributes to how intensely feedback—both positive and negative—affects us. It influences how high we go, how low we descend, and how quickly we recover from dread or despair.

This chapter takes a look at our different emotional reactions to feedback and at the role our wiring plays in that. We'll also look at how those emotions influence our thinking, and how our thinking influences our emotions. Understanding your own wiring and tendencies helps you to improve your ability to weather the storm of negative feedback—and to dig yourself out in the morning.

Learning that how you are in the world is due in part to your wiring might feel discouraging—just one more thing that's wrong with you, and one that seems impossible to fix. But it can be freeing, as well. Like your naturally curly hair, high cheekbones, or flat feet, your wiring is no more judgment-worthy than whether your second toe is shorter or longer than the first. If you've spent a lifetime being told that you're either "hypersensitive" or "totally oblivious," this is a moment to step back and say, "Okay, so that's how I'm built. That's how I showed up in this world." Your reactions are not due to a lack of courage or surplus of self-pity.

This doesn't absolve you of responsibility for how you are and how you act. It is simply a true and usefully complicating observation: wiring matters.[1]

A BEHIND-THE-SCENES LOOK AT YOURSELF ON FEEDBACK

Our understanding of the brain is under construction. By "our" we mean the general state of human understanding (not to mention the authors' understanding). Discoveries in neuroscience pour forth, debates proliferate, interpretations shift. Writing about neuroscience is a little like leaping from a moving train: No matter how carefully you time your jump, you're likely to get roughed up. Even so, we think it's useful; dipping into the recent social science and neuroscience research can help us understand why we each react to feedback the way we do, and why others react differently.

One of the brain's primary survival functions is to manage approach and withdrawal: We tend to move toward things that are pleasurable and away from things that are painful. Pleasure is a rough proxy for the healthy and safe; pain is a rough proxy for the unhealthy and dangerous.

But our approach-withdrawal function is too crudely calibrated to navigate the nuanced worlds of modern work and love. The brain gets tangled when it encounters short-term pain that is necessary for long-term gain—that exercising you put off, for instance. And the opposite is also true: Short-term pleasures that produce long-term pain—as with, say, recreational drugs or an extramarital affair—also produce confused approach-withdraw signals ("wine, women, and song" in older days; "sex, drugs, and rock 'n' roll" to baby boomers). These brain-life mismatches are the source of great fascination and endless torment.

What does this have to do with feedback? Like sex, drugs, food, and exercise, feedback is one of these areas that boggle the brain and muck up the approach-withdrawal system. Doing what feels good now (finding a way to make negative feedback stop) may be costly in the long run (you are left, fired, or simply stagnate). And what is healthy in the long run (understanding and acting on useful feedback) may feel painful now.

A lot goes on in both your brain and body when you experience mood-altering feedback, more than anyone yet understands, and certainly more than we can describe in a short chapter. But for simplicity's sake, we can say that your "reaction" to feedback can be thought of as containing three key variables: Baseline, Swing, and Sustain or Recovery.

"Baseline" refers to the default state of well-being or contentment toward which you gravitate in the wake of good or bad events in your life. "Swing" refers to how far up or down you move from your baseline when you receive feedback. Some of us have extreme reactions to feedback; we swing wide. Others remain on an even keel even in the face of disquieting news. "Sustain and Recovery" refers to duration, how long your ups and downs last. Ideally, we want to sustain a boost from positive feedback and recover quickly from a negative emotional dip.

1. Baseline: The Beginning and End of the Arc

Whether we feel happy or sad, content or discontent, is not determined merely by each individual successive moment of life experience—a good thing happens and I'm happy, a bad thing happens and I'm sad. It doesn't work that way. While our experiences affect our mood, we are not blown in a completely new direction by each gust of wind. We feel emotions in the moment, of course, but they occur against a broader backdrop.

As humans, we adapt—to new information and events both good and bad—and gravitate back to our personal default level of well-being.[2] There will be highs and lows, but over time, like water seeking its own level, we are pulled toward our baseline—back *up* after bad news and back *down* after good. The euphoria of first love fades, and so does the despair of divorce. This tendency is best seen with little kids and their toy joy: When they get what they've longed for, they believe they will be happy for the rest of their lives. And for the first few minutes of the rest of their lives, they are. But then the kids—like adults—adapt.

There is enormous variance among individuals when it comes to baseline. This is why our uncle Murray seems perpetually dissatisfied with life, while our aunt Eileen is delighted with everything for no apparent reason. Happiness is believed to be one of the most highly heritable aspects of personality. Twin studies have led to estimates that about 50 percent of the variance among people in their average levels of happiness can be explained by differences in their genes rather than in their life experiences.[3] Famously, studies of lottery winners have shown that a year after claiming their prize, winners are approximately as happy (or unhappy) as they were prior to the windfall.[4]

Why does your baseline matter when it comes to receiving feedback?

First, people who have higher happiness baselines are more likely to respond positively to positive feedback than people with lower self-reported well-being. And people with lower general satisfaction respond more strongly to negative information.[5] Krista has a pretty high baseline, so it's not surprising that she'd find honks of marital support exhilarating, and criticism less emotionally "sticky." Alita likely has a lower general baseline, so she may get less of a boost from the positive patient ratings, and be hit harder by the criticism.

This may seem particularly unfair to Alita. After all, she's the one who needs to hear the positive feedback and get the emotional boost it offers. But don't worry—there are things Alita can do to turn up the volume on the positives and temper the negatives when receiving tough feedback. For now, it's useful simply to be aware that for her, positive feedback may be muffled and negatives amplified.

2. Swing: How Far Up or Down You Go

Wherever our natural baseline, some of us swing far in either direction, even when the input is minor, while others live in a narrower emotional band. These tendencies appear to be present from birth. Some infants are more sensitive than others and can experience a strong physiological jolt even from comparatively small inputs—loud noises, novel situations, or scary drawings, for example.

Of course, newborns aren't subjected to performance reviews, and feedback for adults is rarely accompanied by scary drawings. But it turns out that infants who are what research psychologist Jerome Kagan calls "high reactive" are more likely than others to grow into adults who are high reactives. High reactivity in infants can translate into a big swing for adults. And we can reasonably assume such adults would be likely to be more sensitive to negative feedback.[6] Brain imaging studies suggest that differences in sensitivity may correlate with anatomical differences as well. The adults who had low-reactive infant temperaments had greater thickness in the left orbitofrontal cortex than the high-reactive group while the adults categorized as high-reactive infants displayed greater thickness in the right ventromedial prefrontal cortex.[7]

Whatever is going on inside our cortexes, differences in swing are easy to observe within our conference rooms. When a client sends the same critical comments to both Eliza and Jeron, Eliza is frantic with anxiety while Jeron has no reaction beyond "Well, this means a bit more work." Because Eliza and Jeron are teammates, their disparate reactions create tension. Jeron thinks Eliza is melodramatic and attention-seeking; Eliza thinks Jeron is in denial about the depth of the problem. Now they have feedback for each other about how they are each (mis-) handling the feedback.

Bad Is Stronger Than Good

Whether we are easily swamped or nearly waterproof, there's one wiring challenge we all face: Bad is stronger than good. Psychologist Jonathan Haidt elaborates: "Responses to threats and unpleasantness are faster, stronger, and harder to inhibit than responses to opportunities and pleasures."[8] This observation sheds light on an eternal riddle about feedback: Why do we dwell on the one criticism buried amid four hundred compliments?

Built into our wiring is a kind of security team that scans for threat. When it detects danger—real or perceived—the team responds instantaneously, bypassing our slower, more reflective systems. The amygdala is a key player. This small, almond-shaped bundle of neurons sits at the heart of the limbic system—a part of the brain central to processing emotion. As Haidt explains:

> The amygdala has a direct connection to the brainstem that activates the fight-or-flight response, and if that amygdala finds a pattern that was part of a previous fear episode . . . it orders the body to red alert.
>
> . . . the brain has no equivalent "green alert" . . . threats get a shortcut to your panic button, but there is no equivalent alarm system for positive information. Bad news is emotionally louder than good, and thus will have bigger impact.

So why are you still obsessing over that oblique comment your mother-in-law made during an otherwise lovely holiday visit? Because she unwittingly activated your red alert system—the one that evolved more than 100 million years ago[9] that was later used to detect snakes, saber-toothed tigers, and other life-threatening creatures that lurk. Long after your mother-in-law has left, your emotional brain remains ready for her to pounce.

3. Sustain and Recovery: How Long Does the Swing Last?

Whether you swing wide emotionally or barely budge, the last variable is duration—how long it takes you to return to your baseline. Do you recover quickly from even the most distressing feedback, or are you brought low for weeks or months? And how long do you sustain the high of good news? When a grateful customer e-mails to extol your expertise, do you have a bounce in your fingertips for the rest of the day? Or just until you read your next e-mail? Researcher Richard Davidson has found that the amount of time that we sustain positive emotion, or need to recover from negative emotion, can differ by as much as 3,000 percent across individuals.[10]

Surprisingly, negative feedback and positive feedback are mediated by different parts of the brain; in fact, they appear to be mediated by different *halves* of the brain. And those different halves of the brain can be differently good at their job. This subject gets complicated quickly, but there are some simple insights that emerge from the research on this front.

Negative Recovery: Righty or Lefty?

It's crucial to have a red alert system for threats, but due to the high number of false alarms encountered in everyday life, it's just as crucial to have a way to turn the alarm off.

The amygdala is a key player in the alert system, but it's no lone cowboy. The frontal cortex runs the show, working to integrate the emotional response with the actual content of the feedback. The frontal cortex can contain or intensify the stampedes that the amygdala starts.

Sitting just behind your forehead, your prefrontal cortex is the seat of higher-order reasoning, judgment, and decision making. Like other parts of your brain, it is divided in two, with a right and left side. When you experience negative feelings like fear, anxiety, and disgust, your brain shows increased activity on the right side. When you experience positive feelings like amusement, hope, and love, your brain shows increased activity on the left side. Researchers have termed this the "valence hypothesis," suggesting that people who have more activity on the right side ("cortical righties") tend to be more depressed and more anxious; cortical lefties tend to be happier.[11] (We shouldn't overstate current scientific consensus; this "locational" theory of emotion is not without controversy.)[12]

With the help of imaging devices like functional MRIs, which reveal how the brain responds to particular stimuli, neuroscientists are beginning to understand how recovery from negative emotion may work. Surprisingly, it's the left side—the *positive* side—that seems to be responsible here. While the amygdala is fanning the flames of fear and anxiety, activity in the left side of the brain exerts a calming influence. Strong activity on the left is associated with quicker recovery from upset.

People who are faster to recover not only have more activity in the left side; they also tend to have more connections ("white matter" pathways that connect brain regions to one another) running between the left side of the prefrontal cortex and the amygdala.[13] This appears to create more bandwidth along which the positive messages can travel to the amygdala. People with numerous connections effectively have a superhighway to deliver reassuring signals, while those who are slower to recover have narrow country roads.

The bottom line is that people whose brain wiring and organization are more right-sided, or righties, are slower than lefties to recover from negative feedback. Recovery is slower whether the feedback is small (you forgot to take out the garbage . . .) or large (. . . and therefore I'm leaving you).[14]

If we hooked up Alita to an fMRI while she read the criticism about keeping patients waiting, we'd likely see activity in her amygdala and right prefrontal cortex increase. "There's danger!" yells the amygdala. "It's a disaster!" confirms the right prefrontal cortex. In contrast, activity in Alita's left prefrontal cortex—the more positive side—would show comparatively less activity. "Let's all just calm down. Lots of patients appreciate the time you spend with them," says the left, but too faintly to be heard above the bluster of disaster and doom.

Alita is likely a cortical righty. Compared with a less sensitive colleague, she'll feel more physiologically aroused, more anxious, more depressed. It will be harder for her to find hope or humor (which are mediated more by the left side) and more difficult for her to calm herself down.

Krista's fMRI in the same situation would likely show a different pattern. Initially, she might feel anxious, angry, or hurt (Krista's amygdala will light up, too), but her strong left prefrontal cortex will soon kick in, quieting down the quick emotional response: "Relax, don't overreact. Most of your patients *love* you, and anyway, motherhood is all about learning patience, so you're giving them a head start. C'mon, let's go have some Mexican food."

While a fast recovery time has real advantages—those who are resilient are more likely to respond to setbacks with energy and determination and less likely to suffer from depression—being at the extreme end of this scale presents its own challenges as far as feedback is concerned. Because negative feedback has less emotional resonance for

Krista, it may not adequately catch her attention or even stick in memory. She may be dismissive of suggestions or lack motivation to work on improving. Those around her may see her as callous to the concerns of others, not because she doesn't care, but because she doesn't always realize how serious their concerns are. And anyway, she's moved on.

Sustaining Positive Feelings

Recovery measures how quickly you emerge from the abyss of upsetting feedback. Sustain measures how long positive feedback has you walking on air.

What's going on in the brain that helps us sustain positive feelings? We need to zoom in on a cluster of neurons inside the ventral striatum called the nucleus accumbens. This region sits just in front of your temple and is part of the mesolimbic pathway—sometimes called the "reward pathway" or "pleasure center"—which is responsible for releasing dopamine, which in turn prompts feelings of pleasure, desire, and motivation. Connected to that upbeat left side of the prefrontal cortex, the nucleus accumbens creates a circuit in which positive experiences trigger a dopamine response, which triggers more positive feelings, which triggers more dopamine.[15]

Both Krista and Alita feel an uptick in joy when given a positive boost, whether it's a honk of marital support or the cry of a newly delivered baby boy. But Krista's nucleus accumbens *stays* active, continuing to release dopamine and maintaining the emotional high long after the honk fades. For Alita, the positive feelings evaporate in minutes.

Just as we can retrigger negative feelings by recalling negative feedback, we can extend our positive sustain by recalling positive feedback—replaying that appreciative comment from a customer or reminding ourselves that no matter what happens at work, we've got nine kids who love us at home. Or perhaps remembering that no matter what happens at home, our kids aren't allowed to follow us to work.

Our sustain and recovery tendencies can create virtuous and vicious cycles. If you find it easier to sustain positive emotion, you can ride the boosts you get from happy moments large (*We landed the account!*) and small (*That was a great cup of coffee!*). You might reread positive feedback from your child's teacher or from a grateful constituent when you need a reminder that you're doing something right. Positive feedback sticks, and helps you turn the corner to recovering your equilibrium. This sense of control over your emotional state means you feel more confident about your ability to cope with whatever life throws your way. You will tend to be optimistic that the future will be bright and confident that regardless, you'll manage things well. That's a pretty good definition of peace of mind.

But when positive sustain is weak, it's harder to remember what you're doing right, and pessimism seems the more realistic outlook. If you've been low and had trouble recovering, you may doubt your ability to pull yourself up the next time you stumble into a particularly troubling time. This can produce a challenging combination of pessimism and self-doubt. This is where baseline, swing, and sustain come full circle and together constitute what is sometimes referred to as temperament.[16]

Four Sustain/Recovery Combinations

Krista has both quick recovery and long sustain. Her nature enables her to bounce back quickly from adversity and to luxuriate in life's joys. Alita is the opposite on both fronts; she takes longer to recover from negatives and has more trouble sustaining positives.

But these aren't the only two sustain/recovery combinations, because how long you sustain negative feelings operates independently from how long you sustain positive ones. From a purely physiological point of view, there are four combinations of sustain/recover tendencies. The chart below doesn't address whether you receive feedback skillfully, or whether you find it helpful and important to learning. It merely suggests different variations on how you might experience feedback, given your wiring. It's an oversimplification, but the categories are illuminating.

	Long Sustain of Positive	Short Sustain of Positive
Quick Recovery from Negative	Low Risk, High Reward "I Love Feedback."	Low Risk, Low Reward "No Big Deal Either Way."
Slow Recovery from Negative	High Risk, High Reward "I'm Hopeful but Fearful."	High Risk, Low Reward "I Hate Feedback."

WIRING IS ONLY PART OF THE STORY

The danger when talking about brain wiring and temperament is that we take our wiring as fixed and assume it is destiny. It's neither.

There are genetic bases to our temperament; understanding this helps us understand ourselves, and this offers insight into why others are different from us. But while aspects of our temperament are inherited, there is ample evidence that they are not fixed. Practices such as meditation, serving others, and exercise can raise your baseline over time, and life events that involve trauma or depression can have a profound impact as well. This growing understanding of neuroplasticity is a thrilling reminder that even wiring changes over time in response to our environment and experiences.

THE MAGIC 40

Perhaps more important, our wiring—whether fixed or not—tells only part of the story. Research suggests a 50-40-10 formula for happiness: About 50 percent of our happiness is wired in. Another 40 percent can be attributed to how we interpret and respond to what happens to us, and 10 percent is driven by our circumstances—where we live and with whom, where we work and with whom, the state of our health, and so forth.[17] Whether these are exactly the right proportions is obviously debatable, but what's certain is that there is a lot of room to move in that magic middle of around 40 percent. That's the piece we have control over—the way we interpret what happens, the meaning we make, and the stories we tell ourselves.

Indeed, University of Pennsylvania researcher Marty Seligman suggests that for some people, these interpretations and responses can help turn post-traumatic stress into post-traumatic growth.[18] Our interpretations and responses to what happens to us—and to the feedback we get—can help turn upsetting feedback and even failure into learning.

But there's a catch.

Our emotions have so profound an influence on how we interpret what happens and the stories we tell about it that, in the wake of upsetting feedback, our upset itself distorts what we think the feedback means. Our boss offers us some gentle advice that is as harmless as a kitten. But in the flush of anxiety, the advice appears to us as threatening as a tiger, poised to rip us apart.

EMOTIONS DISTORT OUR SENSE OF THE FEEDBACK ITSELF

If we're going to get better at handling tough feedback, we have to understand how emotions interact with, and distort, the stories we tell about what the feedback means. Is it really just a kitten, or is it a tiger? Or is it something else altogether?

OUR STORIES HAVE AN EMOTIONAL SOUNDTRACK

As we discuss in chapter 3, we don't live our life in data, but in stories—big stories, like who we are and what we care about and why we're here, and smaller stories, like whether we embarrassed ourselves at the company picnic last weekend.

And these stories are made not only of thoughts but of feelings. We don't experience them as separate. We don't think: *Here's a thought and here's a feeling.* At any given moment we have a seamless awareness of our life. It's similar to the way a music soundtrack works in a movie. When we're absorbed in a good movie, we don't notice the swell and fade of the soundtrack. The music adds to the suspense, the excitement, the poignancy of the plot, yet we are as unaware of the music as we are of the projector.

Most of the time that's a good thing. A movie is better when we get lost in it and the same is true in life. When we are at our most engaged, most creative, and most energized, we achieve that delicious state of unselfconsciousness called "flow."[19] But when things go wrong, it's worth slowing things down to observe the effect our emotions are having on how we tell the story.

THOUGHTS + FEELINGS = STORY

Someone behind you honks when the light changes. You don't think: *That person behind me honked.* You instantly embellish that thought into a story: *Dude! Obnoxious people like you are what's wrong with this town these days.*

How you *feel* in that moment has a big impact on the story you tell yourself. If you are already in a dark mood, you'll tell a darker story. If you're frustrated, you'll tell a frustrated story. If you're sitting at the light feeling like a loser, and the guy behind you honks, it's just another example of you being a loser. You can't even drive right. That guy sees right into your sad, incompetent soul. *Thanks, pal, but I already know.* If you're newly in love, you'll feel patient and generous: *Oops, sorry about that, I was doing a little daydreaming there at the light. But ain't life grand?*

In these examples, the feeling comes first. The feeling colors the story and influences how we perceive the characters in it. But there's a second pattern between thoughts and feelings, and confusingly, it's just the opposite: Sometimes the thought is first, and the feelings follow.

For instance, I may have started my journey feeling just fine, but then I looked at the clock and saw that I might miss my flight. A story unfolds in my mind about how the rest of the day will play out—I'll miss my flight by seconds, I won't make the meeting this afternoon, my client is going to be annoyed, my boss will be apoplectic. And now—*because* of these thoughts—I'm on edge. In this case, the feelings follow the thoughts.

Jonathan Haidt gives us a glimpse of the biology behind this intertwining of thoughts and feeling:

Not only does [the amygdala] reach down to the brainstem to trigger a response to danger but it reaches up to the frontal cortex to change your thinking. It shifts the entire brain over to a withdrawal orientation. There is a two-way street between emotions and conscious thoughts: Thoughts can cause emotions (as when you reflect on a foolish thing you said), but emotions can also cause thoughts. . . . [20]

There's a key insight that follows from this observation that is relevant for feedback: If our stories are a result of our feelings plus our thoughts, then we can change our stories by working to change either our feelings *or* our thoughts. So there are two ways in.

HOW FEELINGS EXAGGERATE FEEDBACK

Let's start by looking at the predictable ways that feelings distort our stories. Knowing those patterns is crucial to being able to tell a less distorted story.

When it comes to feedback, strong feelings push us toward extreme interpretations. *One* thing becomes *everything*, *now* becomes *always*, *partly* becomes *entirely*, and *slightly* becomes *extremely*. Feelings skew our sense of the past, present, and future. They distort our stories about who we are, how others see us, and what the consequences of the feedback will be. Below are three common patterns of distortion.

OUR PAST: THE GOOGLE BIAS

Today's upsetting feedback can influence the story we tell about yesterday: Suddenly what comes to mind is all the damning evidence of past failures, earlier poor choices, and bygone bad behavior.

It's a little like using Google. If you Google "dictators," you're going to pull up 8.4 million sites that mention dictators. It seems that dictators are everywhere; you can't swing a cat without hitting one. But that doesn't mean most people are dictators or that most countries are run by dictators. Filling your head with dictator stories doesn't mean there are more dictators, and ignoring dictator stories doesn't mean there are fewer.

When you feel lousy about yourself, you are effectively Googling "Things that are wrong with me." You will pull up 8.4 million examples, and suddenly you are pathetic. You see "sponsored ads" from your exes, father, and boss. You can't recall a single thing you've ever done right.

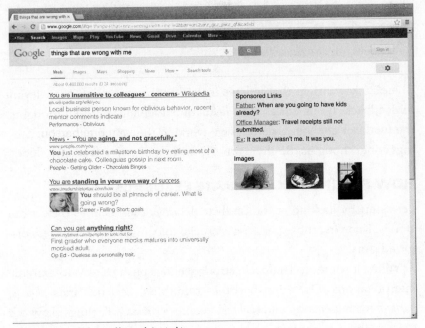

Google search parody designed by Sarah Seminski

We all have our own ways of experiencing these distortions. Marc describes how the "Google bias" manifests for him:

> The feedback could be small, but if I'm feeling vulnerable, it's as if I fall through the floor, plunged into the basement where all the things I've ever regretted are collected. It's as if they are happening all at once, right now. I feel guilty about the people I've hurt and ashamed of the selfish things I've done. When I'm not in the basement I literally don't think about it. But when I'm there, it's the only reality, my failures surround me, and I can't believe I was ever happy.

Of course, when you feel good, the Google bias tilts in the other direction, offering up the successes and the wise and generous choices that have led inexorably to your bountiful life. You rock and always have. Either way, when it comes to your stories about yourself, you get what you Google.

OUR PRESENT: NOT ONE THING, EVERYTHING

When we feel happy and healthy, we are able to contain negative feedback to the topic or trait under scrutiny and to the person doing the "scruting." We are hearing the feedback as it was meant. If you are told you sing off key, you think, *Okay, this person thinks I sang that song off key.* The feedback is about singing one song. And it's from one person.

But if you're in the grip of strong emotion, negative feedback floods across boundaries into other areas of your self-image: *I sing off key? I can't do anything right.* We rush from "I have trouble closing certain kinds of deals" to "I'm no good at my job," and from "My colleague has a concern" to "Everybody on the team hates me."

Flooding can also drown out any positive attributes that might lend balance to the picture. Whether you sing off key has no bearing on your long-standing commitment to improving your community's social services, your tenacious dedication to your daughter, or the astonishing quality of your slow-roast short ribs. But when we get flooded, that's all washed away.

OUR FUTURE: THE FOREVER BIAS AND SNOWBALLING

Feelings affect not only how we recall the past, but how we imagine the future. When we feel bad, we assume we will always feel bad. You feel humiliated by the shoddy presentation you gave at the joint venture launch and assume that you will feel precisely this humiliated up to the moment of your death.

And perhaps worse, we engage in catastrophic thinking, and our stories can eventually snowball out of control.[21] A specific and contained piece of feedback steadily turns into an ever more ominous future disaster: "I had mayonnaise on my cheek during the date" becomes "I will die alone."

What's so amazing about these distortions is how real they appear to us in the moment. Common sense suggests that the bigger the gap between our thoughts and reality, the more likely we would be to notice that the two are misaligned. But unless we are consciously looking for it, we can't see the gap when we're in it, so the size is irrelevant.

The strong feelings triggered by feedback can cause us to distort our thinking about the past, the present, and the future. Learning to regain our balance so that we can accurately assess the feedback is first a matter of rewinding our thoughts and straightening them out. Once we've gotten the feedback in realistic perspective, we have a real shot at learning from it.

In the next chapter, "Dismantle Distortions," we'll look at strategies for straightening out distorted thinking, so that we can more accurately assess the feedback we get.

Summary: SOME KEY IDEAS

Wiring matters.

- Baseline, Swing, and Sustain/Recovery vary by as much as 3,000 percent among individuals.
- If we have a lower baseline, the volume will be turned down on the positives, and up on the negatives.

Emotions distort our stories about the feedback itself.

- The Google bias magnifies the negatives and collapses the past and the present.
- One thing becomes everything and everyone.
- The forever bias makes the future look bleak.

8

DISMANTLE DISTORTIONS

See Feedback at "Actual Size"

One of the biggest blocks to receiving feedback well is that we exaggerate it. Fueled by emotion, our story about what the feedback says grows so large and so damning that we are overwhelmed by it. Learning is the least of our worries; we're just trying to survive.

In order to understand and assess the feedback, we first have to dismantle the distortions. This doesn't mean pretending that negative feedback is positive or adopting untethered optimism. It means finding ways to turn down the volume on that ominous soundtrack playing in our minds so that we can hear the dialogue more clearly.

SETH TAKES A RELAXING VACATION

Seth is a counselor who works with children who have experienced trauma and loss. He needs to address some performance issues with a supervisee, and asks his boss to sit in on the conversation. During the meeting Seth is watching the clock; he's catching a flight to Atlanta tonight to celebrate his recently widowed father's birthday tomorrow. Seth has spent hours planning the party, and both father and son have been looking forward to the weekend all month.

Toward the end of the meeting, Seth's boss suddenly pipes up. He laughs and says reassuringly to Seth's supervisee: "Well, we *all* have trouble with being organized. I mean, geez, look at *Seth*!"

It's a kick in the teeth. Seth has always struggled with being organized and now here it is, trumpeted by his boss, in front of a subordinate, no less. He is instantly nauseated and can't think straight. He looks dumbly at his supervisee, his face burning. The meeting ends, but Seth has no recollection of how. Shame and despair darken his thoughts: *I'm a complete mess. I'll never succeed in this job. My personal life is a mess, too, and no wonder.*

Feeling desperate to fix the situation, Seth decides to cancel his trip and stay the weekend to try to get his life organized. How could he even have scheduled such a trip? What kind of idiotic judgment was involved in deciding to jet off across the country to a party?

In the end, Seth goes. Why? Because his plane ticket is nonrefundable, and wasting money (additional evidence of idiocy) feels even worse than wasting time. He spends the flight consumed with anxiety.

From sheer exhaustion Seth manages to get a decent night's sleep, and the next day he is absorbed by the party preparation and the party itself. He ends up having a wonderful time. Seth and his father talk wistfully of his recently departed mom; their conversation stretches deep into the night, and the time he spends with his father becomes one of Seth's fondest memories. He wouldn't trade it for all the money in the world.

In retrospect, Seth finds his initial reaction to his boss's comment incomprehensible. It seems obvious to him now that his boss was merely trying to use humor—whether joke or jibe—to make a connection with the supervisee. Seth can't explain why his boss's comment set off such an explosion in his mind.

But we can. Like Alita, Seth is on the sensitive end of the wiring spectrum. He is easily triggered, and once triggered, his strong feelings shape and distort the story he tells about what the feedback means. As a result, he loses his balance. When he eventually regains it, Seth has trouble figuring out what, if anything, he has learned from the incident. He's hesitant to go back to his boss and discuss the matter, because he worries that he'll just get triggered again.

FIVE WAYS TO DISMANTLE DISTORTIONS

In order to learn from upsetting feedback, we need strategies to counter the distortions that we bring to it, whether during the feedback conversation itself, beforehand (in preparation), or afterward (in reflection). Below are five strategies that help.

1. BE PREPARED, BE MINDFUL

As Seth's story illustrates, we don't always have the chance to prepare for feedback. Sometimes it calls ahead, other times it just shows up at the door. Feedback has its own etiquette.

But when we're able, it's useful to think in advance about the conversation—to consider how we will feel and respond if we hear things that we disagree with or find upsetting. This can give us a preview of our reactions and allow us to think about issues of identity and well-being while we are still feeling balanced.

Know Your Feedback Footprint

Each of us has our own set of reactive behaviors in response to criticism, our own feedback footprint: Bryan blames others; Claire switchtracks; Anu cries; Alfie apologizes; Mick chatters; Hester goes silent; Fergie agrees while quietly resolving never to change. Reynolds lawyers up, emotionally speaking, and Jody becomes awkwardly friendly. And at least sometimes, Seth panics.

We each have our own personal stages of acceptance and rejection as well. Some of us kick and claw in the moment but over time come around to accepting the possibility of change. Others move in the opposite direction: Initially they assume that everything they're hearing is valid and true, but on reflection, they dismiss much of it. Some people postpone engaging and decide they will figure things out later—and then make sure never to think about it again. Others obsess over the feedback and stop only when a new obsession takes hold.

Regardless of whether your reactions are productive or debilitating, it's enormously helpful to be aware of your particular patterns. It's especially important to figure out how you tend to respond during that first stage—I run, I fight, I deny, I exaggerate—so that you can recognize your usual reaction and name it to yourself in the moment. If you name it, you have some power over it.

Figuring out your patterns is as simple as asking yourself this question: "How do I typically react?" If you're like most people, as examples come to mind, you'll dismiss each as an exception to how you *actually* are. But those exceptions aren't exceptions: They *are* how you are. If you're having trouble discerning your footprint, ask those around you. As they describe your defensive behavior, you can notice yourself getting defensive about it. Then you'll know.

Inoculate Yourself Against the Worst

Your footprint will show up strongest when the feedback is toughest. If you're about to get some news—perhaps you're awaiting word from colleges or funders or the Nobel Prize Committee—a useful way to manage your own tendencies is to imagine that the news is bad. Think through in advance the worst that could happen, try it on emotionally, and reason through the possible consequences. If that sounds like advice to be pessimistic, it's actually the opposite. It is a reminder that whatever the outcome, you'll be able to manage.

This exercise has a few benefits. First, it acts as an inoculation. When you get inoculated, you receive a tiny bit of the virus, easily handled by your immune system. If you are then exposed to the real thing, your body recognizes the threat and knows how to deal with it. In the same way, when actual bad news arrives you'll think, *Yes, this is what I feared might happen. I've seen this before. I'll be okay.* The feelings that come over you and the images in your head are a bit more familiar and a bit less shocking.

Second, you can think through in a balanced and unhurried way what the news might mean for you and what actions you would take if you received it. If your start-up doesn't get funded, you'll regroup and restart the process, or you'll go with the scaled-down Plan B. You might talk to people who have endured similar setbacks. The guy down the street worked for years on his life's dream only to have his proposal shot down by every potential investor he met. Contact that guy and ask him some questions: How did he survive? What helped? What did he learn? Were there any unexpected benefits to the rejection? How does he think about it now?

Notice What's Happening

During the feedback conversation itself, periodically check in on your-self and slow things down. Self-observation awakens your left prefron-tal cortex—which is where the pleasures associated with learning are located.

Seth has been working to improve his awareness of what's happen-ing in the moment: "As quickly as I can, I now think to myself, 'Okay, this is that thing I do, that triggered thought pattern I get into, and that sick feeling I get.' And that one thought really helps. I'm not fighting or resisting my thoughts and reactions; I'm just noticing them. Once I think, 'Yep, this is the part where I have my overreactions,' I actually start to calm down."

2. SEPARATE THE STRANDS: FEELING / STORY / FEEDBACK

As you get better at slowing things down and noticing what's going on in your mind and body, you can begin to sort through your reactions. You'll get better at distinguishing your emotions from the story you tell about the feedback, and distinguishing both of these from what the feedback giver actually said.

Whether you do this sorting during the conversation or on reflection afterward, "separating the strands" is crucial to winding back the dis-tortions that creep into your interpretation of the feedback. It's like sep-arating the soundtrack from the scene when watching a movie. You are pulling apart the different threads so that you can see each element more clearly, and observe how each is affecting the other.

You do this by asking yourself three questions:

- *What do I feel?*
- *What's the story I'm telling (and inside that story, what's the threat)?*
- *What's the actual feedback?*

What do I feel? As you observe how you feel (or remember how you felt), try to *name* the feeling: anxiety, shame, anger, sadness, surprise. Work hard to notice how the feeling *feels*—physically—the same way you would describe the physical symptoms of food poisoning or the flu. Seth elaborates: "I feel a jolt of adrenaline that is by now very familiar to me. It's what I imagine an electric shock feels like. And then I often feel sick to my stomach and slightly faint. It's intensely unpleasant."

What's the story I'm telling (and inside the story, what's the threat)? As you notice your story about what the feedback means, don't worry about whether it's true or false, right or wrong, sensible or crazy; for now, just listen to it. Pay special attention to the threat. It could be about a bad thing that might happen as a result of the feedback, or about what this means for how others see you or how you see yourself. Seth examines his reaction to his boss's comment: "I've always worried that my boss has a kind of free-floating disapproval of me. So when he made the 'disorganized' comment, I thought, 'I knew it!' and then my thoughts snowballed: 'This job is the best opportunity I'll ever have and I've messed it up. I mess up everything and I can't stand it.' So there are a few threats in there: that my boss disapproves of me, that I will lose my job, that I won't be able to live with myself. Ultimately, that I'll just be unhappy all the time."

What's the actual feedback? Our mind takes what was said and immediately tells a story. It's important to peel back that story and ask yourself, what exactly *was* the feedback? What was said? With Seth, it was his boss's single comment about "everyone" being disorganized, including Seth. Everything else going on in Seth's mind beyond that was his own story—his assumptions about what his boss must have *meant*, his fears about losing his job, his concern about how he would live with himself.

The point is not that everything we add to the story is wrong. But we have to be clear about what we've added, and be aware of our patterns over time for the kinds of things we tend to add. Once we see the strands clearly, we can begin the work of assessing whether our story is reasonably aligned with the actual feedback, or whether and how it's distorted.[1]

Our Stories Shadowbox with the Past

Sometimes the threat in the story is obvious; other times it's harder to see. The feedback seems small or inconsequential or there doesn't seem to be any threat at all. And yet, on receiving the feedback, we become angry or despairing.

This happens when today's little story gets linked to larger stories from our past.

There's often a kind of "last straw" dynamic to this. Over the years, you've gotten bits of feedback that have piled up. Each individual piece of feedback seems like nothing—just another weightless comment—and you've kept it all in proportion. Until now. This most recent bit of feedback is suddenly, unaccountably, more than you can bear.

Your neighbor complains that you don't keep your lawn as well manicured as you should. You snap: "Fine. Don't look at it." You storm off and are seethe for the rest of the day.

Why has your neighbor's feedback set you off? Because you've been told your whole life that you are slightly oblivious to social norms—that manners matter, that you should tuck in your shirt, and that you should wrap your gifts. You usually shrug off such comments; you know in your heart that you have your priorities straight about what really matters in life. But this comment was the last straw.

This often happens when we have open wounds. Your colleague suggests you speak with more authority in meetings, and you flip out. You were bullied as a kid; you rode the bench on the soccer team because you were not aggressive enough on the field; your partner broke up with you because you never seemed to have an opinion. All unrelated life events, but each aggravates the same wound that never quite healed. On the face of it, your colleague's comment was small and contained, and offered with respect and care. But while the feedback is mild, the wound is deep.

So, are you overreacting to the current feedback? Yes and no. Yes, your emotional reaction is out of proportion, and when you calm down you will be able to see that. But it is a reasonable emotional reaction to the pattern your brain is recognizing; it's the latest chapter in a long story. And while your current quarrel is with the wrong person—it's really with your bully or your coach or your ex-partner—inside your head it's all part of the same frustrating mess.

The goal in untangling the strands of emotion, story, and feedback is to see what you've woven in that does and doesn't belong there. And the more clearly you see that, the better able you are to keep the feedback in perspective.

3. CONTAIN THE STORY

As we try to make sense of the world, there are a number of rules about the way the world works that we normally (if unconsciously) follow. They're like laws of physics for stories. For example, we know:

- *Time:* The present does not change the past. The present influences, but does not determine, the future.
- *Specificity:* Being lousy at one thing does not make us lousy at unrelated things. Being lousy at something now doesn't mean we will always be lousy at it.
- *People:* If one person doesn't like us it doesn't mean that everyone doesn't like us. Even a person who doesn't like us usually likes some things about us. And people's views of us can change over time.

In the wake of strong feelings, these rules are forgotten, and the feedback expands in all directions. As we saw in chapter 7, each thing becomes everything, nothing is contained, and we are knocked off balance.

But we can rebuild and reinforce the distinctions that matter. One way to do that is by noticing which of the above rules your story is violating and revising your story to be consistent with them. If the feedback is about right now, am I turning it into always—always was, always will be? If the feedback is about a specific skill or action, am I turning it into all of my skills and all of my actions? If it's from one person, am I imagining that it's from everyone?

When you notice that the feedback has stampeded over whatever barriers should keep it in place, you have to round up the feedback, and drop it back into the area where it belongs. Below, we offer three useful tools to help you do that: the Feedback Containment Chart, the Balancing Picture, and Right Sizing.

Use a Feedback Containment Chart

Filling out a Feedback Containment Chart helps you to see the feedback (so you don't deny it), while at the same time helping you to contain it (so you don't exaggerate it). Asking, *what is this feedback not about?* gives you a structured way of staying balanced.

Feedback Containment Chart	
What is this about?	**What *isn't* this about?**
Whether *this* person still loves me.	Whether I'm lovable, whether I'll find love.
Whether I'm as productive as I might be on the publications front.	Whether I'm a good clinician, a smart colleague, a valued team member.
Whether my first YouTube video was as good as I wanted it to be.	Whether I will ever make a video that gets positive response.
Whether I'm patient with the kids in the evenings.	Whether my kids know I love them, and whether I'm patient much of the time.

For example: You apply for your dream job and don't get it. Your first thought is: *I'll never get a job I like.* Now, break it down into the two columns in the chart. What is this *not* about? It doesn't predict your future. It doesn't tell you if you'll get the next job. It doesn't say that you will never work in your chosen field.

As you rope off the things it's not about, it's easier to see and learn from what it *is* about. Maybe there are qualifications the employer is looking for that you still don't have. Or maybe you have them but aren't presenting yourself in quite the right way. Figuring out what the feedback is actually about, and then doing something about it, takes work, but it becomes easier when you realize that you need to work on one or two discrete things, and not everything.

Draw the Balancing Picture

You know logically that you are overreacting to one negative student comment in a series of generally high ratings, but you find it hard on an emotional level to keep that comment in perspective. It helps to get visual: You can illustrate the balance as a drawing, a pie chart, a Post-it collage on your bathroom mirror, a macaroni sculpture.

Below, we see how Alita and Krista choose to depict balance. When Alita draws a representation of the range of patient feedback, she's shocked at how different the balance of positives and negatives feels when rendered this way. Krista's task, in contrast, is to remind herself that she's gotten feedback at all.

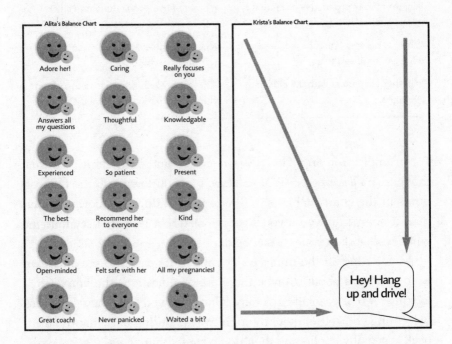

When you visualize the feedback in these ways, you literally *see* the proportions rather than just intuiting them. Your drawing is not some final "truth" about the feedback. But seeing it in front of you, looking so different from how it feels, helps you loosen up your story, and let go of exaggerated conclusions or unfounded fears.

Right-Size the Future Consequences

Feedback is not just about how you see yourself; it often involves real-world consequences. If you fail your pilot's license test, it's not just a blow to your self-confidence; it prevents you from flying. When that guy you like shows up at the holiday party with his new special someone, you might feel bad about yourself—but also, you won't be kissing that guy anytime soon. And getting a poor evaluation at work is not just about your performance, it's about your paycheck. If you didn't get a raise, that's not a "distortion" in your thinking. There's a dollar amount printed right there on your check. It seems that in regard to the consequences of feedback, there isn't much play in the joints.

But there is. While consequences are "objective," we still have our story about what the consequences *mean,* and this is where distortions and assumptions creep in. If you decide that not getting a raise means you're a "failure," well, that's a ridiculously broad conclusion to draw from the circumstance.

In addition, when in the grip of upsetting feedback, we often fail to distinguish between consequences that *will* happen and consequences that *might* happen. Your boss was clear that you're not getting a pay raise. But having your spouse leave you because you didn't get that pay raise is only something that *might* happen (and presumably the chances are small). Yet in the moment of receiving the bad news, the chances don't *feel* small. So you worry about it as if it *will* happen. We all do this on occasion—as if we didn't have enough to worry about already.

As Harvard psychologist Daniel Gilbert notes in *Stumbling on Happiness,* "[w]hen people are asked to predict how they'll feel if they lose a job or a romantic partner . . . they consistently overestimate how awful they'll feel and how long they'll feel awful."[2] And that's further compounded by our tendency to *under*estimate how resilient we are likely to be in the face of actual loss.

Let's take an example: Recently retired, you've just been diagnosed with severe arthritis in your shoulder. You can no longer swim, and this is no small matter. Until the arthritis, your daily swimming regimen was your big hobby and a great source of joy. So the diagnosis is terribly disappointing, and apparently there's nothing you can do about it. The consequences are what they are: no more swimming.

When you imagine what all this will mean for you, you picture your future life as being the same as your current life, except that where once there was swimming, there's now a gaping hole. What will you do for fun, exercise, and community? You assume the answer is, *you will do nothing*. But that's unlikely. Something will replace swimming, and whatever it is will serve many of the same purposes that swimming served.

In fact, ten years ago you hurt your lower back, which ruled out playing tennis. At the time, tennis was your greatest love and you despaired of ever finding something as healthy and fulfilling. And then you started swimming.

So when we think about the consequences of feedback, the goal is not to dismiss them or pretend they don't matter. The goal is to right-size them, to develop a realistic and healthy sense of what might happen and respond in line with these reasonable possibilities. After all, our predictions about life are just predictions, and they are often just plain wrong.

4. CHANGE YOUR VANTAGE POINT

Anything that helps you see a dark situation from a different point of view is beneficial. Here are a few ways to step outside your default perspective.

Imagine You're an Observer

Feedback packs an emotional punch because it's about *you*. If the exact same feedback were directed at, say, your sister, you might be able to explain to her that it is not so terribly serious and offer her advice on how to cope. Not just because you're trying to be helpful, but because from your perspective, she really is overreacting: "Mom said that to you? It means nothing. That's how she is these days. Why do you even care? You're an adult!"

Exactly. But if Mom had directed that comment at you, well, that would be different. You'd begin to wonder, *Why would Mom say that? Is she upset with me? Maybe she's disappointed with how my life has turned out. Does she still love me? Did she ever love me?* When you share your fears with your sister, she's incredulous: "What?! That one stupid comment is still bugging you? Why are you worrying about that? It meant nothing. That's how she is these days, and anyway, you're an adult!"

We can use this difference between being the object and the observer to our advantage. When we get feedback—when we are the object—we can imagine how we might react if instead we were the friend, the sibling, the observer. Try it as a thought experiment. You'll be surprised by how dramatic the difference in perspective is—even when you know it's just a thought experiment. Once you've shifted perspectives in this way, you can take your own advice. Why *are* you still thinking about that comment your mom made? That's just how she is now.

Of course, you can also solicit actual advice from a friend. That disturbing e-mail from your colleague? Show it to your friend and see if it sounds as damning to them as it does to you. Are you giving it too much weight? Too little? Some friends are better than others at offering this kind of support, but anyone who's not you is a good start.

Look Back from the Future

Try looking back on your life from the vantage point of ten or twenty or forty years from now. Ask yourself how significant today's events are likely to seem in the grand scheme of things. You might still find the current feedback challenging or the news regrettable, but in your final days, you're much more likely to regret the time you spent fretting. Today feels big right now, but from the perspective of many days hence, it will look pretty small.

Cast the Comedy

It's been said that comedy is tragedy plus time. The sooner you adopt that viewpoint, the better. Humor—even or especially gallows humor—offers a release from the emotional tension of a miserable moment, inviting you to see yourself and your life as an amusing play, with the usual array of hapless characters and interesting plot twists. If you can see humor in the situation, it means you're succeeding in gaining perspective.

The ability to laugh at yourself is also an indicator that you are ready and able to take feedback. Laughing at yourself requires you to loosen your grip on your identity. You have to align yourself with the world and to let go of trying to align the world to you. Your friend points out that the e-mail you sent him correcting his grammar had spelling mistakes. Your first instinct is to defend yourself: "Well, I was rushed when I sent you that e-mail. Obviously I know how to spell those words." But notice what happens when you think about it this way: *Ha! You got me.* It takes so much less energy.

Humor forces your brain to shift into a different emotional state. It taps that positive left side of your prefrontal cortex, where amusement lives. When you think something is funny, you are helping to disrupt the panic and anxiety that are taking hold, and to calm down those upsetting signals.

Juliet, emotionally wrung out, puts down her wineglass and smiles. "So . . . boy meets girl. Boy deceives, betrays, and dumps girl. Girl will never date another bad boy because she has finally learned her lesson. Wait, who's that super-hot drummer over there?"

At least that names the problem.

5. ACCEPT THAT YOU CAN'T CONTROL HOW OTHERS SEE YOU

How others see us and how we see ourselves are inevitably intertwined. We need others—their perspective on us—in order to see ourselves clearly. Their view may be only one piece of the puzzle, but it's an important piece. It's like the horseradish in the cocktail sauce: You don't want to eat the horseradish alone, but the sauce won't taste right without it.

So understandably, we care how others see us. But at the end of the day, we have to accept the fact that how others see us is something we can't control. Others' views of you may be incomplete, outdated, unfair, and based on absolutely nothing. Or most annoying, they may be claiming something about you that is actually true only about them. *I'm nasty and self-serving? Really? You're the one who's nasty and self-serving!* In one stroke, you are falsely accused and they are falsely exonerated.

We can become obsessed with the desire to get others to admit they are wrong and to change their views about us. How can we accomplish this? We can't. No matter how wrong and unfair their view of you might be, you can't control what others think. You love watching football because of the chesslike intricacies of the strategy involved, but your coworker insists it's your adolescent attempt to mask your insecure masculinity. You figure that if anyone would know why you like football or whether you feel secure about your masculinity, it would be you. But your coworker is equally sure that she's the authority on these particular subjects.

You can discuss it; you can offer counterexamples, supporting evidence, and notarized statements from your therapist or your dad or the pope. But you can't *make* her think something different about you. Maybe she will and maybe she won't.

The good news is that others aren't actually spending as much time thinking about you as you might imagine. Most people are simply too obsessed with themselves to be obsessed with you. So while you're sitting at home trying to figure out how your ex-spouse could be so horribly wrong about the kind of person you are, your ex-spouse is sitting at home watching Luke on *America's Got Talent*. Sure, she once called you a pathetic excuse for a human being, and she may still think that. But she's not dwelling on the matter.[3] And neither should you.

Have Compassion for Them

When someone levels an unfair attack at you or has spent a lifetime withholding approval, compassion is not the first response that comes to mind. And yet empathy can have a profound effect on how we see another person and hear their feedback. When your dad yet again fails to register any appreciation for an accomplishment that means a lot to you, remind yourself what *his* dad must have been like. Better still, think about your dad as the wounded little boy he must have been, and give that little boy a hug.

Speaking of little boys, when yours gets off the bus crying because a kid called him stupid, don't tell him he's not. That's just asking him to choose between your story and the mean kid's story. Help him find his own story in which to stand. Help him think through the actual evidence, what might be going on with the other kid, and what is actually true. If he can see for himself that he's not stupid, then he'll see that someone else's saying so doesn't make it so.

So don't dismiss others' views of you, but don't accept them wholesale either. Their views are *input,* not *imprint.*

WHEN LIFE COMES DOWN HARD

Okay, book, I've tried some of the things you're talking about here, and they're not helping. I'm not just upset and worried. I'm depressed and afraid—and it's worse than you know.

Well put. Us too, sometimes.

DROWNING

If we were designing a human learning system from scratch, we might be inclined to eliminate the most painful feelings. Let the toddler stumble and the teenager fumble, but don't let it hurt when they do. Your spouse leaves? Do a quick exit interview to find out how you can improve, buy yourself a killer pair of shoes, and head out on the town that very evening in search of your next exciting partner.

Of course, we're not built that way, not even close. And often enough we wonder: Do these strong negative emotions serve any useful purpose in our lives?

Sometimes they do. Emotional distress can send us under the covers for weeks, but it can also cause us—*force* us—to reevaluate ourselves and our lives in ways that we otherwise simply would not. Strong negative emotions can keep us in a rut, but they can also help us break out of one. In fact, we often learn the most from the feedback that in the moment is the most distressing.

But for some of us, that distress turns into long-term anxiety or despair, and we can become depressed, nonfunctioning, or suicidal. All those distortions that Google our problems and make it appear that things will never get better settle in for an extended stay. From the outside we look fine, and so we get well-meaning advice from friends about maintaining a good attitude, looking on the bright side, and staying active. But when we are really struggling, that sort of counsel is as useless as yelling "just float!" to someone who is drowning.

It is true that studies show that most people who experience trauma (for example) come out the other end intact, and in fact, some percentage experience post-traumatic growth. That should give people who have experienced trauma a clear, empirical reason to be optimistic, and it tells the rest of us that we need not be quite so fearful of the bad things that might happen to us.

But if we're not okay, then we're not. Some combination of predisposition and experience has broken us, and no matter how hard we work to keep the feedback balanced and contained, it just isn't helping.

When you are at your lowest, solace may come in the form of friends, family, community, or God. You may find relief in medication, therapy, or hospitalization. Exercise and meditation often do help, as does devoting your time and energy toward something larger than yourself.

We are proponents of all of these.

ASK FOR SUPPORT

Often the first step is reaching out and asking for help. That takes humility and courage. You might think those around you should know you're having trouble, but they may not. You might have to say the words: *I need help. I need you to be supportive right now.*

Ask those around you to be supportive mirrors. They can see that you're still lovable, and that what you're going through now isn't the whole story about you. They can see beyond the current pain to the place where things will get better. Their picture of you is clear-eyed and balanced, not distorted by the anxiety or shame or depression that clouds your own view.

Have faith in them. When that ex-spouse shows up at your door with an unflattering portrait she painted of you, supportive mirrors will stop you from hanging it over the fireplace in your living room. When your boss recommends that you have the words "I'm incompetent" tattooed to your forehead, they'll gently steer you away from the tattoo parlor.

If you can't find self-acceptance right now, get self-acceptance by proxy. Allow your mirrors to cast your vote for you. And allow them to help you find ways to make meaning out of the pain you're experiencing by doing something useful with it in the next chapter of your life. That's the subject of the next chapter of this book.

Summary: SOME KEY IDEAS

Before we can decide what we think of the feedback we get, we need to remove the distortions:

- *Be prepared, be mindful* — recognize your feedback footprint.
- *Separate the strands* — of feeling / story / feedback.
- *Contain the story* — what is this about and what isn't it about?
- *Change your vantage point* — to another, to the future, to the comedy.
- *Accept that you can't control how others see you.*

Don't buy their story about you wholesale.

Others' views of you are input, not imprint.

Reach out to supportive mirrors who can help you see yourself with compassion and balance.

9

CULTIVATE A GROWTH IDENTITY

Sort Toward Coaching

In chapter 7, we looked at how our wiring affects how we react to both positive and negative feedback, and how our emotional reactions affect our ability to see the feedback clearly. Whether we're elated or despairing, our emotions can warp our perception of the feedback as surely as a fun house mirror. In chapter 8, we talked about how to straighten out the feedback so that you can understand it in perspective.

But even "actual size" feedback can destabilize our sense of ourselves. Feedback can contradict or undermine the story we tell about who we are, or it can confirm our worst fears about ourselves. Learning profitably from feedback is not only about how we interpret the feedback; it's also about how we hold our identity. In this chapter we'll examine how to build an identity that is robust, not brittle, feedback friendly rather than feedback averse.

FEEDBACK CAN ROCK OUR SENSE OF SELF

Visiting Mom in the facility was always heartbreaking. Saying goodbye at the end of each visit and walking away as she watched on, sad and confused, was almost more than you could bear.

After your mother's dementia diagnosis, your dad cared for her, and you helped out as much as possible. But as incontinence set in and the falls grew more frequent, you found yourself lying awake nights sick with worry. The toll on your father was becoming intolerable, and the risk of something tragic happening only increasing. Eventually you helped talk your father into putting your mom in a full-time care facility, for her safety as much as for your dad's sanity. It was the right thing to do. Wasn't it?

Not according to your mother's best friend, Rita, who told your father that she will never speak to either of you again. When you hear this, you are filled with shame.

IDENTITY: OUR SELF-STORY

Identity is the story we tell ourselves about ourselves—what we're like, what we stand for, what we're good at, what we're capable of. *I'm a strong leader; I'm an involved grandmother; I'm rational; I'm passionate; I'm always fair.*[1] When feedback contradicts or challenges our identity, our story about who we are can unravel.

> *You see yourself as smart, hardworking, and politically savvy. But after ten years of focused pursuit, you've just been denied tenure. Now who are you? And now what?*

> *Nothing is more important to you than being a good son. Rita's condemnation slices through you like a white-hot knife, cutting deep into your sense of self.*

> *Your husband delivers an ultimatum—it's me or the dog. You are confused to realize you prefer the dog. Does that make you a bad person?*

It's not just big, important feedback that can knock us sideways. The everyday stuff can trip identity as well: Your best buddy gives his playoff tickets to someone else. The customer you helped out for an hour yesterday called back today and requested to speak to another representative. Even positive feedback can be disorienting: You were comfortable with the image of yourself as the "starving artist." With the sudden acclaim for your latest work, you wonder whether you've become a sellout.

We can even be triggered by information that isn't about *us.* The girl you used to work the register with at KFC was named head of NASA and your nursery school nemesis just announced he's taking his company public. You feel happy enough for them, yet somehow worse about yourself. Because identity stories are influenced by how we are doing relative to those around us, our peers become the yardsticks we use to gauge how we measure up.[2]

IS YOUR IDENTITY BRITTLE OR ROBUST?

Imagine two people with similar natural abilities, life experiences, and brain wiring. You might assume that their identities, and ability to absorb feedback without losing balance, would be about the same.

And they might be. But not necessarily. *Our ability to metabolize challenging feedback is driven by the particular way we tell our identity story.* Some people tell their identity story in ways that cause their identity to be brittle, while others tell their identity story in ways that allow it to be robust. Those in the latter group are predisposed to treat feedback not as a threat to who they are, but as a core aspect of who they are.

There is good news in this: While some of us do it naturally, we can all *learn* to hold our identity in ways that make us more resilient. We can't control the feedback life throws at us, but we can make some specific shifts in assumptions that can improve our ability to take it in, stay balanced, and learn from it. Two shifts are crucial. We need to:

(1) Give up simple identity labels and cultivate complexity; and
(2) Move from a fixed mindset to a growth mindset.

We'll look at each of these in turn, and then give you three practices that can help you make these shifts amid the business and busyness of everyday life.

GIVE UP SIMPLE LABELS AND CULTIVATE COMPLEXITY

While our identities are built from the endless complexity of our life experiences, we tend to hold these identities as simple labels such as I'm competent, I'm good, I'm worthy of love. These labels serve an important function: Life can be messy and confusing, and simple identity labels remind us of our values and priorities, of what we're trying to live up to. If I'm a man of my word, well, that settles it. I may be tempted to break my commitment, and I can even justify doing so . . . but that's not who I am.

Yet simple labels also present a problem. They are simple because they are "all or nothing." That works fine when we're "all." But when we get feedback that we are *not* all, we hear it as feedback that we are *nothing*. There's no "partly all" or "sometimes all," or "all, except for . . ." If we're not good, we're bad; if we're not smart, we're stupid; if not a saint, then a sinner.

No wonder feedback feels so threatening and we are so easily knocked over. We've set ourselves up with identity stories that operate like a light switch, and even minor feedback can flip that switch. If we're not ablaze in glory, we're lost in the dark.

KEEP IT OUT OR LET IT IN?

When all-or-nothing identities bump up against negative feedback, they are often overturned: The feedback becomes headline news in the latest issue of *The Daily Me*: "Hardworking Academic" becomes "Fool Who Wasted Years Chasing Tenure." "Good Son" gets replaced by "Heartless Child Fails Mother." The feedback is the headline in our identity story, and all the other things we know about ourselves get shoved to the back page. And in this way, the feedback gets exaggerated.

In our struggle to cope, we spot the other choice: Keep the feedback *out*. If we can figure out why the feedback is flawed or off base, *if we can do some skillful wrong spotting*, then we can "deny" the feedback and preserve our current sense of self. We're safe. We're still "all." Our identity story remains intact.

All-or-nothing identities present us with this choice: Either we can exaggerate the feedback, or we can deny it. And often, we end up toggling between the two. We shift back and forth between accepting and rejecting, but find no stable place to land. ("If I accept this feedback, it means I'm a bad person. Maybe I am. But that can't be right. I'm going to reject this feedback. But why would they say it if it weren't true? Maybe it is right. But I know myself better than they do, and if it were true, it would just be too upsetting, so it can't be true. On the other hand . . .") And on we go, flipping like a fish on the deck of a boat.

Neither choice feels right because neither choice *is* right. The answer doesn't lie in finding just the right way to jerry-rig the balance between exaggeration and denial. The answer lies in how we hold our identity in the first place.

EMBRACE IDENTITY NUANCE

So, while simple labels help orient us in the world, they don't hold up well against the complexity of the world. You're a man of your word, but what if your choice is between keeping your word to your supervisor and keeping your word to your stepson? Or maybe you see yourself as "fair," and fair is fair, right? But what seemed fair last week suddenly seems less fair now that you've talked to others who are affected by your choice.

So the simple labels are too black-and-white to be the whole story about who you are. You are someone who cares deeply about being trustworthy or fair or responsible, and there are a thousand examples of your being each of these. And some examples of your falling short. That's reality.

Your mom died about six months after the placement in the full-time care facility, and you still struggle with whether the decision was the right one. You had good reasons to suggest the move to your dad. At times you can't conceive of any other way it could have gone, while at others, you think it was a grave moral lapse, the worst thing you've ever been involved in. In your mind, you juxtapose images of your mom's being there for you throughout your life with her bewildered expression as you leave the facility. Maybe you could have moved home to help, or brought your mother to your place and hired a full-time nurse. People do that. Why didn't you?

Here's the bottom line: As long as you tell your self-story in these black-and-white terms, you will find no peace. You can't choose between whether you're a good person or a bad person. Whichever you select, there is evidence for the opposite conclusion.

It wasn't a Disney movie. No fairy godmother or flock of bluebirds was going to come along with stardust and wand-waving solutions. It was complicated, and your feelings about it complicated. You were trying to figure things out for your mom, and also trying to support your father. You wanted your mother to be surrounded by love, but you also wanted her to be safe and taken care of. You were trying to figure out how to do right for each of your parents in the face of a hundred unknowns.

There are some things about how you handled the situation that you're proud of. You saw your mother almost every day. You made her photo books about her life, filled with pictures of the early days—the ones she could still remember. And there are some things you are less proud of—opportunities missed, flashes of impatience. Your father probably didn't get enough of your time and attention. And certainly it took a toll on your own family in those final months.

As your story of the situation and yourself becomes more nuanced, you wonder whether there is something to learn in Rita's view. You get up the courage to call her, and she agrees to talk. She tells you how she feels, and you understand. You tell her how you feel, and she doesn't. Rita has some implicit rules about these things—rules you probably shared yourself until you'd been through the experience with your mother.

Rita insists your behavior was selfish, and that may be where you learn the most. You don't know if "selfish" is the right word, but self-interest was certainly involved. By placing her in a facility, you no longer had to worry about your mom's falling; you didn't have to clean up accidents, or worry that she wasn't eating enough. You didn't have to be concerned about your father collapsing from the stress of caretaking. The idea that self-interest was involved in your decision clashes with a core part of your identity, to be sure. You always saw yourself as someone who would do *anything* for those you love. But now you recognize it's not that simple.

With this acceptance comes sadness, but also a kind of balance.

THREE THINGS TO ACCEPT ABOUT YOURSELF

The sadness and the balance. That's not unusual. There are things about ourselves that are hard to accept, but when we do, we're more grounded. Tough feedback is less likely to knock us over; we can take it in as being at least part of the story.

No one is perfect, and all things being equal, it's better not to believe you are—not just because it makes you less likable at parties, but also because it makes it harder for you to learn from feedback. In *Difficult Conversations* we offered three things to accept about yourself, and we include them here: You will make mistakes, you have complex intentions, and you have contributed to the problem. Accepting these is a lifelong project, but working on them makes hard feedback easier to take in.

You Will Make Mistakes

If you have any doubts about this, just ask your spouse. In fact, your particular spouse may be all the proof you need.

This is not the first you've heard that people make mistakes—even brilliant, generous, otherwise awesome people. But it's an easy truth to forget when someone is pointing out a specific mistake we have made. If you think that that would be precisely the easiest time to remember it, you'd be mistaken. When a mistake is pointed out to us, our first instinct is to defend ourselves or explain it away. *Mistake? Not mine, not at all. I was given the wrong date for that meeting, and anyway, I had decided I didn't need to attend.*

Accepting the fact that you will make mistakes takes some of the pressure off. Any given mistake may still have the capacity to shock and dismay you, and the degree to which it highlights your blockheadedness is unfortunate. But you can be confident that people make mistakes like these, and that some of those people are you.

You Have Complex Intentions

This observation gets less airplay than the one about mistakes, although it's probably even harder to accept. Mixed in with our positive intentions are less noble ones—we can be self-promoting, vengeful, shallow, vain, greedy. We get tired and cut corners. We try not to lie, but forgive ourselves for occasionally landing just shy of the full truth.

When we receive negative feedback about our intentions, without exception we take exception. We had good intentions. We know we had good intentions because that's what good people have. We kept that assignment for ourselves because we were the best person for it. The fact that we've always wanted to go to Hawaii had nothing to do with it.

Pursuing a certain amount of self-interest is a requirement of being alive, and occasionally that self-interest will conflict with someone else's self-interest, and occasionally that will be pointed out to you. It may be hard to see or hard to admit. You shouldn't stop striving to improve, but accepting what "is" can be an enormous relief.

You Have Contributed to the Problem

It's easy to do relationship math such that we are the wronged party in the equation. And when we're the wronged party, we don't have to bother listening to feedback. You e-mailed the wrong documents, and now somehow you've got feedback for *me*? I don't think so. When you attached the wrong documents, you earned yourself a lifetime membership in my "I-don't-have-to-take-feedback-from-you-about-this-problem club."

Of course, that math doesn't usually add up. As we saw in chapter 6, in most situations we've both contributed to the problem. We've each done or failed to do things that got us into this mess. If we are going to learn from the experience and address the problem, we have to look at the whole picture. Which means we've got to close down the no-feedback club. Just because we have feedback for them ("Send the right documents") doesn't mean they don't have feedback for us ("Don't tell me 'the attachments look good' if you haven't even looked at them").

Accepting that we're not perfect also means giving up the idea that being perfect is a viable way to escape negative feedback.[3] It's a seductive thought, but it doesn't work; you can't behave your way out of ever receiving feedback. You can't outrun it, and you will collapse trying. Accepting imperfection is not just a good idea, it's the only choice.

YOU'VE BEEN COMPLICATED ALL ALONG

The first step, then, in keeping or regaining balance and improving your odds of learning from feedback is to recognize that your identity label is a simplification. You can more easily metabolize tough feedback when you move away from the all-or-nothing instinct. You aren't going from good to bad, or even from good to complicated. You've been complicated all along.

SHIFT FROM A FIXED MINDSET TO A GROWTH MINDSET

Now that you've gotten out of the simple label business, let's take a look at another aspect of how you hold your identity: Do you consider your traits and abilities fixed and finished? Or are they always evolving and capable of growth?

Professor Carol Dweck of Stanford University says this distinction in how we think about ourselves has important implications for our ability and desire to learn from feedback. Where did she learn this? From kids.

PUZZLING KIDS

Dweck began her research with a simple question: How do kids cope with failure? To find out, she brought children to her lab and had them engage with progressively tougher puzzles. As the puzzles got more challenging, the kids grew frustrated, disengaged, and finally gave up.

Except some didn't. In fact, to Dweck's surprise, a few of them became more energized as the challenges increased. One boy licked his lips excitedly as he tried first one approach and then another, saying, "I was hoping this would be informative!" Dweck herself was puzzled and somewhat amazed. *What's wrong with these kids?* she wondered. *Why aren't they giving up? Why aren't they taking in the feedback from their puzzle struggle and getting upset that they're failing?*[4]

Dweck talked with the children to find out how they were making sense of things and concluded that the ones who gave up quicker thought along these lines: *The first puzzles showed I was smart. These new ones are making me look (and feel) dumb.* In contrast, the kids who persisted thought this: *These new harder puzzles are helping me get better at doing puzzles. This is fun!*

The reason some kids kept trying had nothing to do with their interest in or aptitude for puzzles. It came from each child's mindset. The kids who stopped assumed their puzzle-solving skill was a fixed trait. They had a certain amount of it, the way a water molecule has a certain number of hydrogen atoms. The kids who kept going viewed their puzzle-solving ability as a flexible trait that could change and grow.

FIXED VERSUS GROWTH ASSUMPTIONS

If you have a fixed mindset, every situation you encounter is a referendum on whether you have the smarts or ability that you think (or hope) you have. "Fixed" kids do fine when the puzzles are easy. But when they start to struggle, they hear the puzzle whispering to them: *Not enough puzzle smarts. You are not up to this task.* They become discouraged, impatient, embarrassed. Better to quit than to continue to face what they lack.

In contrast, the kids with growth mindsets assume that puzzle smarts aren't something you either have or you don't. They assume that it's a skill that can be developed, and moreover, they see struggling with a tough puzzle as just the challenge they need to improve. As Dweck explains, "Not only weren't they discouraged by failure, they didn't even think they were failing. They thought they were learning."[5] For them, the puzzle is not an evaluator, but a coach.

It's as if the growth-mindset kids were doing the puzzles in a room called the "Learning Room," and the fixed-mindset kids were doing the puzzles in a room called the "Testing Room." Which room would you rather live your life in?

Dweck observes that many of us believe that our core traits, assets, and character—our identities—are "carved in stone."[6] The way we were talked to as children (and the way we often talk to our own children) reinforces this tendency: "He's a born leader," "She's very bright," "You've always been a very kind person," "You're a natural athlete." Our identity stories calcify around what we have and what we don't. And we buy into the obvious implication: Effort is unlikely to move the dial. How we are described is how we are, and the rating is permanent; it doesn't come out in the wash.

BUT AREN'T SOME TRAITS FIXED?

It's reasonable to wonder: Isn't the fixed mindset just an acknowledgment of reality?

It's true that some traits are less influenced by effort than others. Fish are better than you at breathing underwater, and it's not because of their can-do attitude. And each of us finds that some things come more easily than others: Math and running feel natural to you, drawing and patience still don't.

Researchers argue over the precise degree to which various traits are fixed or elastic, and have offered both thrilling evidence of growth and dispiriting stories of limitations. But the bottom line is this: People do get better when they apply themselves, and people apply themselves when they believe they can get better. This is true whether we are excruciatingly bad at something or preternaturally good.

And effort matters most with the qualities in life that matter most— things like intelligence, leadership, performance, confidence, compassion, creativity, self-awareness, and collaboration. These all grow with attention and improve with coaching.

IMPLICATIONS FOR HOW WE RESPOND TO FEEDBACK AND CHALLENGE

The fixed and growth assumptions we carry have profound implications for how we see ourselves, how we hear the feedback we get, and how we respond to it.

The Accuracy of Our Self-Perception

Part of learning and growing is having a decent handle on your current capabilities. That tells you what strengths you might capitalize on and nurture, as well as what weaknesses you need to work on or work around. Dweck reports that those with growth mindsets are "amazingly accurate" in gauging their current abilities, while people with fixed mindsets are "terrible" at estimating their own proficiencies.[7]

Why might this be? If your traits are fixed, it should be easier to get an accurate read on your abilities. After all, they're not a moving target.

But it's more complicated than that: Although your mindset may be fixed, the daily incoming data about you can fluctuate wildly. *Yesterday I was brilliant; today, a dolt. Last week I was competent; this week I seem to be a real screwup.* It can be hard to match up this broad range of data with your simple, fixed sense of yourself. It's not surprising that you'd be confused.

If you've got a growth identity, it's easier to understand the mixed data. It's information, not damnation. Instead of hearing *Last week I was competent; this week a screwup,* you hear *Last week I was on top of things; this week I'm dropping balls.* It's not who you are, but something you did. Growth identity folks aren't thrown by the contradiction and are motivated to seek accurate information in order to adjust and learn.

How We Listen to Feedback

Our mindset—and resulting identity stories—has a significant impact on what we pay attention to and what we don't. Researchers Jennifer Mangels and Catherine Good brought both fixed- and growth-mindset undergraduates into a brain lab at Columbia, where they were hooked up to EEG monitors and then took a test that drew from general knowledge of literature, history, music, and art. Each student was then told two things: whether they got each question right or wrong, and the correct answers for the questions they missed. The fixed-mindset students paid close attention to whether they got each question right or wrong, but lost interest when informed what the right answer was. The growth-mindset folks, in contrast, listened closely to the right answers. They didn't ignore the evaluation, but they were also hungry for coaching—how they could do better the next time. And indeed, when retested, the growth-mindset students outperformed their fixed counterparts.[8]

How We Respond to Struggle
Can Create Self-fulfilling Prophecies

This may help to explain why, in the wake of failure, those with growth mindsets tend to bounce back sooner. They see a shortfall as an opportunity to grow and redouble their efforts as a result. After a setback at school, growth-identity kids said they planned to study more or study differently the next time, while kids with fixed mindsets were more likely to say that they "felt dumb, would study less the next time, and seriously consider cheating." Perhaps driven by humiliation, people with a fixed mindset are also more likely to lie to others about their performance and withdraw after failure. They give up earlier, letting setbacks become settling points.[9]

The Framing Matters

Although Dweck says that about half of us tend to have fixed-identity assumptions, the way we tell the story matters.

In fact, a single sentence can nudge us in the right (or wrong) direction. In another study, Dweck and colleagues had fifth graders work on an easy puzzle. Upon successful completion, half the children were told: "Wow, you're really smart!" The other half were told: "Wow, you worked hard at that puzzle!" Then both groups were asked what they would like to do next: a harder puzzle or an easier one.

Guess which group opted for the challenge? You guessed it.

One thing to learn from this study is that praising our kids for their intelligence is, surprisingly, counterproductive to their learning. We're better off extolling their effort if we're hoping to encourage them to take on new challenges.

But wait a minute, why does this work? By the numbers, about half of those kids who were admired for working hard had fixed mindsets. And yet they opted to take on the next challenge as readily as their growth-mindset groupmates. Perhaps the reason is that praising effort rather than ability doesn't trigger their fixed-identity anxiety. Or perhaps it's that working hard is a trait they feel confident they can replicate; whatever happens with that next puzzle, their hard-working-ness could shine. But the bottom line is that by focusing on a trait that emphasized the *learning process*, these kids were just as willing to take risks and take on a challenge.

MOVE TOWARD A GROWTH IDENTITY

So how *do* you prod yourself from fixed assumptions to growth? The first step is to be aware of your own tendencies. Are you more inclined to live in the Testing Room or the Learning Room? Do you experience challenges as threats to your identity or as opportunities for growth? Is failure the end of the game or just another play in an ongoing game?

Look at the chart below and think about which assumptions resonate with you.[10]

Identity Questions	Fixed	Growth
Who am I?	I'm fixed. I am who I am.	I change, learn, grow.
Can I change?	My traits are fixed—effort doesn't really change the fundamental truth about people.	My capabilities are always evolving. Effort and hard work pay off.
What's the goal?	Success. The outcome is what matters.	The process of learning is what's rewarding. Success is a by-product.
When do I feel smart/capable/successful?	When I do something perfectly, and when I do it better than others.	When I struggle with something and then start to figure it out (others' abilities are less relevant to my own potential).
Response to challenge	Threat! I may be exposed as not up to the challenge.	Opportunity! I can learn something and improve.
Most comfortable environment?	Safely within my abilities and comfort zone.	Just outside my abilities to stretch my capabilities.

If you're confused about whether a particular trait or ability is capable of growth, that's okay, too. These aren't easy questions. But just because the answer is not a clear yes does not mean it's a clear no. Try experimenting: Set out to change a habit or improve one of your skills. Find a coach and get your hands dirty. Force yourself to try things you aren't good at, and when you fall on your face, make a list of three ways you could do better next time. Rinse and repeat, and see what happens.

For instance, after your experience with your mother and your conversation with Rita, what have you learned that will change how you handle a comparable situation with your father? How will your experience influence what you teach and expect from your own children? If you can see things you will work at, if you can see things you have learned and might change the next time, then you're on your way to holding your sense of self as capable of growth and change. The experience teaches you rather than labels you.

And through it all, remember that negative feedback is not a rebuke to the growth-mindset assumption. A growth mindset is not without setbacks and disappointments. You'd hoped you were farther along this learning curve than you apparently are. Your payoff for effort is smaller than you'd hoped it might be. A growth identity is not about whether you get terrific or troubling feedback. It's about how you hold whatever you get.

· · ·

Let's turn to three specific practices that can help you cultivate a growth identity.

PRACTICE #1: SORT TOWARD COACHING

Some feedback is primarily evaluative (your grade, your blog ranking). Other feedback is intended as coaching. The giver's only purpose is to help you learn or get better at something. But as we saw with our twin batters Annie and Elsie in chapter 2, even feedback offered as pure coaching can reasonably be heard as evaluation. *Try it this way* (coaching) contains the implicit message *So far, you haven't been doing it as well as you might* (evaluation).

As feedback receivers, we are always sorting feedback into coaching and evaluation bins. Your choice of bin makes a huge difference in your ability to take in feedback productively. The reason is this: While identity is easily triggered by evaluation, it is far less threatened by coaching. It's almost like getting a free pass. You can learn without enduring the arduous task of reevaluating who you are.

Elsbeth is on break after finishing the first half of a three-hour presentation. The client approaches her and comments that it's going well, but suggests she amp up the energy level.

Is this coaching or evaluation?

If Elsbeth takes it as coaching, she might think to herself, *I should have another cup of coffee and figure out how to make this next segment more interactive.* . . . If she takes it as evaluation, her identity is hooked: *Am I boring you and everyone else? People usually love my sessions! But maybe I'm not up to an audience this senior.* . . . Elsbeth is left struggling with her self-image, unable to engage with coaching that might actually improve the next part of her talk. Identity triggered, learning blocked.

Hear Coaching as Coaching

Sorting toward coaching is not always easy. But there's one kind of feedback that should not give us any trouble: feedback that is specifically *offered* as coaching. In that case, everything lines up in favor of hearing it as such. It's what they intend, it's what will be helpful.

Yet too often we get it wrong and still sort coaching into the evaluation bin.

> *Your friend shows you a better route to the airport, but you hear it as a judgment that you don't know your way around the city.*

> *Your unit head tells you about a new app for time management, but you hear him criticizing you for procrastinating.*

> *Your partner tells you what she finds romantic, but you hear her saying you are clueless and self-absorbed.*

We snatch defensiveness from the jaws of learning.

As feedback conversations get more emotional or the stakes grow higher, it gets easier to hear evaluation, and tougher to hear the coaching.

Try this exercise: Think of feedback you've received in the past several months, big or small. Say, for example, that your friend asked you why you let your children stay up so late.

First assume that the feedback was intended as evaluation. What would the feedback say about you? You're overpermissive? A bad parent?

Now imagine that the feedback was intended as coaching—something you might learn from. In that case, you'd probably have a conversation with your friend about what they've noticed and what they're concerned about. It might be something you've already considered or something you haven't. It's another set of life experiences for you to consider when you make parenting choices.

If you run through this sorting exercise a few times, you'll notice three things. First, you'll see that with some effort you *can* hear most feedback either way. Second, if you're successful in hearing it as coaching, you'll notice that your identity reaction is diminished or gone. And third, you'll start to notice patterns—your own tendencies. Not uncommonly people have this insight: *Wow, I oversort toward evaluation way more than I realized.* Whether you do that only one out of ten times or eight out of ten times, each of those oversorts is a potential meltdown that didn't need to happen, and feedback you could have been learning from. There are enough real challenges in life. You don't need to create imaginary ones.

When Coaching and Evaluation Get Tangled

Of course, sometimes the person giving the feedback intends a mix of evaluation *and* coaching, or, more commonly, just hasn't thought about it clearly. In intense personal relationships this can be especially confusing, and it takes real effort to sort things out.

A grown daughter, Lisa, tells her mother, Margaret: "When I was eight and Dad left, I felt like you had abandoned me, too. You were so consumed with your new job and your new social life—with 'finding me a new dad.' I don't think you realized how hard it was for me."

Margaret hears Lisa saying, "You were a bad mother," and is devastated. She feels the feedback is unfair and defends herself: "Lisa, I worked *so hard* to make things okay for you. It was a terribly hard time for both of us, and I was really struggling emotionally and financially."

This conversation is a good example of how identity and feedback collide and of the fallout that results. Margaret sees herself as a good parent—it's a core theme in her identity story. She hears Lisa saying that she was a failure as a mother, and is thrown into the dilemma of either accepting what her daughter is saying (and seeing herself as a failure) or arguing with Lisa's characterization in an attempt to keep the feedback out.

It's important to ask: What does Lisa want? What is her purpose in bringing the subject up? Does she want her mother to admit she was a bad mother? No. Lisa is hoping for three things: She wants her mother to understand how she felt growing up; she wants acknowledgment from her mother that some of her mother's choices contributed to Lisa's pain; and she wants a better current relationship.

Clearly, there is evaluation and judgment here, and anyone in Margaret's position would hear it. But the core of what Lisa is trying to communicate is coaching. Her goal is not for her mother to feel judged, but for her mother to *learn* about Lisa's views and feelings. And in time, Lisa wants an improved relationship with her mother.

We can test the assertion that Lisa intends coaching by looking at different ways Margaret might respond and imagining which would be most satisfying to Lisa. If her mother says, "Okay, maybe I was a bad mother," that is unlikely to do Lisa much good. In contrast, Margaret might say, "Wow, I never realized how I was affecting you during that time. It's hard for me to hear that I was doing things that were hurtful to you. I'm so sorry." Of course, this will be a longer conversation, but likely to be more satisfying to Lisa. And at some point they can begin to discuss how they'd like their relationship to be now.

Placing the conversation in a coaching frame may help lessen Margaret's emotional pain, but that's not the reason it's important to do.

Margaret should hear it as coaching because it's at the heart of what her daughter intends. Hearing coaching helps Margaret to move away from her own internal identity reaction and work to hear what her daughter is really saying.

PRACTICE #2: UNPACK JUDGMENT
FROM THE EVALUATION SUITCASE

Some feedback, of course, is straight evaluation, and it's this that challenges our identity most directly. *I'm breaking up with you; you didn't get the job; the neighbors won't let their kid play at your house because they disapprove of your "home environment."*

As we figure out how to hear evaluation, it's helpful to break evaluation itself down into three constituent parts: assessment, consequences, and judgment.

> *Assessment* ranks you. It tells you where you stand. At the track meet your assessment is clear: You ran the mile in five minutes, nineteen seconds, placing you fourth in the forty- to forty-five age group.
>
> *Consequences* are about the real-world outcomes that result from the assessment: Based on the assessment, what, if anything, is going to happen? As a result of your race time, you qualify for the regionals, but do not yet qualify for the nationals. Consequences can be certain or speculative, immediate or down the road.
>
> *Judgment* is the story givers and receivers tell about the assessment and its consequences. You are delighted by your performance—it's better than you expected this morning. Your coach is disappointed by your performance and thinks you should have done better.

By looking at the components of evaluation this way, you can figure out what about a given evaluation is triggering your identity. In the racing example, it's not the assessment or the consequences; it's your coach's judgment. You see yourself as someone who doesn't let others down. Learning that your coach is disappointed challenges that aspect of how you see yourself. Not in a huge way, but it's something you notice.

Breaking it down also helps you focus on what you want to discuss with the feedback giver: Are you in agreement with the assessment but not the judgment?[11] Are the consequences clear and fair? Why does your coach have a different judgment about your time, and what can you learn from that?

Accurate assessment is valuable and the consequences are important to understand. Others' judgments? You may find certain judgments illuminating; other judgments you'll rightly dismiss. It's one person's interpretation, and you've got your own interpretation, thank you very much.

PRACTICE #3: GIVE YOURSELF A "SECOND SCORE"

Let's imagine you get a negative evaluation. The assessment seems fair, but the consequences are painful. You get rejected—by that potential employer, that girl, that graduate program, that team, that client.

Now what?

Whatever else you do to cope, imagine that there is an invisible second evaluation. After every low score you receive, after each failure and faltering step, give yourself a "second score" based on how you handle the first score. In every situation in life, there's the situation itself, and then there's how you handle it. Even when you get an F for the situation itself, you can still earn an A+ for how you deal with it.

There are two pieces of good news here. First, while the initial evaluation may not be fully within your control, your reaction to it usually is. And second, in the long term, the second score is often more important than the first.

Mel and Melinda, two aspiring performers, work hard on their first YouTube video, which they hope will be their ticket out of the mundane world of their day jobs. They write it, direct it, act in it, and edit it. They compose and perform the music. The final product exceeds their expectations. It's brilliant. They post it.

It gets savaged. The comments are uniformly thumbs down, and several are needlessly personal and cruel. And it's getting a paltry number of hits.

Mel is crushed, angrily accusing the world of being too stupid to understand what he and Melinda are trying for. Melinda is just as upset, but as she licks her wounds, she wonders what they can learn from the experience.

A few weeks later Melinda watches the video and notices for the first time that, although the ideas are clever, the execution has problems. The lyrics are hard to make out, the jump cuts are too jumpy. She shares her observations with Mel, who responds that creative people would be able to see past the problematic execution.

Melinda has a different response: She's determined to get good—scary good—at the *craft* of making these short movies. She reads everything she can find on social media and takes an evening class on film editing. Over the course of the next year she develops and posts several new videos and starts to pick up subscribers to her channel. Eventually she reworks the original video and posts it to a mostly thumbs-up reception.

Both Mel and Melinda got a thumbs-down first score; only Melinda got a thumbs-up second score. In this example, as is so often the case, a good second score is what really matters.

To be clear, we're not just saying that it's good to be resourceful and resilient. We're suggesting that you make getting a good second score part of your identity: *I don't always succeed, but I take an honest shot at figuring out what there is to learn from the failure. I'm actually pretty good at that.* You might even have a kind of Second Score Scorecard set up in your mind. That will make this particular part of your identity easier to keep track of. The scorecard reminds you that the initial evaluation is not the end of the story. It's the start of the second story about the meaning you'll make of the experience in your life.

A strong second-score identity can help you deal with even the most challenging life events. Heather recalls the day her longtime girlfriend left her, and the weeks and months that followed: "All I had control over was my reaction, and I got up every morning and went to work. I treated everyone around me respectfully. Actually, working to 'handle it well' gave me something to focus on and to feel good about. And I do."

As we mentioned in the previous chapter, handling something well doesn't mean denying pain or that you emerge unscathed. Heather isn't saying, "Now that my girlfriend has left me, I'm happier than ever!" It's

First Score	Second Score
Performance Review:	
Meets Expectations	Exceeds Expectations
	Did a decent job of asking questions rather than withdrawing. Got clarity on expectations. Putting time in to improve my product knowledge, which is one place I fell short.
Review of My Restaurant:	
2 stars	4 stars
(and a generally negative review)	Didn't blame others. Didn't overdwell. Set a good example for kitchen and waitstaff. Changed some menu items. Retrained and replaced some waitstaff. Pretty confident we've corrected some issues that were flagged fairly.

about facing whatever you're dealing with head-on. If you find yourself unable to sleep and fighting bouts of anxiety and loneliness, then handling it well means having the courage to admit that you need help and asking for it. Even as Heather's identity as someone who is worthy of love took a hard hit, she found growth: "I learned that I could deal with a tough loss with grace and resilience."

That's not nothing.

Summary: SOME KEY IDEAS

Our ability to take in and metabolize feedback is affected by how we tell our identity story. Shift from:

- Simple all-or-nothing to realistically complex.
- Fixed to growth — so that you see challenge as opportunity, and feedback as useful information for learning.

Three practices help:

1. Sort for coaching. Hear coaching as coaching, and find the coaching in evaluation.
2. When evaluated, separate the judgment from assessment and consequences.
3. Give yourself a second score for how you handle the first score.

FEEDBACK IN CONVERSATION

10

HOW GOOD DO I HAVE TO BE?

Draw Boundaries When Enough Is Enough

Martin started in the oil business straight out of the Marines, working his way up on the rig. He is now considered one of the best drillers in the business. After a long shift, Martin crawls into his bunk and pulls out his unfinished development plan. It's overdue. He needs to send it shoreside tonight or risk an escalated round of pestering.

> **Item 23b:** *Please list your personal goals for the coming year. Include benchmarks for how you will measure your attainment of those goals.*

Martin groans. *After thirty-one years in the business, I need yet another round of hungry new goals?* He smiles and writes: "My goal is to complete another year safely and productively. And to get you to leave me alone about my goals."

No benchmarks necessary.

FINDING BOUNDARIES, SETTING BOUNDARIES

Most of this book explores how to get better at receiving feedback—taking it in and understanding it fully before deciding whether to accept it. But this raises a question: Is it okay not only to turn down feedback, but to say, "I don't even want to *hear* it"?

It is.

In fact, being able to establish limits on the feedback you get is crucial to your well-being and the health of your relationships. Being able to say no is not a skill that runs parallel to the skill of receiving feedback well; it's right at the heart of it. If you can't say no, then your yeses are not freely chosen. Your decision may affect others and it will often have consequences for you, but the choice belongs to you. You need to make your own mistakes and find your own learning curve. Sometimes that means you need to shut out the critics for a while so you can discover who you are and how you are going to grow. Writer Anne Lamott puts it this way:

> . . . *Every single one of us at birth is given an emotional acre all our own. You get one, your awful Uncle Phil gets one, I get one. . . . And as long as you don't hurt anyone, you really get to do with your acre as you please. You can plant fruit trees or flowers or alphabetized rows of vegetables, or nothing at all. If you want your acre to look like a giant garage sale, or an auto-wrecking yard, that's what you get to do with it. There's a fence around your acre, though, with a gate, and if people keep coming onto your land and sliming it or trying to do what they think is right, you get to ask them to leave. And they have to go, because this is your acre.*[1]

This chapter is about that acre, fence, and gate, and how and why you might ask your givers to step outside on occasion.

THREE BOUNDARIES

Rejecting feedback can be as easy as saying no thanks or walking away or simply saying nothing. They offer, you decline, and it's over. But sometimes it's more complicated than that. You say no, but the unwanted feedback keeps coming. It's not just bothersome but destructive. This is when it helps to be explicit about boundaries. Here are three kinds of boundaries to consider:

1. I MAY NOT TAKE YOUR ADVICE

The first is the softest: I'm willing to listen. I'll consider your input. But I may not end up taking it.

Is this any fence at all? If the choice is always yours, why would you need to describe this first boundary out loud? Because the person giving you the feedback or advice may not share your opinion that it's optional. You ask your future mother-in-law to suggest florists for the wedding. You choose a different florist, and she gripes: "Why do you even ask my advice if you don't care what I say?" In the dance between receiver and giver, when you don't follow the giver's lead, you may step on some toes.

It can be confusing terrain. If you reject my advice, are you reject-ing *me*? Some advice givers hear it that way, even if it doesn't mean that to you. When you solicit suggestions you know you may not take, you can avoid heartache by saying so up front. Don't say to your mother-in-law: "Which florist should we use?" Be more precise: "We're thinking about several different florists. Are there any you'd add to our list?"

Another challenge is the line between a suggestion and an order. Choosing to disregard feedback may have consequences. You can continue to turn up late for your shift at the hospital . . . and your boss can fire you. If you're unsure if the coaching is optional or mandatory, discuss it explicitly. And if you decide not to take the coaching, don't assume the giver knows why. Explain your reasons carefully.

2. I DON'T WANT FEEDBACK ABOUT THAT SUBJECT, NOT RIGHT NOW

With this second boundary, you are not only establishing your right to decide whether to take the feedback, you're establishing your right to be free of the topic altogether: "I don't even want to hear it. Not right now (and maybe not ever)."

Your sister has badgered you to quit smoking for years. You've tried and failed and tried and failed. Now that your uncle is dying of a smoking-related illness, the whole family has joined the chorus. You understand where they're coming from, but right now you need them to back off. There just isn't anything more to say on the subject, and you don't have the emotional energy to continue the conversation.

3. STOP, OR I WILL LEAVE THE RELATIONSHIP

This third boundary is the starkest: If you can't keep your judgments to yourself, if you can't accept me the way I am now, then I will leave the relationship, or change its terms (I will come home for the holidays, but I'm not staying with you). Simply being in the relationship, buffeted by your judgments, is doing damage to my sense of self.

HOW DO I KNOW IF BOUNDARIES ARE NEEDED?

It starts with an agitated feeling or thought: *I'm overwhelmed; I'm a failure; this isn't working; this is too much; I can never do anything right; I'm not good enough.* And then a question: *Should I draw a boundary here?* But how can you tell the difference between someone who is genuinely trying to help you (or trying to share a real concern about how you are in a relationship) and a relationship that is in some fundamental way out of whack or unhealthy?

There is no pat formula for determining the difference between a legitimate request for change and one that indicates a deeper problem. The feedback giver may not mean harm, may not be trying to control you, and may even care deeply about you. They may not know any better, or may have issues of their own. But that doesn't change the feedback's impact on you, as it eats away at your self-acceptance bit by bit.

Below are a set of questions that will help you sort out your own thinking about whether a boundary is needed in a particular context or relationship.

DO THEY ATTACK YOUR CHARACTER, NOT JUST YOUR BEHAVIOR?

They don't say, "I found that frustrating," or, "Here's an idea that would help." Instead they say, "Here's what's wrong with you," or even, "Here's why you'll never amount to anything." Whether or not it's explicitly spoken, the message is that you are not attractive or ambitious or good enough, you are not worthy of love, respect, and kindness the way you are now.

IS THE FEEDBACK UNRELENTING?

Your executive coach is trying to help you feel more comfortable hobnobbing with the bigwigs in the C-suite, but he is making you more self-conscious and anxious, not less. You've discussed the fact that it's not helping, but instead of adjusting his approach, your coach opens the spigot wider.

Unhelpful feedback is useless; relentless unhelpful feedback is destructive. You've asked the person to stop, cease, desist, shut up, go away. Yet the coaching and advice pour forth.

WHEN YOU DO CHANGE,
IS THERE ALWAYS ONE MORE DEMAND?

Some feedback givers are always looking for the next thing to fix, whether it's about the house or the car or you. But more ominously, it may be that the act of telling you what to change is the end in itself. They are in charge, you are their charge, and those clear roles keep things in order.

This need for control could be motivated by their own fear: If your partner didn't always have you scrambling to be worthy of their love, you'd notice there was nothing in the relationship for you. If your supervisor didn't withhold his respect, you'd realize that he's not particularly worthy of *your* respect. Or maybe they need to feel in charge because they just don't know how to play any other role. Whatever the cause, the effect leaves you in a constant state of not good enough.

DOES THE FEEDBACK GIVER
TAKE THE RELATIONSHIP HOSTAGE?

The formulation here is this: Of course it's your choice whether or not to take my feedback, but if you don't, it means you don't love or respect me. They tie something small to something big, which is a ploy to get their way on every small issue that comes along. This tactic strips you of your autonomy while pretending you're free to do as you please.

Your mother-in-law conveys an implicit message: If you don't choose the florist I recommended, you're the one who ruined our relationship. It sounds ludicrous because it is. But it's worth being aware that the intention behind this approach is not always manipulative. People sometimes seek attention by holding the relationship hostage because they don't have the skills to express their feelings of insecurity, anxiety, or hurt in any other way. You can be compassionate about the giver's needs without becoming their hostage.

ARE THEY ISSUING WARNINGS—OR MAKING THREATS?

Here's the difference: A warning is a good-faith attempt to explain possible legitimate consequences ("If you're late to dinner, the spaghetti will be cold"), whereas the purpose of a threat is to manufacture consequences that will induce fear ("If you're late to dinner, I will throw the spaghetti at you"). These are warnings:

"If your people management skills don't improve, we can't keep you in this position."

"If you don't disclose this in the filing, I'm required to inform the commission."

"If you come home drunk again, I'm moving out."

As you can see, the variable is not whether the consequences warned of are severe; it's whether they are legitimate. In some cases, the warnings are final; they're ultimatums. It is not a happy situation that things have come to this. But the other person is giving you information about real consequences so that you can make informed choices.

Threats have the same "if-then" structure, but spring from a different motive: to induce fear or dependence, to lower self-esteem or confidence, to control or manipulate. And the consequences are manufactured for that purpose:

"If you don't do as I say, I'll see that you never work in this industry again."

"If I leave you, no one else will ever love you."

A warning is when someone tells you the other shoe may drop; a threat is when they make sure it will squash you.

IS IT ALWAYS YOU WHO HAS TO CHANGE?

Things seem okay until you notice a troubling pattern. Whenever there is conflict between you, whenever you need to solve a problem that has arisen, you are the only one who takes responsibility for anything. You apologize, you stay late, you absorb the budget overruns. If you are always the one who has to change, who has to give in, who has to go the extra mile, then your roles may be stuck. Negotiating a shift from blame and one-way feedback to mutual accountability and willingness to look at the system between you is fundamental to the sustainability of a relationship, whether it's based in work, love, or friendship.

ARE YOUR VIEWS AND FEELINGS
A LEGITIMATE PART OF THE RELATIONSHIP?

This may be both the simplest and most important of the criteria. Regardless of anything else, is the feedback giver listening to you and working hard to understand how you see things and how you feel? And once they know, do they *care*? Are they willing to modify how they share their feedback, requests, and advice based on how it affects you? Do they respect your autonomy to make up your own mind and to reject their advice? If your feelings and views aren't part of the relationship, there is a problem.

WHERE BOUNDARIES WOULD HELP:
SOME COMMON RELATIONSHIP PATTERNS

The relationship doesn't have to be certifiably dysfunctional for you to decide that feedback within the relationship is not working for you. Let's look at three examples of how the challenges described above form common relationship patterns.

THE CONSTANT CRITIC

Constant critics provide running commentary that is a stream of evaluation—sizing you up and letting you know the score. They are your father, your older sister, your best friend, your devoted coach, your demanding boss. They just want to help. And they do this with all the subtlety of an auctioneer.

Conversations between Hunyee and her mother have always been fraught. As a child Hunyee was relentlessly corrected, coached, and chastised. As an adult she knows that the minute her mother arrives she will begin assessing the state of Hunyee's closets, cooking, weight, and wardrobe. Hunyee knows that her mother loves her, and even recognizes that her constant criticism is the way her mother expresses that love. In fact, it's the way her mother expresses everything; without criticism, there would be only silence.

But it still leaves Hunyee feeling raw and hurt. Even in her mother's absence, Hunyee hears her voice in her head, goading and condemning. This is not the legacy her mother intends, but without some change, it is the one she will inevitably leave.

There are constant critics at work as well. Jake, a successful investment adviser, prides himself on his mentoring relationship with Brodie, a young analyst. Jake's standards are uncompromising, but he's lavish with coaching and advice, rare commodities at this particular firm. Unfortunately, this is not how Brodie sees it. He feels like he can do no right. Every move he makes is criticized, every report is ripped apart, every effort inadequate. Brodie, a pretty tough character himself, now dreads coming to work.

HATE-LOVE-HATE RELATIONSHIPS

Psychologists tell us that the most addictive reward pattern is called "intermittent reinforcement." Video games and gambling use this approach. We win just often enough to keep us playing. When we do win, we're desperate to win again; when we lose, we are even more desperate to play until we win. Winning love and approval may be the reward we crave most.

Jasmine is caught in a relationship in which approval is dangled and promised but withheld. Just when all seems lost, approval is briefly bestowed—and then withdrawn again, starting the cycle afresh. This is one important reason why someone might stay with a damaging partner, coach, boss, or family member. They hate the hate, but it makes their need for the love even more intense. Feedback giver and receiver are both caught up in a powerful dynamic that is not healthy for either and is particularly damaging to the receiver.

RENOVATION RELATIONSHIPS

Henry was thrilled by all the attention Isabella paid him. Even her little "suggestions" had an intoxicating effect; they were, after all, evidence of how much she cared about him. He'd found love, and all this self-improvement was a bonus.

Until it wasn't. At first her suggestions for change seemed reasonable. She had ideas for how he could "freshen up his look," and he figured it wouldn't hurt to be a sharper dresser. But then the feedback spread to other aspects of his life: work out more, stop reading those comics, don't act like such a nerd in front of my friends, don't take things so personally, have some ambition, make my hobbies your hobbies.

Henry tried. He was genuinely eager to be the person Isabella wanted him to be. But in time he grew anxious and unhappy and told Isabella so. She explained that she was just trying to help him grow, noting that Henry wasn't making it easy since he was so hypersensitive to feedback.

Henry decided to get some outside perspective and discussed the relationship with his friend Rollo:

Henry: I mean, maybe she's right. Maybe I am too sensitive. If I'm going to be in a serious relationship maybe I have to be more mature myself. Maybe I really do need to change. Maybe I'm being selfish or maybe I'm kind of stuck.

Rollo: That's possible. But what I'm struck by is how unhappy you are. Have you told Isabella how all her advice and criticism is affecting you?

Henry: Yeah, I've told her. Several times.

Rollo: How does she respond?

Henry: She said the real problem is that I'm just too sensitive to feedback.

Rollo: And you were honest about just how unhappy you are?

Henry: I was. The whole thing is really eating away at me and I've told her that.

Rollo: To me, that's the big problem here. From what you've said, it sounds as if she's trying to turn you into someone else. But even putting that aside, it sounds like your feelings are not part of the equation, and what you need is not part of the relationship.

Henry: Hmm. So you're saying that regardless of whether she's too critical or I'm too sensitive, it's a problem that she doesn't seem to care how I'm feeling.

Rollo: It's a giant red flag.

Henry has become so preoccupied by whether he is able to please Isabella that he isn't noticing just how little his needs and feelings matter to her.

Keep this front and center: No matter what growing you have to do, and regardless of how right (or not) the feedback may be, if the person giving you the feedback is not listening to you and doesn't care about its impact on you, something is wrong. Rollo has this exactly right. It's fine to try to figure out whether the giver is too critical or you're too sensitive, but if the other person isn't listening to you and your feelings, the answer is beside the point. You are worthy of love, acceptance, and compassion—right now, as you are, full stop. This may be tough to see from inside an unbalanced relationship. But it's the bottom-line truth.

BUT WAIT, DOES THAT MEAN . . . ?

Is there something wrong with hoping your significant other does pick up some better habits, loses some weight, or finally finishes college? No. It's fine to wish that for them, and to coach and support them so they can get there. The key question here: Is it something *they* want? Or something only you want? If they genuinely do want this change, you're in the clear. Make your intentions discussable, and most of all, make sure to listen.

TURNING AWAY FEEDBACK
WITH GRACE AND HONESTY

The biggest mistake we make when trying to create boundaries is that we assume other people understand what's going on with us. Surely they know we're overloaded or unhappy or struggling, and that their feedback is making things worse. But often they don't. We may not have told them, or if we have, we were indirect or unclear or they just weren't listening. It's true that they haven't exactly gone out of their way to figure us out, but that's not within our control, and frankly, it's par for the course. They'll never be as interested in figuring out our boundaries as we are.

BE TRANSPARENT: ACTUALLY TELL THEM

With increasing frequency, Dave, a cop in his mid-forties, asks people to repeat themselves and misses what is said in meetings. His coworkers have started to notice. "My partner kept nudging me to get my hearing checked, so I finally did," says Dave. "Turns out my hearing has really deteriorated, and I need a hearing aid."

Yet six months have passed, and Dave hasn't gone back to be fitted for one. "I've been wrestling a bit," he admits. "I'm having trouble thinking of myself as someone who needs a device that, fairly or unfairly, I've always associated with the elderly. I know my resistance isn't rational. I'll get there. I just need time to update my self-image."

Dave hasn't told anyone on the force about the test or the result. He doesn't feel that he needs to: What matters is that he's on top of things and is dealing with it.

But his coworkers don't know that. So they're left with the impression that he's ignoring them. When they repeat their concerns, Dave responds to them—in his head. *It's being handled*, he thinks to himself, *so why do you keep bothering me about it?*

All he needs to do is explain things out loud: "I got checked. I need a hearing aid. I'm going to get one. It's a hard adjustment to make. I'll do better if I'm not pestered." That won't fix his hearing problems, but it will go a long way toward fixing his feedback problems.

BE FIRM—AND APPRECIATIVE

Dave's story is an example of someone *taking* feedback. It's at least as important to be explicit and clear when we reject feedback. We can do that best by being both firm and appreciative.

PJ struggles with severe stage fright, and her university department head has a habit of rushing up to her just as she is about to begin lecturing and whispering, "Don't be nervous!" Which makes PJ panic. But she handles the feedback conversation well:

> PJ: Anxiety is a real struggle for me. I know you're aware of that, and when you say "don't be nervous" I know you're trying to help. The impact, though, is it actually makes me more nervous, rather than less.
>
> Department Head: Well, of course I'm trying to help. Anything to give you that extra boost of confidence! So when you get up there, there's no need to be nervous!
>
> PJ: Okay, but that does end up making me more nervous.
>
> Department Head: Well, it shouldn't. You're fabulous!
>
> PJ: Here's the impact it has on me. It reminds me that I have this anxiety problem. What would help me is to hear how you've been able to cope with anxiety when you speak publicly. But I'd like to hear about that on days when I'm not lecturing.

PJ does a graceful job of acknowledging and appreciating her department head's good intentions, while being firm in her request that she not get coaching right before she lectures. Being firm and being appreciative are not opposite ends of a continuum. You can be clear about both.

REDIRECT UNHELPFUL COACHING

Sometimes we assume we need the starkest kind of boundary because of the pain we're in. Our instinct is to shut it all down: No judgment. No coaching. No nothing—or it's good-bye.

But you may have noticed that PJ does something that can make drawing boundaries easier: She redirects her coach's energy and interest toward something that may actually help.

You might experiment with loaning your giver a corner of your acre, and tell them what you'd love to see there. Hunyee to her mother: "I have so much to learn from you. When you visit, would you teach me to make your amazing dumplings?" This suggestion is good for Hunyee, of course, but it might meet her mother's interests as well. Her mother yearns for a role in her daughter's life, and her criticisms may be a misguided attempt to establish such a role. She wants to be useful and to feel valued by her very capable adult child.

Letting givers know what they *can* help you with may be the incentive they need to cut down on the advice you don't want to hear about. And it lays a helpful foundation for erecting other boundaries if you need them.

USE "AND"

In setting up boundaries, you want to reject feedback clearly and firmly, while at the same time affirming the relationship and showing that you appreciate the intention.

The temptation is to link these two thoughts with the word "but." Hunyee to her mother: "I love seeing you, *but* if you're going to come to my house you need to stop criticizing every single thing." "But" suggests a contradiction between the two thoughts. The first part would be true, but for the second. *You love seeing me but what?* "But you criticize me too much." *So therefore you don't actually love seeing me.*

Human emotions don't necessarily cancel each other out. I can love spending time with you and still be anxious that you're coming. I can genuinely appreciate your mentoring and decide not to take your advice. I can be sad that I'm hurting you and proud of myself for doing the right thing. Contradictory feelings sit side-by-side in our hearts and minds, clacking against each other like marbles in our pocket.

Using "and" to describe our feelings isn't just about word choice. It gets at a deeper truth about our thoughts and feelings: They are often complex and sometimes confused. We figure we can draw clear boundaries most easily with a simple bottom-line message—yes, no, not right now—and so our impulse is to keep the complexity or confusion hidden. But often sharing complex feelings along with the message actually makes establishing the boundary easier.

Raul's parents believe that an engineering degree will give their son a secure life, without the hardships they have endured. His passion for music? A "frivolous hobby."

Raul respects his parents and has worked hard to understand their perspective and worries. He shares many of those worries himself, profoundly so. And still, he has decided to pursue music. But how to tell his parents? "When I tried to imagine having the conversation," he says, "my blood ran cold. Rejecting their advice would mean turning my back on them; following their advice would mean turning my back on myself. I don't want to be the ungrateful, wayward son. And I don't want to be an engineer."

Nothing was going to make this conversation easy, and Raul couldn't control how his parents would react. What unlocked the dilemma for Raul was realizing that he could share both sides of the "and"—the multiple, competing, and confusing thoughts and feelings that are no less true for being simultaneous. With his heart in his throat, Raul sat down with his parents and held forth with a series of ands: "I've been afraid to talk to you about this *and* it's important to me to be honest with you." "I've decided to major in music *and* I know this makes you worry about my future." "I'm also very fearful of the struggle I may face *and* I need to try." "I know this is hard for you *and* I hope you will still be supportive of me."

He braced for their reaction. If this were a Hollywood movie, his parents would have smiled and offered a cheerful embrace. But there was no swelling soundtrack. In his father's face there was disappointment, in his mother's there was worry. Raul himself was anxious—but at peace with himself. He'd made a hard decision that felt right to him and had explained it to his parents as clearly and respectfully as he knew how.

When you share the complexity or confusion, you are adopting what we call the "And Stance." It's a powerful place to stand, and you can use it in any situation where you've listened to someone's input and have decided to go in a different direction: "I think what you've said makes a lot of sense. *And* I've decided that those aren't the skills that are the most pressing priority for me right now." Fill in your reasoning and be willing to field questions to make it a two-way conversation. It's your boundary, but the conversation belongs to both of you.

BE SPECIFIC ABOUT YOUR REQUEST

Hunyee ultimately says this to her mother: "Mom, I love you and I know you want the best for me. And your comments about my weight and housekeeping and clothing are incredibly upsetting to me. If you're going to stay with me, I need you to keep them to yourself. Is that a request you can honor?"

Hunyee is making a specific request. She's not saying, "Quit being so critical," or "I need you to back off." These requests would reflect how she's feeling, but they are unlikely to help, for two reasons. First, they set up the terms of a fight. She's giving her mother feedback but tripping all her truth, relationship, and identity triggers at the same time. Her mother will be likely to argue about whether it's "true" that she's critical, or switchtrack because she feels unappreciated. She'll be distracted as she wrestles with whether she's a "good mother" and a "good person."

And second, the request is too general. "Back off" and "Quit criticizing" are too vague, especially since Hunyee's mother may not be aware of her behavior in the first place. Remember that some of this is habitual behavior that's probably in a blind spot, and as such needs more than just a label.

So when setting boundaries, be specific about three things:

- **The Request.** What, exactly, are you asking of them? Are you putting a particular topic off limits (my new spouse, my new weight), or a behavior (my ADHD, my football watching)? If they need examples of what you're talking about, describe them as you recall them, along with their effect on you.
- **The Time Frame.** How long is the boundary likely to be in place? Do you need time to sort things out for yourself, to

adjust your self-image, to take care of other priorities first, to find your feet as a new stepparent or new leader? Let them know if the boundary is time limited, and if not, how they might check in with you about it without violating the boundary. ("Can I ask how things are going with that thing I'm not supposed to mention?")

- **Their Assent.** Don't assume that they understand you or agree. Instead, ask. When they say, "Yes, I will honor your request," it's not just about you anymore. They're making a commitment, and that enlists their identity and reputation in living up to their promise.

These conversations are harder in hierarchy, but with some thought, you can often find an acceptable way in. At the investment firm, Brodie probably isn't going to say to his boss Jake, "Now you listen here, pal. I'll have no more of your constant criticisms!" But he might feel comfortable saying that he appreciates having a mentor who cares so passionately about his progress, and at the same time, is feeling a bit banged up as a result of their conversations. Or he could request that Jake focus on one or two skills rather than on everything.

DESCRIBE CONSEQUENCES

Finally, it's only fair to let them know what's at stake. You are telling them to keep their judgments to themselves, or else.

Or else *what*?

Earlier we talked about the difference between threats and warnings. Your purpose here isn't to make a threat, it's to issue a clear warning. You need to let them know what happens if they can't or won't observe the boundaries. They are free to accept your request, or not—you can't control their choice and shouldn't try. But you are free to make adjustments to the relationship on your end, as needed. Here's an example of how you might describe consequences:

"You know I've struggled with smoking, and I'm all too aware of the causes of Uncle Marv's illness. Right now I'm overwhelmed with my new job and I can't also handle side comments and knowing looks and disapproval when I step outside to have a cigarette. I know you mean it to be caring, but that's not how it's feeling. If you can't leave the issue behind for now, I'll make sure to visit Marv at times when I know you won't be here."

With any boundaries you set, don't be surprised if others stumble here and there as they work to honor the boundary. Don't lie in wait for a single slipup. They've had lots of practice being critical of you—they should receive a lifetime achievement award, in fact—and those habits are hard to break. Expect to have to give a couple of firm reminders, try to keep a sense of humor about lapses, and appreciate progress where they are making it. Of course, if they can't or won't work at it with you, then it's up to you to protect yourself.[2]

YOU HAVE A DUTY TO MITIGATE THE COST TO OTHERS

You've decided not to change. You've listened carefully to your children, but are not yet ready to move out of the home you've lived in for sixty years. You've heard the concerns from your team and are still going forward with your plan to reorganize the department. Your husband's ex-wife wants you to get rid of your "germy" cat out of concern for her visiting children, but you've decided to keep both the cat and the germs.

End of story?

Not so fast. We don't always get to go our merry way, and bollocks to those who don't like it. Being in a relationship—whether at work or at home—means being cognizant of the cost of our behaviors and decisions to those around us. If you're not going to change, you still have a "duty to mitigate." That means you need to do what you can, within reason, to reduce the impacts of your actions (or inaction) on others.

INQUIRE ABOUT, AND ACKNOWLEDGE, THE IMPACT ON THEM

Ask how your choice affects others you live and work with. After much thought, and discussions with several doctors, Larry decided that, for now, he is not going to take medication for his ADHD. This has consequences for him, of course, as he struggles to organize his life and get things done. It also has consequences for his family and for his coworkers at the construction site. Talking with them about the implications will, in large part, determine the success of his efforts and of these relationships. In what ways will his decision frustrate his family as they need to prod, prompt, and remediate? What concerns do his crew members have for efficiency or safety, and what processes can they put in place together to ensure a secure work environment? The decision to take or not take the medication is Larry's; the consequences of that decision are shared.

COACH THEM TO DEAL WITH THE UNCHANGED YOU

Jackie knows she can dominate any discussion, and that she should leave more room for others. After working at it—fruitlessly—for the last year, she decides to give up for now. "I know I can be overbearing," she tells her teammates. "I tried to change. It was a lot of effort for almost no benefit. So I give you all permission to cut me off. Red-card me, or throw me in the penalty box. I don't mean to dominate discussions but I imagine I'll continue to do it without realizing it. I promise I won't think you're being rude; I need the help, and I'll appreciate it."

PROBLEM SOLVE TOGETHER

The idea isn't to shut down discussion, but to open it up and to problem solve about how to minimize the cost of your decision not to change.

Your children don't want to worry about you living alone. Making modifications to the house, moving a bedroom downstairs, hiring some help, or getting a life alert system may help reduce their anxiety and make you safer. Your staff is concerned about the impact on customers while you're all in the middle of a reorganization, so sit down together to map out how you'll ensure continuity of service.

Consider the issues between Mark and his younger brother, Steve. For three decades Mark has been on Steve about his flakiness. The latest clash concerns Mark's season tickets for the Steelers: "When I offer you one of my tickets, you're always like, 'Yeah, man, I'll be there!' But half the time you show up late, and sometimes you don't show at all."

Steve can't argue with his show rate, but he knows himself well enough to know that there's little chance he's really going to change. Mark could keep knocking his head against the wall, or he could stop inviting his brother to the games.

But there's a third option: Mark and Steve decide to assume that Steve *isn't* going to change, and problem solve about how to minimize the aggravation to Mark. These days when Mark extends an invitation, they discuss specific details regarding Steve's assurances that he'll make it on time ("Are you double-booking yourself? What else is going on that day? Do you need a ride?"), and the cost to Mark if Steve bails. Sometimes Steve thanks him for the invite and suggests Mark ask someone else. At other times, recognizing that Mark is really only asking him so they can spend some time together, Steve makes an alternate suggestion that they go golfing or out for a beer instead.

So Steve has set his boundary—I really don't think I can change— and he's worked with his brother to reduce the impact on Mark. This allows them to move on from the fantasy future of a changed Steve and to enjoy who each of them is now. Paradoxically, the clarity of Steve's boundary has made it easier for the brothers to spend time together.

Summary: SOME KEY IDEAS

Boundaries: The ability to turn down or turn away feedback is critical to healthy relationships and lifelong learning.

Three kinds of boundaries:

- Thanks and No — I'm happy to hear your coaching . . . and I may not take it.
- Not Now, Not About That — I need time or space, or this is too sensitive a subject right now.
- No Feedback — Our relationship rides on your ability to keep your judgments to yourself.

When turning down feedback, use "and" to be appreciative, and firm.

Be specific about:

- The request
- The time frame
- The consequences
- Their assent

If you're not changing, work to mitigate the impact on others.

- Ask about the impact
- Coach them to deal with the unchanged you
- Problem solve together

11

NAVIGATE THE CONVERSATION

In 1995, *Toy Story* hit theaters and forever changed animated movies. Although the technology had been in development since the mid-1970s,[1] *Toy Story* was the first feature-length film to use computer animation to bring the characters to life. Rather than drawing each frame anew, computer animators create what are called "keyframes"—or key moments—in the action. The computer then fills in the movement between the keyframes. The animator's assistant, called the inbetweener, then refines the 'tweening to create smooth and natural action.

KEYFRAMES OF THE CONVERSATION

The concept of keyframes is useful for talking about feedback conversations. Whether we are givers or receivers, we can't "script" the conversation, and when we try, our counterparts have an irritating tendency not to follow the lines we've written for them. But we can recognize some keyframes—stages and moments in the conversation that can serve as landmarks. If you can identify the conversation keyframes, you can do your own 'tweening.

• • •

Much of this book focuses on our reactions to receiving feedback. We've included communication advice along the way, but in this chapter we take a closer look at how to handle the conversation itself. What should you say or do to maximize the chances you will learn something valuable?

THE ARC OF THE CONVERSATION: OPEN-BODY-CLOSE

Broadly, feedback conversations are made up of three parts:

Open: A critical piece, oddly often skipped when we jump right in without getting aligned: What is the purpose of the conversation? What kind of feedback would I like, and what kind is my giver trying to give? Is the feedback negotiable or final, a friendly suggestion or a command?

Body: A two-way exchange of information, requiring you to master four main skills: listening, asserting, managing the conversation process, and problem solving.

Close: Here we clarify commitments, action steps, benchmarks, procedural contracts, and follow-up.

Below we examine each part in more detail.

OPEN BY GETTING ALIGNED

Your performance review has been on the calendar for months, but that dressing-down you got this morning was—as far as you know—not. Whether the feedback is scheduled or spontaneous, clarifying a few things up front in the conversation is crucial.

CLARIFY PURPOSE, CHECK STATUS

Below are three questions that will help you and your giver get aligned.

1. Is This Feedback? If So, What Kind?

That birthday sweater from your mother that is a size too small might be a mistake—or a message. Not being put on the project team could be a resource allocation decision—or it could be feedback.

Ideally you would have this thought: *Oh, this isn't just a regular conversation. I might be receiving feedback. I'd better get into my receiving-feedback mindset.* As unnatural as this sounds, doing so will help prevent the reflexive retorts or hasty retreats that can hurt your relationships and diminish the opportunity for learning. If you're aware, you can make conscious choices about how to respond.

If it is feedback, is it evaluation, coaching, or appreciation? You won't always know, and your giver won't either. So, ask yourself this: What kind of feedback would be most useful to *me* right now? If at the age of eighty-three you're finally letting another human being read your first short story, don't just say "Give me some feedback" if what you actually need to stay motivated is encouragement: "Can you just tell me your three favorite things about it?"

Also ask yourself this: What is your giver's purpose? What do *they* think you need? Listen for the real underlying issue. Their feedback might sound like forward-looking coaching for you ("You'd be better off if you didn't work so much. . . . ") when what they really want you to hear is a deeper concern about how they're feeling ("Your relentless pace is having a negative impact on the team"). Be alert for challenging mixes (coaching with evaluation) and cross-transactions (I wanted coaching but you're giving me appreciation). You may have different purposes, and that's okay as long as you're both aware of that and talk them through.

2. Who Decides?

You can have a good back-and-forth, you can disagree and problem solve—even if one of you is the ultimate decision maker. But you both need to be clear who that is. The graphic design you did for the Chicken Farmers' Convention is the best thing you've ever done, but the organizers—your customer—would like the chicken to be more realistic looking. You believe this will distract from the iconic power of the chicken. You wrangle back and forth and arrive at an impasse. Who decides? Were you getting the customer's input so that you could render the final design, or were they getting your input so that they could make the final call?

It's often unclear whether feedback is a suggestion or a command. When your boss says that you should wear a tie to the event, is he giving you some helpful career advice ("You can always take a tie off"), or is he issuing an order ("Wear a tie or you're fired")? You may or may not choose to comply, but you'll certainly want to know which category the feedback falls into.

There's a related common mistake: Two people engage in a conversation as if they need to reach an agreement, when in fact agreement isn't necessary. Ending a relationship, for example. If you break up with someone and they give you feedback that you are a terrible person, the two of you don't need to reach consensus on this point. They think you acted badly, and you believe you acted thoughtfully, and that's where it can remain. You are the decision maker about the relationship's ending; you are each your own storyteller about why it ended.

3. Is This Final or Negotiable?

If the feedback is an evaluation, determine its status: Is it final or provisional? If your performance rating is final, it's important to know that up front. If it's provisional, then you may be able to influence the final outcome. Often, receivers waste time trying to influence a decision that has already been made and cannot be reversed. If it's a done deal, spend your time understanding it and talking about effective ways to handle the consequences going forward.

YOU CAN INFLUENCE THE FRAME AND AGENDA

We often assume that because we're on the receiving end of feedback, our role is simply to react to the feedback giver's opening, like returning a serve in tennis. But regardless of how the other person starts, you can use your turn to frame the conversation constructively and to offer an agenda.

If the giver launches directly into the middle of a conversation, you can say: "Can we take a minute to step back so that I'm clear on our purposes? I want to be sure I'm on the same page as you." If they level an accusation that strikes you as off base and are in a stubborn "I'm right" frame, reframe the issue as a difference between you: "I want to hear your perspective on this, and then I'll share my view, and we can figure out where and why our views are different."

The opening is important because it sets the conversation's tone and trajectory. MIT researchers have found a correlation between skilled interaction during the first five minutes of a negotiation and good out-comes.[2] Research on married couples done by John Gottman shows that if the first three minutes of a fifteen-minute conversation are harsh and critical, and not corrected by the recipient, the outcome is negative 96 percent of the time. A key factor in happy marriages, Gottman says, is a couple's ability to change course, to make and respond to "repair attempts" that break the cycle of escalation between them.[3]

Remember, correcting course up front is about process, not sub-stance. You're not telling the feedback giver what they can or can't say; you're working to clarify the mutual purpose of the conversation and suggesting a two-way exploration. This helps you get aligned for the rest of the conversation.

BODY: FOUR SKILLS FOR MANAGING THE CONVERSATION

There are four skills you need to navigate the body of the conversation: listening, asserting, "process moves," and problem solving.

Listening includes asking clarifying questions, paraphrasing the giv-er's view, and acknowledging their feelings. *Asserting* is a mix of shar-ing, advocating, and expressing—in essence, talking. Don't confuse asserting with "asserting truth" or with being certain. You can be asser-tive about your point of view even as you are aware that it's *your* point of view and not necessarily the entire story; you can be assertive about your ambivalence; you can be assertive about feeling doubt. We're us-ing the term "asserting" because it captures a sense of leaning in, of sticking up for yourself, though without being combative.

The third skill involves *process moves*—hinges that turn the conversa-tion in a more productive direction. You are acting as your own referee, stepping outside the conversation, noticing where you and the giver are stuck, and suggesting a better direction, topic, or process. Getting good at the oft-neglected art of process moves can have a huge impact on the success of your interactions.

Finally, *problem solving* turns to the question: Now what? Why does this feedback matter, and what should one or both of us do about it? You assert that I am too risk averse. And maybe I am, but not to the degree you suggest. It's important that we discuss this, but merely talking it through doesn't end the matter. We need to make a decision together about whether to invest in this new venture, and that will require problem-solving skills.

We present these four skills in a stepwise fashion, starting with listening and arriving triumphantly at problem solving. But real conversations are rarely so neatly ordered. They tend to jump around, and that's okay. The order in which you use the skills is less important than *that* you use them. All the listening in the world can't make up for failing to assert the one issue that matters to you, and there's nothing you can assert that will make up for failing to listen to what really matters to them. And if there are problems to be solved, but you put them off, the glow of understanding will soon fade, and you'll wonder what all that talking actually accomplished.

LISTEN FOR WHAT'S RIGHT
(AND WHY THEY SEE IT DIFFERENTLY)

Advice about listening is white noise. It's so common and so boring that we no longer even hear it. But if you're drifting off, this would be a good time to wake up. Listening may be the most challenging skill involved in receiving feedback, but it also has the biggest payoff.

Your Internal Voice Is Crucial

If you think you and your giver are having a one-on-one chat, think again. You have each brought along your "internal voice," the running stream of thoughts and feelings you have during the conversation in reaction to what's going on. (Your internal voice is going even now. See if you can hear it. It might be saying, "What? I don't have an internal voice!")

Our internal voice is often fairly quiet, especially when we're absorbed in what someone is saying. But when we disagree with what they're saying, or feel emotional, our internal voice gets louder and demands more of our attention. And when we're listening to ourselves, we can't also listen to others.

You might figure that this is not much of an obstacle for you—you weren't even particularly aware of your internal voice, so how in the way could it be?

Very in the way. Your fellow board member is saying something about how you're out of touch with the younger generation of employees, and you're thinking *that's just not true!* Now your colleague has moved on to say something else, but your internal voice is still making arguments about how wrong his first point was. You don't know what his new topic is exactly, but it's probably wrong, too.

Triggered: From Assistant to Bodyguard

Your internal voice is like a personal assistant whose job it is to make sure no one bothers you: "Sorry, Ms. Goldstein is busy right now. She's absorbed in her own thoughts about how unfair you always are to her. You might try coming back later."

When you're triggered, your internal voice goes from mere assistant to armed bodyguard. When your boss, the head chef, yells, "If you can't keep up, get out of my kitchen!" your internal voice leaps to your defense and shouts back (in your head): "If you'd equip this #*@$! kitchen properly, maybe I'd have a chance!" The chef might get past your usual assistant, but no one is getting past your bodyguard.

When Empathy Shuts Down

Recent brain research on empathy suggests that this bodyguard dynamic isn't all in our heads. Or rather, it actually *is* in our heads.

Tania Singer of the Institute of Cognitive Neuroscience in London uses fMRI to examine the neural processes that seem to correlate with empathy. Using couples, Singer and colleagues examined the brain activity of one partner (the female) under two conditions. First, Singer administered an electric shock to the woman, transmitted via an electrode taped to the back of her hand, as she lay in the MRI machine, and mapped her brain activity as she processed the experience of being shocked (we're not sure Singer gets a lot of repeat volunteers). Next, Singer administered the same kind of hand-shock to the woman's partner, who was seated nearby and in view. Here's what's interesting: When watching her *partner* get shocked, the woman demonstrated the same pattern of brain activity as when *she herself* had been shocked.

The patterns weren't entirely identical. When the woman was observing her loved one being shocked, the parts of the brain that register physical pain did not light up (she did not feel the physical pain itself). But the parts of the brain that register the emotional experience of being shocked did light up. This phenomenon is called a "mirror neuron response," and it suggests that human beings are wired for empathy.[4]

Extending her research, Singer wondered whether we *always* empathize with others' pain or perspective. The answer is no. Singer had people watch a game in which some participants played fairly while others played unfairly. Observers had a mirror neuron response when watching fair players get shocked, but had no mirror neuron response when the unfair players were shocked. In fact, in some subjects who watched unfair players receive shocks, the part of the brain connected to pleasure and revenge lit up instead.[5] The bottom line? We are wired for empathy, but only toward those who we believe are behaving well.

What does this have to do with feedback? When we are receiving feedback that feels unfair or off base, when we feel underappreciated or poorly treated, our empathy and curiosity may be neurologically turned off. So listening during a tough feedback conversation won't come naturally. Even those of us who are generous listeners in other contexts may have trouble finding curiosity when we're feeling triggered.

What Helps? Listen with a Purpose

If we're going to be able to listen more effectively, it's going to have to be both *on* purpose and *with* a purpose. We'll have to find or create some curiosity—some tiny nudge that says that maybe the feedback in question isn't entirely unfair, that maybe the giver sees something we don't, or at the very least, their view is their view, and it might be useful for us to know. Put simply, instead of wrong spotting, we need to listen for what's right, and be curious about why we see things so differently.

Prepare to Listen

Before getting feedback (if you have time to prepare), have a conversation with your internal voice. There are a few things the two of you need to get straight. Your task is not to scold your internal voice ("Don't get defensive") or tamp it down ("Think whatever you want, but keep quiet"). Just the opposite. Your internal voice gets loud because it wants your attention. If you give it attention, it quiets down. So tune in to what it's saying, and work to understand it.

Trigger	Internal Voice
Truth	"That's wrong!" "That's not helpful!" "That's not me!"
Relationship	"After all I've done for you?!" "Who are you to say?" "You're the problem, not me."
Identity	"I screw up everything." "I'm doomed." "I'm not a bad person— or am I?"

Find the Trigger Patterns

When you tune in to your internal voice, you'll notice that there are patterns; when we're triggered, we don't think just anything, we think specific and predictable things. Knowing that gives us some traction on the challenge of handling our triggers. There are endless variations, but each kind of feedback trigger—truth, relationship, and identity—produces its own characteristic internal voice patter.

And Then Negotiate

Once you identify your patterns, have a conversation with yourself. Your goal is to hear your internal voice, learn to identify its triggered reactions, and then engage it to help you feel curious. That conversation with yourself might go like this:

> You: During the feedback conversation, you're going to be telling me that what the giver is saying is wrong.
>
> Internal Voice: Right. Because it will be wrong.
>
> You: What will be wrong about it?
>
> Internal Voice: All the usual things. They talked to the wrong people, they're interpreting it all the wrong way. They saw that one mistake we made, but don't appreciate all the other things we get right day in and day out. I could go on.
>
> You: Good to know you're looking out for us. Let me ask you this: What might be right about what they're saying?
>
> Internal Voice: Are you not listening to me? I just explained that what they'll be saying will be wrong.
>
> You: I *am* listening. We'll be mindful of those concerns. Even so, I'm wondering what might be right about their feedback.
>
> Internal Voice: Well, I suppose they could see things we don't see. That's been known to happen. And their interpretation may be different, but it could be valid. Also, they've been around the block a few times. There's that.
>
> You: So there's something to listen for.
>
> Internal Voice: I suppose there's a bit of mystery, yes. . . .

Not exactly Shakespeare, but you get the idea. Talk to your internal voice. Acknowledge and appreciate it (they're your own thoughts, after all). Remind it that understanding doesn't equal agreeing. Negotiate it toward real curiosity. And finally, give it an assignment: *I need you to be intensely curious about what they're saying. Help me dig in and understand. What's right about what they're saying? Why is it that they see things differently?*

Below is a chart that lists the common internal voice patterns and offers ideas about what you're listening for and what questions you might ask.

Internal Voice	Listening For	Questions to Ask
TRUTH		
That's wrong! *That's not helpful!* *That's not me!*	**Data** they have that I don't, and interpretations they have that aren't the same as mine. **Impacts** I'm having that I may not be aware of because of my blind spots.	*Can you give me an example?* *What did that mean to you?* *What are you worried about?* *What do you see me doing that's getting in my own way?* *How did that impact you?*
RELATIONSHIP		
After all I've done for you?! *Who are you to say?* *You're the problem, not me.*	**Switchtracks** that put a second topic on the table about our relationship. **Systems** between us—what are each of us contributing to the issues, and what's my part in that system?	*Help me understand your feedback. Then I want to talk about how/when/why you're offering it and some of my relationship concerns.* *What am I contributing to the problem between us?* *What is most upsetting to you and why?*
IDENTITY		
I screw up everything. *I'm doomed.* *I'm not a bad person—am I?*	What's my particular **Wiring**—how far do I swing and how quickly do I recover? How do I talk myself through my particular pattern? Can I sort for **Coaching**, focused on the opportunity to grow, rather than the judgment implicit in the evaluation or coaching?	*Can you help me get perspective on your feedback?* *What could I do that would help me improve? What could I change that would matter most?*

Listening's Second Purpose: To Let Them Know You Hear Them

You aren't listening to be polite. You aren't listening because the giver is right or because you're necessarily going to accept or take the feedback. And you aren't listening because your own view doesn't matter.

You are listening to *understand*. The first order of business is archeological: You're digging under labels, clarifying contours, and filling in pieces you didn't initially see. You're assembling all the relevant evidence and background to make sense of the size and shape of the feedback from the giver's perspective. After that you and your internal voice can convene to decide what to do with what you've unearthed—how it fits together with your own view, and whether or not you are going to take their advice.

If understanding is purpose one, letting the giver know you understand (or, just as important, that you *want* to understand) is purpose two. Listening rewards the giver's effort in taking the time to give you feedback, and it leaves them feeling reassured that they have been clear. You may need to have a later conversation about why you've decided not to take it, and that might make them unhappy. But they can't argue that you didn't take the advice seriously or that you didn't understand it. And as a result, they're more likely to listen to you when you explain where you ultimately landed and why.

Surprisingly, interrupting periodically (to ensure that you understand the giver, rather than to assert your contrasting view) can be a sign that you are listening well.[6] So jump in: "Before you go further, can you just say more about what you mean by 'unprofessional'? I want to be sure I'm tracking what you're describing. . . ." Clarifying as you go can be helpful to both of you.

Beware Hot Inquiry

Something to watch for: In an effort to keep listening even when we're upset, our questions may become "hot"—inquiry in punctuation only, heated by the affront and frustration we're struggling to contain. Our feelings leak out into our "questions" and we end up saying things like "Why are you so stupid?" and "Do you actually believe that?" Both of these sentences have question marks at the end, but neither is a real question. Inquiry is determined by the intention of the speaker, and the intention of both these "questions" is to assert and persuade (or vent and attack), not to understand.

Sarcasm is always inconsistent with true inquiry ("No, no, I love getting eviscerating feedback from you. Do you have more?"), as are questions that cross-examine ("But isn't it true that . . . ?" "If so, how do you explain . . . ?"). These are external signs of the wrestling match going on between you and your internal voice. Your internal voice is saying, "Can you believe this guy? Let me at 'em!" and you are replying, "Hold up! We're supposed to be asking questions!" The result is "inquiry" that's loaded with frustration and assertion.

What to do, then, when you are experiencing strong feelings? If you're overwhelmed, don't try to fight through it and inquire. Instead, assert. Replace hot inquiry like this: "Do you actually think that what you're saying is consistent or fair?" with a thoughtful assertion like this: "What you're suggesting seems inconsistent with the criteria you've used for others in my position. That doesn't seem fair to me." You can then circle back to listening: "Are there aspects of this that I'm missing?"

Assert what you have to assert. It makes listening easier and more effective.

ASSERT WHAT'S LEFT OUT

It seems paradoxical to talk about assertiveness in the context of *receiving* feedback. But feedback is not simply a thing the giver hands you and you receive. The two of you are building a puzzle—together. They have some of the pieces, and you have some of the pieces. When you don't assert, you are withholding your pieces. Without your point of view and feelings the giver is unaware of whether what they're saying is helpful, on target, or in line with your experiences. There's no problem solving, no adjusting, and no indication of whether you understand the feedback, how you might use it, or why trying it out is more challenging or risky than they assume.

Your assertions will often be in response to the giver's feedback, but not always. You might be asked to begin a performance review with a self-assessment. But at some point, by definition, you will be getting feedback and you will have things to say in response.

Shift from "I'm Right" to "Here's What's Left Out"

Effective assertion hinges on a key mindset shift: You aren't seeking to persuade the giver that you are right. You're not trying to replace their truth with your truth. Instead, you're adding what's "left out." And what's most often left out is your data, your interpretations, and your feelings. As long as you've made that shift, you can assert anything that's important to you. With both sets of puzzle pieces on the table, you can begin to see where the two of you see things the same and differently, and why.

Common Assertion Mistakes

Below, we look at common assertion mistakes produced by the three triggers—truth, relationship, and identity.

Truth Mistakes

The most common pitfall is slipping back into a "truth" mindset.

> *Pitfall:* "That advice is wrong."
> *Better:* "I disagree with that advice."

Why does this seemingly small distinction matter? Because it keeps the topic of the conversation where it belongs. If you say, "That advice is wrong," the giver will simply respond by explaining again why it's right. If you say, "I disagree with that advice," the giver can't argue with the fact that you happen to have an opinion on the matter. You do. All that is left is to figure out why you see it differently. You might say this: "We had a different approach in the last place I worked, and we had fewer problems than we do here." The giver doesn't know what succeeded at your last job; you don't know what they have tried in the past here. That's the conversation to have.

Talking in terms of difference doesn't mean that facts aren't involved; facts are often at the heart of the conversation. You need to know what the sales numbers are before you can decide what they mean. But deciding what they mean is probably the tougher, and more important, task.

Relationship Mistakes

The big relationship assertion pitfall is switchtracking. You can avoid that by noticing that there are two topics, and giving each topic its own track.

Pitfall: "You're a self-centered jerk."

Better: "I'm feeling underappreciated, so it's hard for me to focus on your feedback. I think we need to discuss how I'm feeling, as well as the feedback itself."

If you say the first line, you'll likely start a fight. If you say the second, you'll likely cause the giver to wonder what crazy books you've been reading. But that's preferable (usually) to the fight.

A second common pitfall is about systems, blame, and contribution:

Pitfall: "This is not my fault. I'm not the real problem here."

Better: "I agree that there are things I've contributed to this. I'd also like to step back to look at the bigger picture together, because I think there are a number of other inputs that are important for us to understand if we're going to change things."

Again, the first response is likely to start an argument about who the problem is. The second signals willingness to take responsibility for your contribution, while pointing out that you are not in this alone.

Identity Mistakes

When we're off balance or overwhelmed, our assertions are more likely to tip into exaggeration.

Pitfall: "It's true. I'm hopeless."

Better: "I'm surprised by all this and it's a lot to take in. I want to take some time to think about it and digest what you've said. Let's come back to it tomorrow."

When you're feeling overwhelmed, it's unlikely that you will represent your views in a clear or balanced way. In your effort to regain some balance, you may take far more than your share of the responsibility for a problem, or simply project amplified hopelessness and insecurity.

Better to be open about the fact that you're surprised by the feedback and want time to figure out what it means for you.

A second common pitfall occurs when your internal voice is hard at work keeping the feedback out:

Pitfall: "That's ridiculous. I'm not that kind of person."

Better: "That's upsetting to hear, because it's not how I see myself or who I want to be."

You can signal that the information doesn't fit with how you see yourself without saying the information is wrong. And you can vow to figure it out without saying the information is right.

BE YOUR OWN PROCESS REFEREE

For many years, when we taught communication workshops, we focused on how to listen and assert. If that approach didn't provide 100 percent of what people needed to know, it seemed close enough.

But we started to notice something interesting. When we observed people who were particularly skilled at communicating, they seemed to be using a third skill that we couldn't quite put our finger on.

Then it hit us. They were not only *in* the conversation, they were also actively and explicitly *managing* the conversation. Supercommunicators had an exceptional ability to observe the discussion, diagnose where it was going wrong, and make explicit process interventions to correct it. It was as though they were functioning in two roles at once: They weren't just players in the game, they were also referees.

Process Moves: Diagnose, Describe, Propose

These people sense precisely where they are in a conversation, including the stage they are in and the common challenges in that stage. They have the ability to diagnose on the fly where the conversation is getting stuck and how to move it forward—not to manipulate things to their own advantage, but for the sake of clear communication. They are willing to be hyperexplicit, perhaps sometimes even awkwardly so, in their effort to get things back on track.

Whatever your natural skill level, you can get better at these kinds of process moves with awareness and practice. We ourselves have gotten better by listening attentively to what process moves sound like, and so can you:

"We're both making arguments, trying to persuade the other, but I don't think either of us is listening to, or fully understanding, the other. I know I'm not doing a good enough job of trying to understand what your concerns are. So tell me more about why this is so important to you and to the shop steward."

"I see two issues here, and we're jumping back and forth between them. Let's focus on one at a time. The first is that you're upset because you think I didn't tell you about my upcoming trip to D.C. and I'm upset because I think I did. The other is that you're worried about how you're going to manage the kids' schedules while I'm gone. Do you agree, and if so, which do you want to talk about first?"

"You're saying I've been treating Mom unfairly, and that any normal person would know that. I disagree with both parts of that: I don't think I treat Mom unfairly, and I don't think 'any normal person' would think I do. I'm not saying my view is right and yours is wrong. I'm saying we see it differently. I wonder if there are aspects of how you see this that I'm not fully understanding, as opposed to simply disagreeing with? What would you add?"

"I'm shocked by this. My internal voice is saying, 'My God, this is not a question of interpretation. That simply did not happen that way!' You seem upset as well and might be thinking the same. I'd like to take a break and come back to this in a couple of hours after we've both had time to calm down."

"Okay, we're deadlocked. We both need to agree on this, and we don't. Your solution is that I should give in. As a process, that doesn't feel fair to me. On the other hand, I don't know how to break this deadlock, so we've got to figure it out. What's a fair and efficient way to decide when we don't agree?"

All of these examples have two things in common. The first is that none of the comments are about the substance of the discussion per se. Each contains an observation about some aspect of the *process* that is stuck or off track. And each contains a suggestion for how to move forward or an invitation to problem solving.

The second is that they all sound slightly awkward—not how regular people talk. And paradoxically, that's one of the reasons these kinds of interventions can be so powerful. A referee stops the flow of the game to make adjustments, and that's precisely the goal of a process move. You are pausing the action of the conversation to step back and consider how it's going and how you might correct course. These moves can short-circuit an escalating cycle of frustration or disagreement, and they give both people a chance to make a purposive choice about how to go forward together.

PROBLEM SOLVE TO CREATE POSSIBILITIES

We've been talking about how to understand feedback and how to metabolize it in a way that is useful rather than destructive or dismissive. But there's often a next question at the heart of receiving feedback well: Now what? What's the point of all this hard work to understand feedback anyway? What are you going to do with it?

This can be a challenging question, especially if you and the giver disagree on what the feedback means or what should happen as a result. When there's conflict over this, you need strong problem-solving skills. To most people's surprise, being good at problem solving is not just a matter of being "clever" or even "creative." There are specific skills—questions to ask, ways to approach things—that make a difference.

Create Possibilities

Sometimes, even when we believe the feedback is right, we feel that there's not much we can do about it. It's dispiriting. It might be feedback about deep-seated personality traits or physical appearance (if you are told you are too tall for the leading man role, your efforts to adjust your height will inevitably come up, well, short). Or taking the feedback would require such major upheavals in lifestyle or habits or workload that you aren't sure they'd be worth the effort, or doubt that you would succeed even if you tried.

But we can often create new possibilities even where there don't seem to be any. We saw an example of this in Alita's obstetrics office in chapter 7. Alita's patients complained that she often ran late. Alita felt not only discouraged, but stuck. Without some major structural overhaul to her practice, running late was going to be a periodic feature of the patient experience.

The patients have a preferred solution for the problem: Run on time. But they have another interest as well. They want to understand *why* appointments get backed up, and each still wants attentiveness when her own time comes. This is why a sign in the waiting room explaining why appointments run late actually meets some of the patients' real concerns. They understand the process. They feel acknowledged. They see that the issue is not that the doctor doesn't care, but that she cares a lot.

Finding possibilities requires two things: attentive listening for the interests behind the feedback, and the ability to generate options that address those interests. This can transform your feedback conversations from arguments about whether the giver's ideas are "the right way to go" to explorations of what they're trying to accomplish and how to get there.

Dig for Underlying Interests

In *Getting to Yes*, Roger Fisher, William Ury, and Bruce Patton make a distinction that is crucial to problem solving: the difference between interests and positions. Positions are what people say they want or demand. Interests are the underlying "needs, desires, fears, and concerns" that the stated position intends to satisfy.[7] Often interests can be met by a variety of options, some different from what anyone sees at the outset.

Advice often shows up as a position: It's the giver's best idea for what to do differently. You often run late? Be on time. You micromanage? Cut it out.

Listening for the underlying interests gives you more room to maneuver. Consider the story of Earl, a social worker who helps disabled children and their families. Earl wears his hair in a ponytail, has a long, scruffy beard, and is missing his two front teeth. Although he is extremely good at his job, his unorthodox appearance caused some families to take some time to feel comfortable with him.

Earl's supervisor suggested that he cut his hair and trim his beard. Earl refused, and countered that people who would prejudge him for his unconventional appearance were no different from people who prejudge a child because of their disability. It was a fair enough point, but it didn't change the fact that Earl's appearance injected tension into an already challenging situation.

Earl's supervisor took this position: "Clean up your appearance." But Earl heard through that for the underlying concern: "We want families to feel comfortable with you more quickly." Earl shared this interest and suggested another way to address it. He asked his supervisor to describe him a bit differently to new families before he met them. In addition to presenting his professional credentials, he suggested that she add a few words about his being a semiprofessional bluegrass banjo player.

This one additional fact about Earl put his appearance into a context that the families understood. Instead of being surprised or put off by his appearance, they were intrigued. Many connected with him on the subject of music and came quickly to appreciate that his appearance attested to his courage to be himself in the world—a lesson he was effectively teaching both them and their children.

When you're at an impasse—when what a giver suggests is difficult for you or even unacceptable—ask about the underlying interests behind the suggestion.

Three Sources of Interests Behind Feedback

The interests behind coaching or evaluation typically fall into one of three buckets, and each suggests a different direction to go in creating options:

Helping you. The giver sees ways you could improve and opportunities to accelerate your growth or learning curve. Or perhaps they want to protect you from potential problems or dangers that they see, but you don't. Their goal is to help *you*.

Helping themselves and the relationship. The giver may be giving you feedback because they feel upset, lonely, angry, disappointed, or hurt by you. Instead of saying, "I feel neglected," they say, "You travel too much." The feedback is about you and your behavior, certainly. But the interests involved are not necessarily obvious: You could make a concerted effort to travel less and then go hunting more. You believe you "took" their coaching; they know you missed the point.

Helping the organization/team/family/someone else. Sometimes feedback is motivated by helping or protecting someone, or something, beyond the two of you. Your boss can't give you a higher rating because it wouldn't be fair to others. Your best friend doesn't really care that you often forget to pay her back, but knows that a mutual friend is really upset when you forget to repay him. So she steps in to raise the issue with you.

To solve the real problem, you have to understand the real interests. And to understand the real interests, you have to dig behind the stated positions and identify which bucket the interests fall into.

Generate Options

Once you've got a handle on the underlying interests (and whose interests are actually involved), you can turn to the next step, which is creating options. Life is easier when you find options that meet your interests as well as those of the feedback giver.

It's useful to be explicit about what you're trying to accomplish. You can name the different interests and invite the other person to think with you about ways of meeting them. The number one reason we don't come up with good options is that we simply don't think to try. So, try.

As in Earl's case, some options solve the whole problem and fully meet whatever the feedback giver's interests are. Other options are "process" options. We'll try it your way and then take stock; we'll trade off; I'll draw the chicken more realistically, and then we can show both to the organizing committee and see what they think. You don't need to have a final determination about the feedback. Whether or not the feedback is fair is as yet undetermined; what you agree on now is a process for moving forward that feels fair to both of you.

CLOSE WITH COMMITMENT

How do we know a feedback conversation is over? Often it's when someone gives up, walks out, shuts down, or when time runs out. Even when the conversation goes well, we often skip a crucial last step: figuring out what we've agreed to and what to do next. If we're not explicit, we often end up disappointed by the lack of progress, or confused about the other person's lofty expectations. Both giver and receiver wonder why they spent so much time on the matter to begin with, when nothing ever changes.

Closing with commitment can be as short as a sentence: "I want to think about what you've said, and let's talk tomorrow." It doesn't mean you have to agree with the feedback or make promises to change. You can, of course, but you can also commit to gathering more information or bringing others into the conversation or seeing how things go in the next two weeks or describing exactly which parts of the feedback you have decided not to take. The goal is clarity. You should both know where things stand.

Depending on the formality of the context, here are a few different kinds of things you can firm up as you wrap up:

Action Plans: Who does what tomorrow? What, if anything, is each party going to change or work on, and what do you each agree to do to make that happen?

Benchmarks and Consequences: How will progress be measured, and when? Consider discussing what impact, positive and negative, measuring will have. Also, discuss the consequences, if any, if benchmarks are not met.

Procedural Contracts: In addition to promises about the substance of what will change, you might make agreements on the process for working on them. When do we talk again, and about what? You may agree to gather more input from the client, the board, the neighbors, the market. We may both vow not to discuss the matter in front of the kids or the customer, or agree to give each other the benefit of the doubt.

New Strategies: Whether at work or at home, the friction that produces feedback often reflects differences between us that aren't going to go away. Rather than finding *solutions* in these cases we should often be looking for *strategies*—new ways of working around each other's foibles and failures, forgetfulness, or fiery tempers. At the end of the conversation, articulate the ideas you've generated for how to accommodate each other more successfully, and again, make sure you each know exactly what you're agreeing to.

Remember: Feedback conversations are rarely one-shot deals. They are usually a series of conversations over time, and as such, signposting where you stand, what you've accomplished, and what you'll try next helps you travel the road together.

PUTTING IT ALL TOGETHER: A CONVERSATION IN MOTION

As we've said, feedback conversations are unpredictable, and you'll need to deftly move among the skills we've described. Let's take a look at an evaluation conversation to get a sense of how you might use these skills in motion.

AN EVALUATION CONVERSATION ABOUT RATINGS AND BONUSES

You're in a year-end conversation with your head of function. The more formal part of the meeting concerns bonuses, raises, and promotions. The meeting also serves as a catchall opportunity to talk about anything important: your thoughts on the previous year, your concerns for next year.

You were given a 4 out of 5 rating for the third year in a row. The bonus awarded for a 5 is approximately double the bonus for a 4. You're not outraged, but you are frustrated. You were told last year that the big differentiator between a 4 and a 5 is whether you're bringing in customers of your own rather than just running the division and serving the customers of others. This year you made that a priority, and brought in twenty-three new customer accounts, with contracts that raised your team's revenue by almost 20 percent.

Let's look at four different ways you might handle the conversation. The first three are variations on doing things less well; the fourth is more effective. We'll imagine in each case that the preliminaries are out of the way and pick up the discussion at the point where you react to your rating and bonus.

Version One

You Say: "This is just unfair. Last year I was told that I'd be rated a 5 if I brought in customers. I did that and now I'm still getting a 4. Does anyone around here care about fairness?"

Analysis: We see four problems: (1) You are asserting that the outcome is unfair, but you won't actually know if it's unfair until you've discussed it further. It could be that you didn't bring in enough accounts, or that they were too small, or that the criteria changed, or that you didn't make it clear to anyone that you'd originated these accounts, or that you misunderstood what was said last year, or that other factors militated against a 5 even though your customer work was good. After further conversation, you might still conclude that the assessment is not fair, but you might not. (2) "Unfair" is stated as a truth rather than as your perception. (3) The comment about anyone's caring is a personal attack based on an attribution that you know little about. It could be that many people do care about fairness, or that several advocated strongly on your behalf. (4) Your comment is inexact. You were not told that if you brought in customers you'd definitely get a 5; you were told

that a big differentiator between a 4 and a 5 is bringing in customers.

Result: Your boss might get hooked by any number of these problems. Before you know it, she'll be defending her identity as a
fair person, and an argument about "how your boss is" won't
help resolve the issue you care about.

Version Two

You Say: "Well, okay. I think 4 is a little low, but I suppose it's fine."

Analysis: This comment is both unclear and passive-aggressive.
You're effectively saying, "I'll raise my concern just enough to
make you wonder what I think, but not so much that I take
responsibility for having raised it or that I'm clear about my
actual view." Talk about it or don't—but don't "sort of" talk
about it.

Result: Your boss will either not notice that you're raising a legitimate concern or be annoyed by the passive-aggressive tenor of
it. Either way, you don't learn why you got a 4 or what you
should change, and it may negatively affect what your boss
thinks of you.

Version Three

You Say: "Wow, I was thinking I'd get a 5. Is there any way it can
be changed?"

Analysis: There's nothing wrong with saying you thought you'd
get a 5, because you did think that. But, again, you don't yet
understand why you got a 4, so a request to change it is prema-
ture. After the discussion you may agree that a 4 is the appropriate rating, or you may think you deserve a 5. If so, with
what you've learned, you'll be able to articulate your reasoning.

Result: Your boss says "no." End of story. End of learning. End of
chance to influence. Or, your boss says she'll consider it, but
has no new information or way of thinking about the matter
that would make any difference.

Version Four: A More Skillful Conversation

Your goal is to assert that you are surprised and disappointed and to explain why. At this point in the conversation you are not asserting that the rating is unfair or requesting that it be changed, nor are you judging the overall system or the people making the decisions.

You want to inquire into several things: You want to learn more about the criteria and how they were applied in your case. You want to understand the relationship between what you were told last year about customers and the current criteria. You want to know if anything has changed, and what other data—about peers, the market, pressures from above—might be relevant.

Once you've gotten a better sense of that information, you may or may not feel the rating and bonus were fair, and you may or may not want to raise that issue. If you do conclude that the rating is unfair, you would express that as your own view, not as an objective fact. You should also be explicit about whether you would like to revisit the actual rating or you are having the discussion simply to help you understand the system, perhaps with an eye toward next year.

We'll assume your boss hasn't read this book and is a little slow to understand what you're trying to do. So you'll have to be persistent.

You: I'm surprised that I got a 4 instead of a 5. But I don't actually know much about the decision-making process or the criteria that are used.

Boss: You think you deserve a 5?

You: Yes, I was thinking that, but as I reflect on it, I realize that that wasn't based on very much information. I was told at last year's review that one of the differentiators was bringing in new accounts, so I worked hard to land twenty-three new customers and that increased our revenue by almost 20 percent. I was assuming that was enough for a 5, but I don't have a clear sense of the criteria. Also, there could be other factors involved that I'm not aware of.

Boss: I think a 4 is very good.

You: Well, I appreciate that. It's still important to me to under-stand better how the decisions are made.

Boss: You think it's unfair?

You: I don't have enough information to judge. Can you tell me what factors are weighed in determining the rating? And can you say what role new accounts and revenue play in the rating?

[The boss explains the rating system at some length, with you interrupting periodically to clarify the process, terms, etc., un-til it's clear to you.]

You: Based on what you've just explained about the criteria, and assuming there were no other factors, I do think I should have received a 5. Do you see it differently?

Boss: In terms of revenue and customers, I would agree. But it's not an exact science. Different people on the compensation committee may take slightly different factors into account.

You: I can only imagine how much work it is to sort this all out. Were there additional factors that are relevant for me?

Boss: A few members of the committee raised questions about your overall commitment. They have no problem with me sharing that, but I didn't mention it to you because I disagree with them. I think it's a nonissue and it would do you a disser-vice to emphasize that or, really, even to mention it.

You: Of course it's upsetting to hear, but it's helpful to know. It tells me that whether or not you or I think I'm dedicated, I'm coming across at least to some people in a way that is raising some questions.

Boss: Well, I suppose I could go back to the committee and see whether there's any wiggle room on your rating. I suspect there isn't, but I can check.

You: Well, how would that be perceived by the committee?

Boss: As you'd guess, there are a number of people who are going to whine about their compensation no matter what it is. But occasionally we really do need to reconsider.

You: Well, for the moment, I'd like to leave the rating alone. Would it be okay if I talked to someone from the committee who has concerns about my commitment? I'd like to learn more about that perception before I decide whether to pursue changing the rating.

The conversation continues as you both explore options and nail down commitments on how to go forward. But you've done a good job of working to understand the feedback and demonstrating a willingness to learn from it.

And the ability to learn from feedback is what will shape your future most.

12

GET GOING

Five Ways to Take Action

Here we include a handful of ideas for getting moving—quick ways to solicit feedback, to test out the advice you're getting, to accelerate your learning, and to gauge your progress.

NAME ONE THING

It's his first performance review under the new system, and Rodrigo's head is spinning with charts, graphs, competencies, and comments. Rodrigo is overwhelmed, and confused about what he's actually supposed to do differently.

At least he doesn't have to contend with chocolate chip cookies.

Subjects in a recent experiment were not so lucky. Participants were asked to skip a meal before arriving at the laboratory. They entered the lab one by one, where chocolate chip cookies had been baking in a small oven, saturating the room with the rich aroma. Half of the subjects were asked to eat two or three cookies, while the other half were asked to refrain from the cookies and instead eat two or three radishes.

Later, all were asked to solve a series of geometry problems, requiring them to trace figures without lifting the pencil; they were given infinite attempts and plenty of paper. Those asked to resist the cookies (and eat the radishes) gave up twice as quickly, after about half the number of attempts as their counterparts. Researcher Roy Baumeister and colleagues say that the attention and effort that goes into resisting temptation (or forcing new, less-appealing behavior) leaves less energy, attention, and persistence available to complete other tasks.[1]

This has important implications for our efforts to act upon the feedback we get to change behavior and habits. Feedback can be accurate, timely, perceptive, and beautifully conveyed, but if it involves too many ideas to keep track of, too many decisions to sort through, too many changes to make, it's simply too much. Our capacity to attend to change is a limited resource. Hence, less is more (more or less).

So keep it simple, and here's how: *Name one thing*. At the end of the day, is there one thing you and the giver (or givers) see as most important for you to work on? It should be something meaningful and useful, but don't get paralyzed by that. It doesn't have to be the one *perfect* thing. That sends you right back to no things. Just a useful thing. A place to start.

ASK: "WHAT'S ONE THING YOU SEE ME DOING THAT GETS IN MY OWN WAY?"

How to elicit just one thing? Don't say, "I'd like some feedback." That's too vague. Instead say: "What's one thing I could work on?" Or, as we discuss in chapter 4, you can sharpen it by asking: "What's one thing you see me doing, or failing to do, that's getting in my own way?" This gives your giver permission to go a little further than usual (hey, you did ask), and it helps them prioritize and cut to the chase.

Of course, emergencies are emergencies; if your hair *and* pants are on fire, the one-thing formula doesn't quite fit. And don't use "name one thing" as a way to simply dismiss someone's concerns. You may not be able to work on ten concerns, but if your giver has ten concerns, they have them. Work to understand and validate them, and then swing back around and set priorities: "You've raised a number of different issues, and we've discussed why each is important. I'm serious about improving, and it's been my experience that the best way for me to do that is to focus on one thing at a time. Let's figure out a good place for me to start."

It's not always easy. When your youngest daughter offers you feedback, she's not going to react well when you tell her you've already received your "one thing" for the month from her older sister. So, depending on how big or challenging the changes, you can work on a few at a time, especially if they are on different fronts. You can be working on being more patient with your oldest and more consistent with your youngest. In aiming for one, you're setting expectations: Let's focus.

LISTEN FOR THEMES

Rodrigo's feedback report contained dozens of comments and suggestions, and three highlighted "areas of improvement." Most of the feedback was vague and label-y (for example, at the mean on "empathy," below the mean on "engagement"). In the end, it was the sheer volume of the feedback that left him at a loss for where to begin.

So Rodrigo put aside the report and set off on his own mission. He chose three people he worked closely with in different roles, and threw in his boss and a coworker he found particularly irritating. He went to each and asked this question: "What's one thing I'm doing that you think gets in the way of my own effectiveness?" He asked follow-up questions to clarify. The longest conversation took ten minutes.

Rodrigo knew that he'd end up with more than "one thing" to consider, but he looked for themes. Here are the headlines based on his conversations:

Let us know where you stand sooner.

You hang back and let others dominate the conversation. Given your unique background, we need you to weigh in earlier.

Be more visible at HQ.

I can't tell when you've made a decision. If you have, tell us so we can move on.

The way I think you shoot yourself in the foot is by being disorganized.

Of the five people he talked to, three went straight to his tendency as a team leader to hang back and let conversation run. Until he received this feedback, that shortcoming wasn't even on his radar. (In retrospect he realized that it had been mentioned in his feedback report, but if you hadn't already been looking for it, you'd never have seen it buried in the data.) In fact, until now, he thought he had the opposite challenge: He worried that he was not giving the team enough input into decisions and was working hard at inclusiveness. After talking to colleagues, he discovered that there were times when he needed to give more direction and be clear about when he had made up his mind, so that they could move on to discussing implementation.

So Rodrigo has decided his one thing for the next month is to work on speaking up and providing more direction. One colleague offered a particularly helpful bit of coaching: "She suggested that I be willing to go a little overboard. If I do, she promised to tell me. If I'm less worried about going too far, I'll improve quicker."

ASK WHAT MATTERS TO *THEM*

One last way to seek out one change that could have a big impact is to ask: "What's one thing I could change that would make a difference *to you*?" Sharon posed this question to her three young boys over dinner: "I've been under a lot of pressure at work, and I keep asking you for more help and understanding. But let's turn the tables. What's one thing I could do differently that would help you guys?"

Sharon couldn't imagine any useful answer to this question. She figured that if there were an easy fix, she'd already be doing it. Eight-year-old Aidan yelled out, "more Skittles," which sparked a fight between Aidan and twelve-year-old Owen, who not unreasonably thought "more Skittles" was a stupid answer. Not a strong start to the conversation.

Then ten-year-old Colin spoke up: "We never go bowling anymore."

This struck Sharon as only marginally better than "more Skittles," but she could see that Colin was serious. "So you miss bowling?" she asked.

"Not that much," said Colin.

Baffled, Sharon said, "So tell us why you mention bowling."

Colin had an answer: "It's the only time the four of us ever do anything together, with *just us*, and we haven't done it for a year." He was right. Foursome time mattered less to his more social brothers, but it mattered a lot to Colin, and Sharon hadn't noticed. Sharon called the alley and reserved a lane.

One question, one thing.

TRY SMALL EXPERIMENTS

Sometimes you are clear about whether you want to take the feedback: Now that I understand what you're suggesting, I think it's a fantastic idea and I can't wait to dive in. Or: Now that I understand what you're suggesting, I'm going to go ahead and say no (painting my living room black—it's not the right look for me). And sometimes we fall somewhere in the middle, unsure if it's a good idea or not. I'll table it for now and I'll come back to it, perhaps if I get reincarnated as someone with free time.

In any event, we try to be analytical about the feedback we get, considering pros and cons, weighing different options, and finally doing what makes sense. But here's the challenge: In any contest between change and the status quo, the status quo has home field advantage. All things being equal, we won't change.

Emily is a good example. Her nonprofit, which supports young parents and teaches parenting skills, was built from the ground up, with hard work and a vision as big as the world. Her message is inspirational and her ideas important.

Reaction to her two-hour public sessions has been overwhelmingly positive. But time and again she gets feedback from coworkers, guest speakers, and parents that her twenty-minute introduction to the organization and its work at the beginning of her talk is too long. She should jump right into the evening's activities.

For five years Emily resisted these suggestions. After all, she was a great speaker, she knew how to motivate people, the workshops got strong reviews, and she'd been successful doing it her way. There was just no reason to change things up until now.

When things are going well, feedback can feel threatening, and not just because it suggests we have something to learn or aren't yet perfect. It's threatening because it is asking us to let go of something that's comfortable and predictable. We're already doing just fine, and even if we're not, at least we're aware of the consequences. I know I'm late for everything, but so far it hasn't had a disastrous impact on my life. The guests didn't have to wait *that* long, and in the end, we got married, didn't we?

DON'T DECIDE, EXPERIMENT

Here's our pitch: Experiment. Try the feedback out, especially when the stakes are low and the potential upside is great. Not because you *know* that it's right or you know it will help. But because it's possible it will help. And because actions so often have unforeseen consequences, and trying new things stirs the pot. And because you (we) don't try new things often enough.

Try It On

Sometimes you can do the experiment in your head.

Harpreet had been teaching for several years when he received a shocking set of comments on a student evaluation: "The professor is arrogant and condescending toward students. He is dismissive of their ideas and concerns."

Harpreet felt ill. This characterization could not be more out of step with his values and self-image. Dedicated to fostering students' growth in his lab, he prided himself on his commitment to mentoring. He decided to discuss the evaluation with his department head. "Look at these comments," he said to her. "I can't understand how a student could say such a thing."

She skimmed the comments and after a moment looked up and said, "Well, try it on." Harpreet was dumbfounded. He sputtered, "I'm not sure what you mean." "Try it on," she repeated. "Assume the student is on to something."

"But the student is *not* on to something," Harpreet protested, sort of joking but mostly not.

"Sit with the possibility for a few days," she suggested. "Not because you already know it fits, but because it's a good way of finding out. If it doesn't, no worries. Take it off. But if it does, even in some small way, then it gives you something to work on."

Trying on a piece of feedback in your mind's dressing room can be uncomfortable, but it's a low-risk way of experimenting. Harpreet did try on the feedback, and after considering it from different angles, he began to see what the student might have meant. While he didn't regard certain comments that he had made as arrogant, he could see now how someone might. This new perspective on himself—not "the truth," but an alternate way of seeing—proved enormously valuable for Harpreet and influenced how he interacted with his students for the rest of his career. And he would not have had access to it if he hadn't taken a genuine run at trying it on as true.

Try It Out

For years your spouse has been urging you to wake up earlier and do yoga before going to work. There are two things you don't like about this suggestion: waking up early and yoga. You can't see how trying it would have any positive effect on your life. And you have a rule: "If you can't see how trying something would help, don't try it." Your spouse thinks you're being lazy, but you know you're just being smart.

And then this thought pops into your head: *I am fifty. If I live to be eighty I will wake up roughly 11,000 more times. If I try yoga and don't like it, I will have 10,999 mornings remaining to wake up at my preferred time.*

So one morning you wake up early and go to yoga. You are surprised to learn that this yoga is different from the yoga of your youth. The instructor said to you afterward, "I hope you didn't injure yourself." But despite this "feedback," you have to admit that you sort of liked it. And you certainly liked the effect it seemed to have on the rest of your day. You decide to go a few more times, just to test this out.

The one downside of this situation is that your spouse gets to be right, and you have to admit you were wrong. But you protest: "I wasn't wrong, because it's different yoga, and there's no way I could have anticipated that." Exactly. That's why such low-cost experiments are so great. You do them even though you have misgivings, because you know that you are occasionally wrong. Not as often as your spouse thinks, perhaps, but occasionally.

You May Be Surprised

Dr. Atul Gawande is an accomplished surgeon, *New Yorker* writer, and professor at Harvard Medical School. You'd figure if anyone was feeling at the top of their game, it would be this guy.

But Gawande wondered if he could improve. So he hired a surgical coach to observe him, looking for ways he might enhance both his surgical technique and his already-commendable outcomes. He figured it was possible the coach would see something he hadn't.

The coach's recommendations surprised Gawande. He had a number of technical suggestions ("When you are tempted to raise your elbow, that means you either need to move your feet or to choose a different instrument.").[2] The coach was also able to point out some of Gawande's blind spots: The way he draped the patient for surgery gave Gawande a perfect line of vision on the procedure but partially obstructed the view of his assistant across the table. This was invisible to Gawande but instantly obvious to the coach. And the coach "pointed out ways I had missed opportunities to help the team perform better," observes Gawande.[3] The impact of the advice was large. After following the coach's ideas—a few at a time over a number of months—Gawande has seen his complication rates go down.

Gawande didn't hire a coach because he knew he needed one, or foresaw these particular improvements. He hired one because there didn't seem to be much downside in doing so, and the upside, though unclear, seemed worth exploring. And it certainly proved worthwhile for his patients and for his team, who saw him model an interest in and openness to continuous learning and improvement.

IT'S NOT ALL-AND-ALWAYS

Lowering the stakes often means reframing the question you are asking yourself when it comes to feedback. If the question is "Should I go to yoga for the rest of my life?" the answer will always be no. If it's "Should I try yoga for one morning and see what I think?" the costs drop dramatically.

Emily heard the advice she was getting—cut out the twenty-minute windup—as an all-and-always suggestion: Do your workshops entirely differently for the rest of time. And by the way, it wouldn't hurt if you admitted you had been wrong all along.

Emily finally changed when she shifted away from the all-and-always frame. While she wasn't yet persuaded that scrapping the twenty minutes spent on the big-picture vision was the right call, she decided to try it for one night to see what happened. She welcomed the new parents and then jumped right into the program.

The results of her experiment? There were a few awkward moments when Emily lost her place without her regular script. And it turned out that there were parts of her standard intro that she wanted to retain. But she did find that the full twenty minutes weren't really necessary: "Next time I'll do five minutes on what they really need to know and hand out something written at the end for those who want more details."

It's not all-and-always. Just some-and-sometimes.

Some experiments will inevitably turn out to be a waste of time—that's why they're called experiments. But in the aggregate, there are significant life rewards for being willing to test out feedback even when you're not sure it's right, or even pretty sure it's wrong. At the very least, it shows the giver you are open to trying their advice, and there are surely relationship advantages to that.

RIDE OUT THE J CURVE

This is the story of Bernardus and the new customer tracking system. Stop us if you've heard it before.

The head of sales has been after Bernardus for months to use the new Web-based database that enables you to enter and retrieve data from anywhere, and share information with everyone. If Bernardus goes on vacation he won't have to spend hours bringing someone up to speed on a particular account; he'll just give them the file name. And he will no longer have to worry about finding those little scraps of paper with numbers and e-mails and cryptic notations describing the customer's priorities and preferences.

It's a wondrous system; Bernardus is convinced of its usefulness. But he can't get himself to actually make the switch. He starts using the system, gets frustrated, and switches midway through a customer call. Or he uses the system for a few days, and then forgets and realizes a week later that he's got hours of data to enter to catch up. His note-taking habits have been years in the making and feel dependent on a pencil and trusty paper, no matter how dog-eared. It's not rational. It is resistant to change.

Sometimes we don't do the right, smart, effective, healthy thing because we don't know what that is. But sometimes we know exactly what the right, smart, effective, healthy thing is, and we still don't do it.

TWO DECISION MAKERS

This isn't a new problem. You remember the story of Odysseus? He's worried about being seduced by the sirens, whose songs have lured many a sailor to shipwreck. Odysseus knows he won't be able to make the right choice once he's in the midst of the straits and hears their alluring song. So instead of relying on willpower exercised in that perilous moment, he has his sailors tie him to the mast ahead of time. Odysseus "precommits" to honoring his current desire, preventing his ability to waver when faced with future temptation.

Homer was on to something about the challenges of making good choices, potentially as useful to Bernardus as it was to Odysseus. Economist Thomas Schelling says much of our puzzling behavior when it comes to (failing to) keep our commitments to ourselves results from a kind of split personality we all possess.[4] We decide on Sunday night that come Monday morning we will finally start that low-carb diet. So far so good. But when Monday morning arrives, we are faced with choices: Should I enjoy my usual breakfast muffin, or restrict myself to eggs and ham? Not green, but without the carbs, almost as unappealing. Well, there's really very little difference between starting that diet today and starting tomorrow, or even next week, for that matter.

So our Monday Morning self violates the agreement made by our Sunday Night self. Mr. Sunday Night wants to stop procrastinating and start the diet. He's disgusted by Monday Morning guy's refusal to change but what can he do? Come Monday morning, Monday Morning guy is in charge.

So Mr. Sunday Night asks himself: *Is there a way that I can not only make the choice to change but also bind Monday Morning guy to abide by my choice?* There is. Mr. Sunday Night can change the terms of the choice so that Monday Morning guy arrives at the "right" conclusion: We're both going to start that diet.

Mr. Sunday Night can do that in one of two ways: He can increase the positive appeal of the desired change or increase the negative consequences of not changing.

INCREASE THE POSITIVE APPEAL OF CHANGE

Let's look first at how to make changing more appealing to Monday Morning guy.

Make It Social

Unpleasant things are less unpleasant when you have company. Find a friend, colleague, coach, or fellow aspiring dieter and suggest doing it together. Agree on check-in times, e-mail reports of trials and triumphs, have (low-carb) lunch to discuss progress. Commiserate. Coach, support, honestly reflect.

An obvious reason that making it social helps is that it makes a task that might not otherwise be fun, fun. Or a little bit fun, anyway. And combining change with human connection recasts the emotional story of the effort. It's no longer "I'm suffering," but "We are getting through it together." Friends have mutual closet-cleaning days; students study together; otherwise solitary writers share office space.

A second reason is that it makes you accountable to someone else. You might be okay letting yourself down, but now you have your friend to think of, too. And finally, walking the journey alongside someone else can provide appreciation. A dieting friend or newly hired personal trainer really understands the sacrifices you are making. They witness your progress, *see* you sweat, cheer your efforts. Their appreciation helps motivate you to stick with it even when you are not particularly in the mood.

Extroverts are probably thinking this makes a lot of sense—they typically get energy from being with other people. Introverts may be hearing this suggestion as just one more burden—not only do I have to diet or exercise, but now I have to *meet* people, too?

You can get the benefits without having to buddy up or join a rah-rah city bicycling club. Online communities provide a place to check in, to get empathy, gather useful tips, and be accountable, without having to get out of your pajamas or endure awkward small talk. Communities have formed on the Web for just about anything you might be dealing with—whether it's getting your spending under control, coping with the stress of caring for your autistic child, or losing weight. Maybe Bernardus can find one—or start one—for finally using that customer tracking software. After all, it *is* wondrous.

Keep Score

Another way to increase the reward of keeping a commitment is to keep score. Keeping score is a primary reason that video games are so addictive—they offer an instant measure of your progress and an invitation to reset and try again.

Shigeru Miyamoto is the creative force behind Nintendo's best-selling video games—the Mario Bros. franchise and The Legend of Zelda. When Miyamoto turned forty, he decided to get in shape. He took up jogging and swimming, and kept elaborate charts of his activity and his weight taped to the bathroom wall. By "keeping score" this way, he shifted his workout regimen from a self-improvement kick to a game.[5]

He did so for himself, and then for the rest of us: Miyamoto's Wii Fit is the third highest-selling console game of all time. A balance board weighs you in, and your workout time and accomplishments are tracked as you jog through island wonderlands or hula hoop. Introducing an element of play can "get people to do things they might not normally do," Miyamoto explains. It's a way to engage your playful self in facing a challenge and solving problems. And keeping score is a way to set up those positive feedback dopamine hits that entice you to keep trying.

Gamification[6] has such pull that it's now being used (not without controversy) for everything from customer engagement to education. Many middle school science teachers in Massachusetts encourage their students to play JogNog, an online game in which students accrue points for answering "towers" of science questions, with their accomplishments ranked nationwide on a real-time leaderboard. Eighth grader Antoine, who had previously declared science class "boring" and "too easy," found himself using scarce weekend screen time not for video games, but to complete thousands of science questions. As he scanned the leaderboard, noting the point gap between himself and the student above him, he mumbled, "Now I have to pass *him*—just to keep my honor." It's not just about science anymore.

The best games strike a "magical balance between the excitement of facing new problems and the swagger from facing down old ones," writes Nick Paumgarten about Miyamoto's Nintendo games. You can't stay motivated if you have to try your hardest all the time. You need to experience the satisfaction of exercising skills you have mastered, interspersed with the new ones you're working hard to improve. It can't be all learning curve. You need the downhills to coast and recharge.

How to capitalize on these insights when it comes to acting on your feedback and working to change? Well, whatever the task you're engaged in, are there ways to keep score? Are there ways to make the process more competitive, playful, or satisfying? If you're working on procrastination, can you create an incentive system for daily pieces of a project accomplished? If you're trying to act on your husband's request that you stop swearing, paying into a quarter jar not only raises your own awareness but makes it fun for your kids to "help." Download an app that will track your food choices and calorie count. Put on a pedometer and see if you can beat yesterday's step total. This type of approach just might persuade Monday Morning guy to leave the muffin behind.

INCREASE THE COST OF NOT CHANGING

So far we've been talking about ways to tip the calculus in favor of change by increasing the appeal of trying to change. Now let's turn to the other side of the scale: how to increase the cost of choosing not to change.

Tie Yourself to the Mast

Here's a thought: What if the choice was "go low carb, or choose the muffin and donate $500 to the American Nazi party"? Well, that sure changes the siren song of the muffin, right?

But why would one of your choices ever be "eat the muffin and donate to the American Nazi party"?

It wouldn't, unless you designed it that way on purpose, by tying yourself to the mast. How would that work? You give a friend $500 to hold for you. If you don't start your diet when you say you will, he agrees, for real, to donate the money to the American Nazi party. It has nothing to do with your diet, but it certainly changes the terms of the choice.

Thomas Schelling finally stopped smoking by using the threat of donating to the American Nazi party on himself. He has helped doctors break their own drug addictions by having them write a letter to the medical board confessing the problem, seal it, and entrust it to a friend who will mail it if they relapse. One more hit of cocaine isn't just one more hit; it's their license, their career, and their reputation.

Recognize the J Curve

As you work to change, there's a pattern that's worth getting to know, because it's so common and has such a profound effect on our behavior and choices. This pattern is important precisely because its tricky shape can otherwise fool you.

When we try to take feedback that requires change or start any new and challenging activity, a common pattern that results is what's called the J Curve. Imagine a graph where the vertical axis gauges well-being (happiness, contentment, etc.), and the horizontal axis represents time. High is happy, low is unhappy. Left is now, right is later.

In terms of happiness we start somewhere in the middle. We're going about things the way we always have and so we're perhaps medium happy. Maybe our usual approach is working reasonably well though it generates complaints (feedback) from others, or maybe we're not happy with the status quo ourselves, but so far we haven't been able to change.

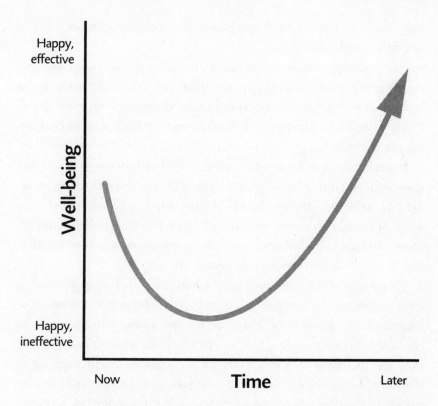

Now, however, we're going to get serious. We're going to finally learn to swim, get out and meet people, cut back on gossiping, leave ourselves more time to get to the airport, provide more mentoring for our team members. As we begin to implement our change we may find that our level of happiness immediately drops. It's uncomfortable. It's awkward. We get worse at whatever we're doing rather than better; we feel vaguely depressed. We begin to slide downward, and we seem only to be heading lower. We not unreasonably take stock: I may not have been thrilled before, but now, as I'm changing, things are taking a turn for the worse. I feel awful. I don't like this change.

That's how things feel now. And we begin to wonder about the future. How is this going to turn out, this new thing we're doing? We've done nothing but head downhill, as if pulled by gravity. Do we keep sledding downward until we crash?

Of course not. We should stop. This effort to change was a big mistake. We cancel the change. Sorry, Mr. Sunday Night, we tried. It just didn't work out.

It's a sad story, but it makes sense . . . *if*, that is, our projection that we are going to continue to go down is correct. But what if we're at the bottom of the curve and are about to head up the happiness slope? What if we are on our way to surpassing our previous level of contentment and skill?

In other words, what if the curve is in the unlikely shape of a J? The truth is, at any time you are changing your habits or approach, or working on a new skill, you are likely to get worse before you get better. And more important, you are likely to *feel* worse before you feel better. In these moments, it's useful to know that a common trajectory isn't further downward, but—eventually—back up.

This suggests that committing in advance to working at something for a specific amount of time—a time that reaches past that most challenging first stage—can be useful. Give it two weeks, thirty days, a fiscal year—whatever seems like a reasonable duration to test whether this new behavior might actually help. Whether you're learning to sleep with a breathing machine to help your apnea, or learning to stop running the experiments themselves and start running the lab, you need to resist letting the dip of the curve erode your resolve.[7]

Understanding the typical trajectory of the J Curve is what ultimately helped Bernardus. His first few weeks with the online database were a minor disaster. He lost data, and it took him longer to input information into the computer than to take handwritten notes. But he started keeping score of the number of customers he successfully entered, and his miss percentage slowly started to improve. Six months later he takes notes in the database while directly on the customer call, and he's starting to enjoy the benefits of having all of his customer information accessible in one place, and on his phone, freeing him from needing to carry his laptop 24/7. Bernardus is now enjoying the upswing of that happiness curve.

All of these ideas can help you to make good on your commitment to implement feedback and to change. By seeing the choice in a new light, or by actually changing the choice, you can change your behavior, and that very often sets in motion a virtuous cycle. And motion—getting going and keeping going—is the goal.

COACH YOUR COACH

When one of the authors was in high school (we won't say which author), he played defensive back on the football team. He saw limited action his junior year, so was excited one Saturday afternoon to be called into the game. As the defense huddled, the defensive captain barked out the formation: "In and Out Zone!" Everyone ran off to their respective positions.

Just prior to the snap, Doug shouted in panic to the captain: "What's an 'In and Out Zone?'" Doug's internal monologue was running like this: *I'm playing varsity football in front of all these people and I have no idea what the defensive formation is. I don't know where to go or what I'm supposed to do. What's wrong with me?*

The captain yelled back: "We don't know! Just guard someone!"

After the game Doug expected the captain—or someone—to ask the coach exactly what an "In and Out" formation involved, but no one did. Apparently, if you didn't understand the formation, you were just supposed to "guard someone." And that's what Doug did, for the rest of the season. At season's end the team had a perfect record: 0-8.

Doug could have said to the coach: "Can we go over the formations again slowly until I really understand them?" But he feared admitting what he didn't know, and anyway, that's not how things worked: The coaches coached, and the players played. Players didn't "coach the coach" to help the coaching staff understand what the players actually needed to learn to get better results.

Here we'll use the term "coach" broadly to mean anyone who gives you feedback. That includes formal mentors, of course, but more often our "coaches" are peers, clients, coauthors, collaborators, bandmates, roommates, friends, or family members. We collaborate to turn out the best product, we ask colleagues to help us get up to speed, we get advice—solicited and unsolicited—from a financial planner or our uncle Phil. Too often, though, we respond the way the players on that football team did: If we don't understand the advice, or how it's being offered to us isn't helping, we don't step back and discuss it. Our colleagues and family aren't even aware that the advice isn't getting through. Or perhaps they are very aware it's not getting through, but they're not seeing that how they're handling it is part of the problem.

That's unfortunate, because coaching your coach—discussing the process of what helps you and why—is one of the most powerful ways to accelerate your learning.

WHAT COACHING YOUR COACH DOESN'T MEAN

"Coaching your coach" does not mean laying down the law about how you wish to be talked to: "When you point out that I come in late all the time, it makes me feel bad, so from now on let's stick with praise." Or: "I'd do a lot better on this eye exam if you tested me with bigger letters."

The goal is not to erect barriers to the delivery of challenging or inconvenient feedback; in fact, it's just the opposite. Your aim is to find ways that you and your coach can collaborate so that communication is clear and efficient and you learn what's most important to learn as quickly as you can. The goal is to work together to minimize the interference.

And that's a negotiation. You'll have preferences, and your coach will have preferences. You'll make requests that won't work from the coach's point of view. That's the nature of these conversations. It's not about making demands; it's about figuring out together what works best.

TALK ABOUT "FEEDBACK AND YOU"

There are plenty of things about how you receive feedback that aren't in your awareness. It's not as if you spend twenty-four hours a day reflecting on your feedback strengths and weaknesses, and in any event, we all have blind spots. But you are probably aware of *some* of the ways that you react to feedback—after all, you're thinking about bringing it up because something about the current process isn't working for you (including, sometimes, that you're getting no coaching at all). Whatever that something is, talk about it explicitly with the person giving you feedback. Here are slices of what that might sound like:

Subtle doesn't work with me. Be really explicit and don't worry about hurting my feelings. You won't.

I tend to get defensive at first, and then I circle back later and figure out why the feedback is helpful. So if I seem defensive, don't be put off. I'll be thinking about what you've said, even if it doesn't sound like it.

I react better when you present your advice as an idea that might help, rather than as "the obviously right answer." In that frame, I notice that I get hooked into arguing about whether it's "obvious" or "right," rather than just considering whether it's worth trying out.

Here's what I've been working on lately, in terms of self-improvement: ___ . That's the area I need the most help with right now, and I've been putting other things on the back burner, even though I know I need to work on them, too.

I'm really sensitive to negative feedback. So don't give it in the middle of a presentation unless it's urgent and immediately actionable.

Put your ideas out there, explain your thinking behind them, and be open to your coach's thoughts about what you've told them.

It's easy, by the way, for coaches to dismiss your requests and concerns by thinking, *Well, sure, there's an ideal way we'd all like to hear feedback, but what really matters is the feedback itself.* And that's partly true—the conversation is not a set of obstacles around which your coach has to maneuver. But often our own observations about how we learn best can make a huge difference in our ability to take in the feedback. We're explaining our particular defensive formation not to block givers out, but to help them get through.

DISCUSS PREFERENCES, ROLES, AND MUTUAL EXPECTATIONS

Sometimes the person giving you feedback actually *is* a mentor or executive coach, or perhaps a peer or friend who is particularly inclined to give you advice. In these cases, it can be useful to talk more broadly about feedback styles and preferences and the challenges of learning.

Three topics should be kept front and center. The first two are about the receiver:

(1) Your feedback temperament and tendencies;

(2) Growth areas you are currently working on.

The third is about the coach:

(3) Their philosophy, strengths and weaknesses, and requests.

On the following page is a set of questions that can move you into helpful territory.

It's also useful to clarify whether the coaching is confidential, how often you will get together, how you will measure progress, and what your priorities and goals might be. Get aligned on where you are going and how you will get there.

The coaches in our lives also include "accidental coaches," like your neighbor who is being a pain. Discussing roles and mutual expectations can be helpful here, too. Let's imagine that your neighbor is upset that your dog periodically finds her way into his garden. The neighbor is "coaching" you to put up a taller fence, stake the dog on a chain, or, ideally, find her a new home far, far away. Your neighbor is conveying his coaching via notes left in your mailbox.

This is not working for you. First, you're not convinced your dog is in his yard as often as the neighbor claims, but it's hard to tell since you often don't learn about it until the following day when you pick up your mail. Plus, you are surprised and put off by the hostile tone of the notes.

Whether this situation deteriorates or begins to right itself has little to do with the dog and everything to do with whether you take the initiative to coach your coach. Pick up the phone, or better yet, walk next door with the express purposes of (1) gathering more data on what's actually going on—how often your dog pays a visit, what your neighbor does when he sees her, and whether there's been any damage or particular behavior that prompts the concern; (2) coaching your neigh-

Grab Bag of Questions for Coach and Coachee

Who has given you feedback well? What was helpful about how they did it?

Have you ever gotten good advice that you rejected? Why?

Have you ever received good advice that you took years later?

What motivates you?

What disheartens you?

What's your learning style? Visual, auditory, big picture, detail oriented?

What helps you hear appreciation?

What's something you wish you were better at?

Whose feedback-receiving skills do you admire?

What did your childhood and family teach you about feedback and learning?

What did your early job experiences teach you?

What's the role of time/stages?

What's the role of mood and outlook?

What's the role of religion or spirituality?

What has been the impact of major life events? Getting married? Getting laid off or fired? Having children? Death of a parent?

What do you dislike most about coaching? About evaluation?

What helps you change?

bor on how he can best work with you; and (3) setting some mutual expectations about how you'll work together.

So you might say, "When you see her in the yard, please call me right away. When you leave a note I don't learn about it until the following day, and that makes it hard to assess why she was out in the first place." You might add, "I was hopeful that our fence was effective, but something isn't working. Give me a little time to explore whether she needs to be retrained, or whether we're going to have to come up with a better solution. I'll give you an update by the weekend." Letting the neighbor know that his concerns have gotten through, and that it will take you some time to learn more and sort out solutions, will help prevent escalation of the conflict.

HIERARCHY AND TRUST

Hierarchy can have an impact on coaching conversations. We've discussed in prior chapters the benefits of separating coaching and evaluation. That's hard to do when the person evaluating you is also the person who coaches you. Sometimes that's unavoidable; you can't have one spouse who coaches you and another who decides whether to stay married. But when they can be different people, they should be. It's best to have a coach who is well insulated from your compensation and career decisions.

But sometimes your coach is your boss, and there is no getting around it. In these cases you might be thinking that a "coach the coach" conversation is off limits: "I'd never talk to my boss about these kinds of things. My boss determines my future. I can't suggest that I'm anything less than a confident, fully competent person."

Certainly, you should make thoughtful choices about what you are comfortable discussing in a particular relationship. But talking about feedback doesn't require you to reveal everything (or anything) about past failures. You don't need to confess, "I was fired from my last two jobs because I made lots of costly mistakes. Can you help me with that?" You can say, "I was hired as a big-picture guy, but there are a lot of details that matter, too. Being more detail oriented is a learning edge for me. It's helpful to me if you point things out in real time so I can correct quickly."

When framing a request for feedback, talk in terms of effectiveness rather than ambition. Don't say: "Feedback on running meetings well is important to me because in five years I see myself as a vice president." Likewise, avoid empty generalities: "Feedback on running meetings is important to me because I think that's a really important skill in today's workplace." Your request for feedback should always be tied to doing your *current* job more effectively: "Feedback on running meetings is important to me because I want to use the team's time as efficiently as I can, given the upcoming merger." This puts the purpose and payoff in current terms that actually matter to both of you.

Here's something else that matters to both of you: Workers who seek out negative feedback—coaching on what they can improve—tend to receive higher performance ratings.[8] Perhaps showing an interest in learning doesn't highlight what you have to learn. It highlights how good you are at learning it.

DON'T BECOME A GIMME-FEEDBACK FANATIC

Of course, like anything, this can be taken to an extreme. Young Dan caught the "coach me" bug, and while his earnest thirst for improving was endearing at first, his repeated requests for feedback quickly became burdensome. "He wants to sit down to talk about his performance after every single client meeting," complained a coworker. "I can't take much more of this."

If you try to draft everyone around you into your personal learning army, you're going to produce burnout—and soon find your colleagues going AWOL. Asking others what they think of *you*, and how they can help *you*, is not the only way to learn. Try asking them questions about themselves: What do they think about the business problem you're facing together? Have they seen a similar problem in the past, and what mistakes have they seen people make in this situation? What gave them the insight to respond to the media the way they did this morning? People enjoy talking about their own thoughts and experiences. By tapping into their wisdom, you can learn as much as you might by asking for explicit coaching.

YOUR COACH CAN HELP YOU GET IN SYNC

Your coach wasn't born a coach, and it's unlikely that they've taken coaching lessons. They're a longshoreman or a lawyer, just like you. So they may or may not be comfortable or skilled in the role of coach, and even the best coaches will have individual strengths and weaknesses.

You might ask your coach what—if anything—they are finding challenging about the work you're doing together. Your coach might say:

I can't always tell what you're thinking when I give you suggestions. I'm not sure if you're agreeing or disagreeing, and whether you feel like you're allowed to say so if you disagree.

The firm wants women to have access to a female mentor, and I'm delighted to be yours. I grew up with three brothers and I have four sons, so this feels like a learning experience for me, too.

For me, appreciation feels like blowing smoke. I don't like getting it and I've heard I'm not particularly good at giving it. But I want to be a good coach, so let's figure this out.

WHEN THE PERSON BEING COACHED IS THE BOSS

As the years pass and you move up the ladder of success, there will be fewer people willing to take the risk of giving you candid coaching. You might get evaluation—market analysts, revenue figures, and the board can be counted on to provide that. And you might get appreciation—applause when you get up to speak, gratitude from subordinates who admire your willingness to give them some time and attention. But genuine, candid coaching becomes increasingly rare.

Being human, we tend to attribute this slow disappearance of coaching to our effectiveness and overall mastery. And to be fair, that's part of what's going on. You're the CEO or COO or C-whatever because you're good at what you're being asked to do, and you've been good at it for a long time. But everyone has shortcomings and weaknesses, and these are more likely to get in your way as the complexity of what you're doing grows. You need help to see your blind spots, which at this stage will not just bite you, but also hurt the organization.

Even if you're head of a global bank or playing in the finals at Wimbledon, you can improve with coaching. We all can. A trusted adviser can help you think through complex choices or prepare for a potential backlash.

Some forms of coaching can, in fact, come only from your subordinates. What do they know that no one else does? They know your impact on them. When they are in meetings with you, they are also in meetings with your blind spots. They see the things you do that get in the way, that undermine your message, that create extra work for them and others. They also hear from their subordinates what others in the organization think you don't understand, don't pay enough attention to, or aren't being clear about.

Our subordinates are such a valuable source of information that it's astonishing that we don't tap their knowledge more regularly. It's like crawling along in a traffic jam and ignoring the fact that you have a direct line to the traffic helicopter above—which can see the bigger picture that you can't from where you sit. They could give you the lowdown on the hot spots, pileups, and shortcuts that would get you the farthest fastest.

It's tough to get information to flow up an organization, and you might have to do a little hydraulic engineering to get it going. Why? Remember that most feedback givers are anxious about raising their concerns, *especially* upward. They worry that they will jeopardize their relationship with you—that you will disagree, be annoyed, become defensive, or retaliate. They also don't want to hurt your feelings, embarrass you, or embarrass themselves by handling the exchange badly.

When we show ourselves to be interested in and receptive to suggestions, it can be enormously refreshing. The boss is self-confident enough to ask for, and really listen to, feedback. Now, here's someone I can work with.

You might consider establishing "reverse mentor" relationships, in which you take on one or several coaches from different levels of the organization so that you can see the world, and yourself, through their eyes. What does this organization look like from the factory floor? What does it look like to the younger generation of workers and customers? What are people worried about in the Caracas or Calgary or Kuala Lumpur branches, and what do their customers think of the new global marketing push? You don't want to be buffeted by everyone else's priorities. You do want to learn how your priorities are and aren't flowing to the extremities of the organization, and what unintended effects they are having—so that you can continually work together to adapt and correct course.

• • •

A final thought on coaching your coach. This may sound immodest coming from the authors, but it can be useful for you and a colleague or family to read *Thanks for the Feedback* together. Not literally at the same time, reading aloud to each other over cups of cocoa. But you can choose a particular chapter and then discuss it over lunch or dinner. You don't need an agenda, and the conversation doesn't have to be about anything specific. Just talk about your thoughts and reactions to what you've read. Use the ideas here as a catalyst for conversation. Pick out a few ideas that make sense and a few that don't, and put them up for discussion. Go to our website, www.stoneandheen.com, and download our *Team Leader's Facilitation Guide*, which provides a wealth of questions to stimulate rich discussion with your team. The guide also offers coaching on how to facilitate such discussions.

If you're interested, send an e-mail to the authors. We'll do our best to respond. Let us know what's useful and what's not. And include a short, clear description of what an "In and Out Zone" defense looks like, if you're able.

INVITE THEM IN

Here's something we haven't said: letting someone far enough into your life to help you *transforms the relationship*. Not just because you learn, but because the interaction itself creates connection and shifts both of your roles inside the relationship. You become someone humble, vulnerable, and confident enough to ask for help; they become someone who has the capacity to help and who is respected and appreciated enough to be asked.

In chapter 10 we looked at why being good at setting boundaries is so crucial. You have to know when and how to keep people out of that emotional acre of yours. But just as surely, you have to know how to let them in—whether it's a well-kept garden or an old junkyard. For many of us, that's the real challenge.

Let's be honest: Everyone's acre is a mix of garden and junkyard. Your garden might be messy or manicured, the presentable bits a small plot or sprawling park. But we all have a few things in the back shed, and we could all use some help in figuring out what to do with that rusting heap of fears and those old cartons of shame we trip over regularly. Letting someone in *there*, just past the garden, is what takes courage. That's where intimacy grows.

How we handle feedback in a relationship has an enormous impact on that relationship. And changing how we handle feedback can often transform that relationship. Let's look at four common variations, where feedback was out of whack and how letting someone in made a difference.

A GOOD LISTENER ASKS FOR HELP

It wasn't until a few years ago that Roseanne noticed that her relationships were lopsided: "People come to me for help. I'm a great listener and good at helping them. And I enjoy it. But I started to see that all my conversations were about other people's problems. I knew what was going on with everyone else, but not even my closest friends knew what was going on with me."

At first she assumed that her friends and colleagues were just self-absorbed. "But now," Roseanne says, "I realize that I'm a 'slow reveal.' I don't easily volunteer information about myself and I never ask for help. I was sending signals I wasn't aware of—waving people off, telling them to stay away." Roseanne had secured the perimeter with her silence.

Roseanne sat with this realization for months. "I knew that this wasn't how I wanted things to be, and I was determined to change. I decided to work on a very specific skill: I was going to learn how to ask for help. And for a long time, deciding was as far as I got. It was actually slightly funny. I'm a person with a million problems, but somehow none of them seemed like quite the right one to get help with. And anyway, how would I know who to ask, or what it was I wanted from them? I was so unaccustomed to getting help that I didn't know where to start."

Roseanne finally came up with a strategy. She decided to ask a friend for help with something she was genuinely lousy at, but which ultimately wasn't that important to her: rethinking her wardrobe. "And holy cow, be careful what you ask for! I hit an artery. It was as if Stacy had been suppressing her opinions about my appearance for years. 'No polka dots after thirty!' was the first thing she said. And then, 'Let's talk about your hair.' Apparently, one way to get feedback is to *ask*."

Over time, with that friend and others, and even with colleagues at work, Roseanne started letting people into the less lovely parts of her acre. She shared some of the scars that lingered from a rough childhood, and her challenges with committed relationships. Some of the feedback itself has been more useful than she anticipated. But more important, she is making deeper connections.

In letting herself be helped she is letting herself be known.

A FRUSTRATED ADVISER OPENS UP

Clay, meanwhile, was having the opposite experience from Roseanne: "A coworker of mine, Nadine, has a thirteen-year-old son. Bryan is wonderful in so many ways—a smart, funny, insightful kid. But he has never been easy. Tantrums like thunderstorms, and recently he's been turning his anger on his parents. Nadine and her husband are at a loss for how to cope, but she doesn't want any kind of advice. She vents about it and then shuts down."

Does Clay have advice? He does. But for as long as he's known Nadine, he's held his tongue: "I don't have kids and because of that I've found that people aren't very receptive to my suggestions on that subject. But before I was a geologist, I worked for several summers at a camp for troubled kids. I have this sense for what sets kids off and what helps calm them down. Maybe because I was that kid myself."

Does Clay's coworker know this about him? "She does, vaguely," he says. "And I've even brought it up by saying things like, 'Oh, yeah, I had a kid in my cabin who did that,' but Nadine cruises by it, never following up."

If we were coaching Clay as an advice giver, there's a lot we could offer him. He could be explicit about what he does and doesn't know. He could say: "I do have some ideas for what might help from my work with kids like Bryan. At the same time, I'm not a parent, and so I don't have that perspective." He could be extra appreciative of the tough work involved in parenting Bryan and explicit about autonomy—that Nadine is free to take or leave his ideas: "You've worked so hard and maybe you've tried these things. At the end of the day, you know him best. . . ."

But this is a book about feedback receiving. And it turns out that receiving feedback was just the thing to unlock the Nadine puzzle. Clay did something he never thought to do before. He asked Nadine for advice. "I was at dinner at her home," he says, "and we got on the topic of my personal life. And for the first time, I described my battles with depression. It turns out that Nadine knows quite a bit about antidepressant drugs, and so I was finding the conversation very helpful. And then out of nowhere, in this conversation about me, she started talking about Bryan. She described a recent episode, and then listened intently as I shared my theory about what might be going on with him. It was literally the first time we've ever discussed it, and she was like a sponge."

There's a coda to this story, as Clay explains: "We've talked about it since, this question of being open to advice. And this blew my mind. She had suspected I'd struggled with depression in my life, and felt like she knew things that would help me, but always thought I was uncomfortable talking about it. So she was having the same experience I was of feeling uninvited to offer help. Wrap your mind around that." Indeed.

PERFECT FEEDBACK FOR THE PERFECT PERSON

Fiona founded and runs a community health center in Kenya. For ten years she's been working around the clock to build partnerships, expand services, and train new staff. She is liked and respected in the region; people come from across Africa to learn about her community outreach model.

Recently Fiona has started to feel restless, and as new opportunities arise, she finds herself with a surprising problem: Despite working hard to train her staff, she has not groomed anyone who could take over the organization if she departed.

Once she became aware of this hole in her planning, she set about in her usual competent way to tackle it. She made lists of skills that that person would need and started to devise strategies for how current staff might acquire them. She also began investigating where she might find new employees who might already be qualified for the role.

And then a friend from another health center asked Fiona: "What are you doing that is disabling your staff from learning?" The implication was clear: After ten years, you should already have at least a couple of people with the know-how to run the center. Fiona was offended: "*Disable* my staff? Are you kidding?" She pointed to all the training and mentoring she had done.

But the question stuck with her, needling and nudging. So one day she went to a junior staffer she knew was capable and observant and asked not whether she was hindering others, but how: "What do you see me doing that disables the staff?"

It turned out that Fiona—like many entrepreneurs—had her fingerprints on everything. In the early days this ensured quality control and consistent messaging. As the organization grew, however, her need to oversee, to direct, to manage, meant that no one could decide anything without her say-so. Staffers couldn't make their own mistakes and never learned to take initiative or trust their own judgment.

The feedback required some tough self-examination on Fiona's part, as well as a number of additional conversations inside the organization. There were three results: Fiona learned to step back and trust her staff with more responsibilities. Her relationships with her staff members were strengthened enough to make that easier to do. And finally, Fiona demonstrated that no one is perfect, not even Fiona. And that allowed everyone to loosen up, step up, and learn from mistakes more easily.

SHIFTING MIRRORS

Amy was just scolded by her boss. In front of others, on a conference call. Again.

She hangs up and immediately dials Hank, her best friend since the time they worked together as night managers at a chain of grocery stores. Amy is now the manager of a rival supermarket across town, and Hank has remained a trusted sounding board. He has heard plenty over the last few months about Amy's new regional boss and chief antagonist, Ivan.

The latest is this: Ivan had scheduled an early call for the store managers in the region to discuss a change in shipping providers. Amy was a few minutes late dialing in, and when she clicked into the call, she caught Ivan mid-sentence saying, ". . . Amy, late as usual."

"He just has it in for me," Amy tells Hank. "It's so unprofessional. There were eighteen people on that call who got to hear his little put-down."

Later on the call they clashed again when Ivan explained that the new shipper would require authorized personnel to sign for produce. Amy pointed out that their other produce suppliers already required signatures. "Not true," Ivan corrected. "Not until now, but we'll need signatures from now on. Everyone should arrange to sign for their produce deliveries."

Amy continues with Hank: "So I told Ivan that I would forward the list of signers I already use. I just wanted to let him know that, obviously, we already had a list. And then, as if I couldn't hear, he said, 'I guess Amy really wants to be right.' It's as if Ivan can't stop himself. He's the most defensive person I've ever met, but doesn't think twice about offending anyone else." Hank listens thoughtfully, and says "yeah" and "wow" every once in a while.

When he hangs up, Hank wonders if he could have done more to help Amy hear the feedback.

We Triangulate for Comfort, but Not Coaching

Amy is doing what we all do when upset by criticism—she's reaching out for support. Venting is natural and cathartic; turning the sting of the moment into the latest "get this" story for friends and coworkers helps us connect with others and regain our balance.

But too often we stop there. We ask our friends to be supportive mirrors so that we can get recentered and feel better. But we miss the opportunity to also ask them to help us sift the feedback itself for anything we might learn.

Of course, from Amy's point of view, Ivan's actions didn't constitute feedback; he was simply being a jerk. But extracting feedback from jerkiness is just the kind of thing friends can help you do.

Hank Has a Hunch

Later that afternoon Amy calls Hank back. She thanks him for being supportive earlier, and then makes a request: "I can usually see where people are coming from, but with Ivan, there's something going on that I don't get. I don't know if I push his buttons or if he's just this way with everyone. I need you to help me with that." She'd like Hank to shift from supportive mirror to honest mirror.

Amy's instinct is sound: In the conflict between Amy and Ivan, Hank actually does see both sides. He gets why Amy was triggered by Ivan's comments. But he's had his own experiences with Amy's wanting to be right, and Hank wonders if this is a blind spot for her. Just because Ivan is difficult doesn't mean Amy is not.

Hank observes that this isn't the first time that she and Ivan have clashed over "who is right." He sees a pattern: It's not just that Ivan is triggering Amy—Amy is also triggering Ivan. "That's true," Amy admits. "But I'm not just going to act as if he's right when he's not, especially if he's making comments about me being wrong in front of other people."

She pauses and then adds this: "You know, there was one other thing going on that I didn't mention." When Amy overheard Ivan's comment about her being "late as usual" she remained civil on the phone. But she couldn't resist sending him a text while the conference call rattled on about trucking and signatures:

Amy: Late? 2 minutes.

Ivan: 5.

Amy: Was dealing with shopper's complaint.

Ivan: Don't care. Don't be late.

Amy: 2 minutes. Maybe 3.

Returning to the call, Ivan and Amy pick up their repartee, this time about signatures and past produce practice, and again, Amy can't seem to sense when the argument has passed its expiration date.

Hank suggests that maybe there's something to this idea that Amy likes to have the last word, and that this is contributing to the Amy-Ivan conflicts. (Of course, that very instinct shows up in her conversation with Hank: "But just so you know, I really was only two minutes late," she adds before they hang up.)

Make Two Lists to Stay on Track

In his effort to be an honest mirror, Hank suggests that they make two lists—what's wrong with the feedback, and what might be right or helpful (which is a version of the containment chart we include in chapter 8). Each time Amy strays back to defending or pointing out the problems with Ivan's approach, Hank tells her to write it down in the "what's wrong" column. He then guides her back to what might be right.

Here's a sample of the notes Amy took on her napkin:

The Feedback	What's "Wrong" with the Feedback	What Might Be Right
"I guess Amy really wants to be right." "late again" "don't be late"	What are we, in seventh grade? Totally inappropriate to say on the call in front of everyone. Should have told me one-on-one. Am I supposed to pretend he's right even when I know he's not? I was two minutes late, but I didn't miss anything. He's overreacting.	I do get sucked into debating the finer points, even when it doesn't matter. The produce thing didn't matter—I just didn't like being told I was wrong in front of others, especially when I knew I was right. Why is it that I need to have the last word? Hmm. Dad? I have been late to the calls a few times. Now I'm noticing that others aren't late. Ideas to change this? Whether I was two or five minutes late matters less than that he noticed. Always better to be on time.

Writing down and discussing what's wrong frees Amy to see what might be right or valid or reasonable. The two sides of the list don't net each other out, and the point isn't for Amy to reach some grand conclusion about her interactions with Ivan, or a verdict on who was more right or more to blame. Amy is digging to learn—about herself and about her relationship with Ivan. That way, when she approaches Ivan with her thoughts, she'll have a more balanced view of what's going on, and a better sense of what might help improve the situation.

■ ■ ■

Feedback isn't just about the quality of the advice or the accuracy of the assessments. It's about the quality of the relationship, your willingness to show that you don't have it all figured out, and to bring your whole self—flaws, uncertainties, and all—into the relationship.

13

PULL TOGETHER

Feedback in Organizations

The supply chain manager for a sheet metal company, Everett likes data.

So he was surprised when he received a load of data in his 360 report that he did not like. The information was confounding, wildly out of line with how he saw himself. He felt defensive—for himself and in the name of good data everywhere. The whole feedback endeavor, he told anyone who would listen, had been poorly executed and pointless.

And then one day—*wham!*—it hit him. "The feedback fell into place," he says. "I suddenly saw myself in a new way, and it explained so many things. Oh, *this* is why I've been struggling; *this* is where I've been wrong; *this* is what has been disrupting my marriage; *this* is where I can change." Everett now supports 360s with the zeal of the converted: "It's the only way to get successful but stubborn son of a guns like me to look at themselves."

But many of his colleagues disagree. Some found their 360 useful, but not overwhelmingly enlightening. Some found it unhelpful, and a few felt it was destructive. Everett finds this attitude regrettable: "No performance management system is perfect, but ours is really quite good. Too many of our top people are complacent. Or maybe they're just afraid to do the hard work of growing."

Pierre is also wrestling with *his* company's performance management system. The president of a retail clothing chain, Pierre took stock of the toll the system was taking on his employees: It absorbed an excessive amount of time and left people feeling demoralized and unfairly treated. "Most of the people who work here are amazing," he observes. "But the system we had in place was just not working. Everyone found it stressful. And performance issues that needed to be addressed still didn't get addressed. We've been searching for a better way but haven't found it yet." Pierre eventually canceled performance reviews altogether. Threw out the whole thing.

Pierre thinks the people are good but the system is broken; Everett thinks the system is good but the people are broken.

THERE ARE NO PERFECT FEEDBACK SYSTEMS

As far as "broken people" are concerned, the first twelve chapters of this book explore just how hard it is for any of us to be perfect learners. Simply being human provides a lifetime's worth of challenges when it comes to seeing ourselves clearly, managing our emotional reactions, and changing long-standing habits. Can people learn and change? Sure. Is it difficult for each and every one of us to do so? You bet.

Just as there are no perfect learning people, there are no perfect organizational feedback systems. There are better and worse systems that are more and less well matched to the needs of any given organization. But anyone choosing and implementing a particular system must grapple with the inevitable tensions and tradeoffs associated with it.

For example, any system that is applied to an organization larger than a few people is going to run into the problem of differences in temperament. The system will be well suited to some, adequately suited to others, and poorly suited to at least a few. And, inevitably, it will be implemented by some managers who are relatively good at feedback and some who aren't. So we will never have ideal execution or full buy-in, and the buy-in challenge can form a reinforcing downward cycle. *That* guy's not putting any time into this, so why should I?

Feedback givers in any system too often see big cost and little benefit. Lucinda, who works in pharmaceutical research, is clear about this: "It takes time away from my primary tasks, and there's no reward or acknowledgment for doing it well."

And she's unsure how to assess her subordinates. She knows that they are not all top performers, but is worried about the costs to morale of negative evaluations: "If I score my people on the rigorous scale we've been given, many of them are going to be disheartened. In a tight labor market, I can't afford to lose any of the talent I've got, or to erode the performance we've achieved. So while forcing me to differentiate this starkly might make things fair across the organization, for me and my team, there's only downside. And from what I hear, other managers aren't paying any attention to the scale anyway. If I did use it, it would be like penalizing people just for being on my team."

Jim feels caught by the performance system at the park service, for a different reason. He's a team leader for search and rescue, where performance is critical to survival. "I've put in the time to recruit and select the best people," he explains. "If I've got the wrong person out there in a blizzard, it's dangerous for everyone. I've only *got* A players, because unlike some of my fellow managers, I've already done the work of having the hard conversations and making the tough calls. A 'forced curve' punishes me for managing well."

CAN'T LIVE WITH IT, CAN'T LIVE WITHOUT IT

From where Jim and Lucinda stand, their feedback systems look pretty flawed: It's risky for any individual manager to give fully honest reviews. If handled poorly by either giver or receiver, such conversations can damage trust, working relationships, motivation, and team cohesion.

But then again, it's risky *not* to. Problems fester, the manager and the system lose credibility, the team underperforms, and high performers resent that low performers aren't pulling their weight yet face no consequences.

Managers feel stuck, and avoidance is ubiquitous. Recall that 63 percent of executives surveyed say their biggest challenge to effective performance management is that their managers lack courage to have the difficult performance discussions.[1] They give artificially high reviews to even mediocre employees, which dilutes the usefulness of reviews for addressing performance or guiding decision making. In one organization 96 percent of employees received the highest rating.[2] And researcher Brené Brown observes that a lack of meaningful feedback was the number-one reason cited by talented people for leaving an organization.[3]

It's easy to complain about the system and the people who populate it. What's hard is to figure out what would help, especially because of the vast range of goals that performance systems are charged with accomplishing:

- Providing consistent evaluation across roles, functions, and regions;
- Ensuring fair compensation and distribution of rewards;
- Incenting positive behaviors and disciplining negative behaviors;
- Communicating clear expectations;
- Increasing accountability;
- Aligning individuals with organizational goals and vision;
- Coaching and developing individual and team performance;
- Helping to get and retain the right people in the right roles;
- Assisting succession planning in key leadership positions;
- Promoting job satisfaction and high morale; and
- Getting it done on time—in the moment, quarterly, annually.

Accomplishing all of these goals can't be done with a single system or even with a combination of systems.

The trend has been to centralize and standardize systems, collecting data on metrics across employees, functions, regions, and markets. This can be helpful, but you can't "metric" your way around the fact that feedback is a relationship-based, judgment-laced process. As Dick Grote observes in "The Myth of Performance Metrics," you can't evaluate the performance of a language translator simply by counting the number of pages he translates.[4] You have to make judgments about the quality of the translation—its success in capturing nuance, meaning, and tone. In addition, as we've explored here, the feedback lives (or dies) amid the trust, credibility, relationship, and communications skills between giver and receiver.

So there are no easy answers. But we assert this: Systems will always be imperfect. We should work to improve them, but that can only take us so far. The greatest leverage is helping the people inside the system communicate more effectively, and as between giver and receiver, it's the receiver's skills that have the most impact. We need to equip receivers to create *pull*—to drive their own learning, to seek honest mirrors as well as supportive mirrors, to speak up when they need additional appreciation or coaching or are confused about where they stand. As each receiver becomes more skilled at receiving—at creating pull—the organization gets better at it, too. We *pull together.*

• • •

Below, we consider this challenge—of imperfect people within imperfect systems—and offer ideas for improvement from three different organizational perspectives: leadership and HR, team leaders and coaches, and receivers.

WHAT LEADERSHIP AND HR CAN DO

We'll start with leadership and HR, since they're the ones we expect to "do something" about the problem of performance management. They're not the only players, but they're the most visible and the most likely to have their hands in the design. Here are three things they can do that help.

1. DON'T JUST TRUMPET BENEFITS, EXPLAIN TRADEOFFS

The task of implementing and championing a performance management system usually falls to Human Resources.[5]

Because these systems are so often and so easily criticized, HR leaders struggle to supply the positive side of the argument: "What's even better than Focused Friday and Work Hard Wednesday? The new performance system!" But that advocacy has unintended consequences in that it causes the roles in the debate to harden: HR and senior management are the cheerleaders. Everyone else is a sneerleader. And as HR sends out more positive messages, the complainers feel obligated to send out more negative ones.

Of course, HR and senior leadership are acutely aware of the real challenges. One survey found that, privately, within senior HR forums, only 3 percent of HR leaders give their own performance management system an A; 58 percent give their system a C, D, or F.[6] They know the challenges better than anyone else, but it's just not their role to talk about those challenges publicly.

Our advice is this: Don't just promote benefits. Also discuss and explain tradeoffs. Here's an illustration of why that matters from a client we met a few years back. Jane, the new head of HR, was hired to fix the organization's performance management system. Jane's predecessor had tried to implement a new system, but after a year of work, the executive committee voted it down and the predecessor left the organization.

Then Jane came on board and examined what her predecessor had sketched out. Jane decided that her top priority would be not just adopting a new performance evaluation system, but adopting the exact system that had been proposed by her predecessor and rejected by the exco. Jane's assistant asked why she was going to the trouble: If you're trying to get fired, why not just post scandalous pictures of yourself on Facebook? It's easier and much more fun.

But Jane had a plan. She called a meeting of the executive committee and began her presentation by stating that she wanted the group to take a second look at the system that had been voted down the previous year. No one was pleased by this suggestion, but when Jane added, "I want to make a list of all of its drawbacks," there was at least the possibility of some amusement.

The exco commenced their critique, and the list grew, with Jane adding a few drawbacks of her own. When the list was complete, she read each item out loud and concluded with this: "Wow." After a pause Jane added: "These are serious drawbacks. No wonder you voted this system down." This was met with some grumbling: *Did she not realize that the plan had flaws until just now? This is the person we hired to fix the problem?*

Then Jane said: "Now let's make a list of the benefits of the plan." The process started slowly but soon gained momentum. Again, she finished by reading each item out loud; several items pointed to the benefits of the proposed new system compared with the current one or with other systems the exco was aware of. When she finished she paused and said: "Serious drawbacks *and* important benefits." And added: "We've looked at many other performance management systems. Every system has its drawbacks. The plan we're looking at now has the fewest drawbacks, and also the most important benefits, given our goals and what we're up against. We should adopt it because it's by far the best fit for us. The minute something better comes along, you can be sure I'll grab it."

The plan passed unanimously. The conversation took about forty-five minutes. When asked what had caused the executive committee to reverse its decision from the previous year, one member remarked, "Last year we were presented only with the benefits of the plan. This year we discussed the drawbacks."

Funny reasoning, maybe, yet it's exactly right. When we are asked to make a choice about a subject we're worried about, and we are presented only with the benefits, we supply the potential drawbacks on our own—some real and some imagined. And then we construct an imaginary way out: Why accept a plan with so many drawbacks when we could accept a plan with no drawbacks? Let's use that one.

Jane found a way to bring the internal voices of the committee members—their fears and concerns—into the room, so they could be weighed and assessed. When you do this, it could be that the drawbacks do outweigh the benefits, but at least people can now evaluate the real choices involved. We aren't choosing between this and some fantasy plan yet to be discovered; we're choosing between this plan and other comparable plans that have both benefits and drawbacks.

In general, when selecting or implementing an organizational system, HR and senior leaders should provide the following to employees at all levels of the organization:

- Clarification of the various goals of the system;
- An explanation of why this system was chosen over other systems;
- Transparency about potential costs as well as benefits;
- A description of the costs of half-hearted participation; and
- An invitation for ongoing discussion, suggestions, and feedback.

When handling complaints or concerns about the system, make sure to listen and acknowledge. Ask for specific suggestions that might improve the system. If you decide to reject an idea that's been proposed, it's crucial to explain why: "We discussed it at length. It fixes this problem over here, but creates this other problem over there. On balance, we decided not to implement it." If you don't explain why, people assume you didn't fully understand the benefits of their suggestions, were just going through the motions of asking for input, or don't care about their concerns or well-being.

HR can streamline the process, but in the end, the dilemmas and time crunch created by having to give and receive feedback are a *shared problem*, not an HR problem. Sharing the problem can generate new ideas, but it also shifts the roles from the standard oppressor-victim dynamic to that of mutual problem solvers.

Ismail, fed up with the state of feedback in his firm, decided to "share the dilemma." He called an all-hands meeting and laid it on the line: "I hear people complaining they don't get enough feedback. I hear people complaining they don't like the feedback they do get. Employees blame managers, and managers blame employees. Everybody blames HR. We've put in the best systems we know on evaluation and mentoring, but let's admit the truth: They're not perfect, and they never will be. No system can make you learn, but no system can keep you from learning either. So the best way forward is for each of us to ask ourselves: What kind of learner do I want to be, and what kind of mentor do I want to be? We're in it together: If you support me in my learning, I'll support you in yours."

Ismail's honesty helped people to see that this was not an administrative problem, but a human problem. He got people involved and talking—not just about the challenges but about taking responsibility for their own learning and for creating possible solutions.

Obviously you can't have everyone who works in an organization involved in designing and implementing feedback systems. But you can invite participation, both formal and informal. It's often useful to invite those who are the loudest voices against performance systems to be part of the process of designing them, both to take advantage of their perspective and ideas, and to enroll them in the challenge of doing something constructive about their complaints.

2. SEPARATE APPRECIATION, COACHING, AND EVALUATION

A single performance management system can't effectively communicate all three kinds of feedback. Each requires different qualities and different settings to be effective.

Evaluation needs to be fair, consistent, clear, and predictable—across individuals, teams, and divisions. We need to understand who is evaluating whom and what the criteria for success and advancement are. We'll need to have thoughtful two-way conversations throughout the year about goals and progress, in time to address problems along the way. The evaluation system needs to be rigid enough to ensure fairness and consistency, yet flexible enough to take account of individual differences in role and circumstance. None of this is new and none of this is easy.

Good coaching requires different parameters to work well. Those who are improving need frequent, close-to-real-time suggestions, and the chance to practice small corrections or improvements along the way. The "one big coaching meeting each year with twenty suggestions" or even "two coaching meetings each year with ten suggestions each" isn't likely to help, because at its core, *coaching is a relationship, not a meeting.* Coach and coachee need ongoing discussion of what the coachee can work on in light of organizational needs and individual competencies. They need people who can be honest mirrors to help them see themselves when they're not at their best, and supportive mirrors to reassure them that they can get better.

As we've discussed, there are at least two problems in mixing coaching with evaluation. First, on the receiving end, my attention will be drawn to the evaluation, which drowns out the coaching. If I think I have lost the bonus I already promised my family, I'm not going to hear your suggestions for how I can tweak my PowerPoint slides. The second concern is that, if I am going to be open to coaching, I need to feel safe.[7] I need to know that admitting mistakes or areas of weakness isn't going to count against me in my job security or career advancement. I need absolute trust that being open in coaching conversations will not adversely affect my evaluation.

Finally, as we've said, too many workplaces suffer from mutual appreciation deficit disorder. Even the most satisfied among us can sometimes feel underappreciated for how much we put into our jobs and for how much crap we put up with along the way. Formal recognition programs are helpful, but we care more about appreciation from our immediate coworkers and supervisors than we do about ceremonial recognition from seven levels above. Rote thank-yous lose currency fast, but an authentic "Hey, watching you handle that complicated task so well is making me rethink my approach to those problems" can mean more than any plaque or gift certificate.

And everyone hears appreciation in different ways.[8] Some hear it in their paycheck, and are baffled why others need more than that to feel valued. Others hear it in a private word of affirmation or handwritten note of thanks, in the patience a mentor shows as she goes over the skill yet again, or in the juicy assignment sent their way. The point here is not that you have to have an "appreciation system" in place; rather, it's about having a cultural norm of appreciation that encourages everyone to notice (1) the genuine and unique positives in the work of others, and (2) how each team member hears appreciation and encouragement so that it can be best expressed to that person as an individual.

The responsibility to get the balance right on all three kinds of feedback ultimately lies with both givers and receivers. Sara, a first-year consultant, found that she was getting plenty of hard-hitting coaching, but had no sense of where she stood. That vacuum meant she struggled not to hear the coaching as evaluation. "I couldn't tell if I was on track, which made all this mid-project coaching from partners feel like stepping in front of a firing squad every time. Finally, I decided to ask. I said to the partner, 'Before you give me your coaching, can you tell me how you think I'm doing? Am I on track based on where I should be at this stage?' He was surprised: 'Sara, you're doing great! You've definitely got a future here—do you not realize that?' I didn't, but the minute he said it, I could relax and focus on his coaching. And now that I could hear his coaching as coaching, it was really quite helpful."

3. PROMOTE A CULTURE OF LEARNERS

In every organization explicit and implicit messages evolve about what is (actually) valued and what is (actually) rewarded. If you want "learning" to be valued, it has to be embedded in what is talked about with admiration, what is highlighted as important in the war stories that are told, what matters when it comes to visible projects and key promotions.

Here are five ideas that help promote a culture of learning.

Highlight Learning Stories

The most visible picture of competence in many organizations is the superstar with God-given talent who delivers consistent results and, with a bit of luck and the right relationships, rises quickly through the ranks. But the reality is often different from the myth. In fact, what many of these superstars are actually doing well is *learning*.

God-given talent is the way her peers tell the story of Sijia. She's attractive, bright, and likable, gets put on the best projects, and is soon included in more senior meetings. Among her colleagues her swift rise is seen as the result of her natural gifts and her skill at playing the political game.

But her colleagues are missing a key part of the story. What they don't see is that Sijia is a proactive and determined learner. She pays attention to what she doesn't comprehend and asks questions. She asks if she can sit in on meetings that will help her understand the customer better, and as a consequence, she gets to observe firsthand how people above her play their roles. Sijia's openness to coaching is evident. She doesn't present herself as perfect; in fact, she's quick to acknowledge her mistakes and what she's learned from them. No one thinks Sijia has all the answers, but her senior colleagues increasingly see her as a trusted partner in tackling the toughest challenges.

Unfortunately her organization isn't fully capitalizing on Sijia's skill at learning. As she moves up, there is no encouragement for her to share her learning approach, and no one in management has done it either. So her peers and younger colleagues attribute her success to luck and brownnosing, failing to observe (or emulate) her single greatest asset.

Part of what defines an organizational culture are the stories and myths about it—the courage or genius or endurance displayed in the face of impossible challenges. These stories tell us what kind of place we work at and what is expected of us. "Mistake stories" that ultimately result in "what we learned" stories are abundant—probably every successful employee and team has some—but they are too rarely shared.

Cultivate Growth Identities

If you want to nudge people out of a fixed identity and into a growth identity, two things help. First, teach them about it. A "growth identity" is not a concept most people are aware of until they hear about it. Hold a session on the difference between fixed and growth identities; let people discuss the topic, ask questions, express doubt. Talk about the differences in how people metabolize positive and negative feedback, and the implications for how to coach one another on teams. Float the concept of honest and supportive mirrors, and get the grapevine to actually grow something beyond rumors—peers helping one another to see their blind spots and process feedback for what's right, not just venting about what's wrong. Get the ideas into the air and onto people's radar.

Second, make the challenge of "pull"—the work required to recognize our triggers and find a way to learn—discussable during feedback conversations. People get better as they practice, and they can practice more productively when both people in the conversation are aware of feedback challenges. Discussing reactions to feedback, confusion, defensiveness, blind spots, and interpretations regarding where the feedback is coming from and going—these should all be part of everyday conversations on how to do things well.

It's important, though, that "growth identity" not be used by feedback givers as a way to shortcut a conversation: "You're not taking my feedback because you don't have a growth identity." A growth identity provides a way of hearing the feedback. It doesn't mean you always take it.

Discuss Second Scores

In chapter 9 we suggested developing a second score that looks at how you deal with challenging feedback. You may not have been happy with your evaluation, or the project you were on may have failed, but we're especially interested in how you responded to that experience. That's what tells us what you're capable of as the challenges naturally get harder and the environment you have to navigate gets more complex.

We recommend against actually "giving" people formal second scores. (*Now they are worried about your evaluation of my reaction to your first evaluation.*) But we do urge you to discuss the challenge and importance of second scores. A feedback giver can encourage a receiver to reflect not only on the feedback itself but on how and what he's doing with it—to reflect on how to maximize his second score.

Create Multitrack Feedback

In foreign affairs the concept of multitrack diplomacy describes the range of players who are involved in creating systemic change and building peace. Track 1 is the official government track—involved in negotiations, summits, sanctions, and treaties. Track 2 is the unofficial but often significant work done by others—community members and grassroots organizations, et cetera.[9]

We've borrowed this concept to describe the two tracks that organizations can put in place to support individual learning. They need to have Track 1 structures that support evaluation and mentoring. Those include performance management systems, mentoring programs, trainings, and the like.

But in many ways Track 2 activities are even more crucial to learning. These include the informal coaching conversations among friends, peers, and mentors; the stories of success and failure; discussions of best practices and skills that did or didn't help; and even an exchange of favorite books. You might have honest mirror and supportive mirror lunches with friends, combining social time with helping each other to learn.

Track 2 gives a formal name to these important informal interactions, and that helps you talk about it and bring it more consciously into the culture of the organization.

Leverage Positive Social Norming

The least appealing part of performance management for everyone involved is the phase called Nagging and Being Nagged. Setting goals, coaching, and completing appraisals are responsibilities that usually sit alongside the more pressing tasks already on everyone's plates, and are often the first to get postponed in the face of more immediate crises. So it falls to HR or team leaders to nag, and to managers and employees to be nagged.

Work by Robert Cialdini suggests we may be going about the whole process wrong. Cialdini is an expert on influence, and he argues that talking about negative behavior often has the unintended effect of reinforcing it as the social norm. If I'm a manager getting chiding e-mails about my late appraisals, I have two reactions. First, I feel underappreciated for all the hard work I'm doing that is the *reason* my appraisals are late. I'm not hanging around in my (apparently spacious) cubicle playing Ping-Pong. I'm swamped with a thousand different projects that the organization needs me to do.

But second, based on the tone of the nagging e-mail, I gather there must be quite a few of us who are late. I figure I'm in good company. If my bad behavior is the social norm, I don't feel particularly moved to take this reminder very seriously. I'll just get another reminder in a week or so, along with everyone else. That seems to be how it works around here. Interestingly, it's when the reminders stop that I might worry I've missed the expected "window" of grace.

Cialdini's studies demonstrate that highlighting *good* norms does more to change disliked behavior than calling out bad norms. Rather than issuing a reproachful "31 percent of you still haven't completed your reviews" it's more effective to crow, "69 percent of you have completed your reviews. Thank you!" Those who have completed the task feel appreciated and recognized for the effort. And those who haven't get the message that they are out of step with their peers.[10]

WHAT TEAM LEADERS AND FEEDBACK GIVERS CAN DO

What can one manager or team leader do to improve an organizational culture?

An organizational culture is really a collection of subcultures, and those subcultures can vary tremendously from manager to manager, team to team, and department to department. You can have significant impact on your own subculture and teammates, and over time, you can invite others to join you. Here are three ideas that help.

1. MODEL LEARNING, REQUEST COACHING

If you had to pick between *preaching* the benefits of being a learner and *modeling* good learning, well, there's no contest. In many ways, the manager *is* the culture: If they're good learners, they set the tone for a learning culture.

The first step in modeling learning, of course, is actually *being* a good learner. That's the hard part for all of us. Compared with that, the next step is easy but often forgotten: make your endeavor to learn *explicit*. Encourage people to discuss your blind spots with you. Shift from blame conversations to joint contribution conversations, and start by asking what you might have contributed to the problem. Hold people accountable by showing them how you hold yourself accountable alongside them. When you conduct performance reviews, help people look at the system and their role in it, and appreciate them for their engagement and efforts to change. Be open about what you continue to find challenging about receiving feedback. Ask for coaching and help, not only from those above you, but from peers and subordinates. All things we've talked about elsewhere, but we say them again here because modeling is the most powerful thing you can do as an individual leader to improve the culture.

2. AS GIVERS, MANAGE YOUR OWN MINDSET AND IDENTITY

Consider the situation Janice is in. Although she has terrific technical skills and a file stuffed with glowing reviews, she's been passed over for promotion into management time and time again. She is confused and increasingly resentful. Why is she being treated so unfairly? The politics around this place are ridiculous.

Janice's supervisor, Ricky, knows that she is *not* being treated unfairly; she simply doesn't have the requisite skills. She is not being promoted because there are well-founded concerns—from Ricky and others—about her ability to manage people. But fearing he would upset her, Ricky has never given Janice this feedback directly. She can't change what she's not aware of. In Ricky's well-intended effort to avoid hurting Janice, he is hurting her and holding back her career. And *that's* treating her unfairly.

Ricky reminds us why managers dread feedback conversations as much as employees do. Givers can struggle with identity issues of their own:

"I'm not good at giving feedback. That's obvious when I try."

"If they disagree or are upset with me, I must not be a good manager."

"They won't like me."

"I don't want them to think I'm being controlling or 'telling them how to do their job' (despite the fact that somebody obviously needs to)."

"I'm a nice person. I don't want to hurt their feelings or appear unsupportive."

Perhaps the most common concern is the last: Hurting someone, regardless of our intentions, conflicts with our self-image as a good and kind person, or a supportive leader. It's true that the receiver needs the feedback: they are long-winded, unresponsive, exude "attitude," or smell bad. Yet raising these concerns makes most of us squirm. Even if it's done in the execution of our role, it feels horrible to hurt or upset others, and we quite reasonably try to avoid it when we can.

Our advice is to notice that what might hurt someone in the short term might help them in the longer term, and indeed, withholding important coaching because it might be painful—to them and to us—can do them real damage over time. We all need empathy and encouragement—supportive mirrors. But we also need clear and accurate information—honest mirrors. When we ourselves are screwing up or shooting ourselves in the foot, we want someone to tell us. Yet we hesitate to tell others. As you think about whether and how to give feedback, make sure to factor in the long-term consequences for the receiver as well as your own short-term identity discomfort.

3. BE AWARE OF HOW INDIVIDUAL DIFFERENCES COLLIDE IN ORGANIZATIONS

Part of the challenge of feedback in organizations is due to differences of temperament and wiring; we all have different baselines, swing, and sustain and recovery. For simplicity, let's assume that in any given population, about half the staff tend to be optimistic, quick-recovery Krista types from chapter 7, and half are Alita types, who swing wide in response to negative feedback and take longer to recover.

Now, just for fun, pair them all up to give each other feedback.

Our sensitivity to feedback can affect not only how we receive feedback but also how we give it. If a manager is highly sensitive to negative feedback, he may not be comfortable giving negative feedback to others; he may assume they'll have the same painful overreactions that he does.

Which may be true. Or not. If you matched an Alita type, who hates critical feedback, with a Krista type, who can't hear critical feedback unless it's extremely explicit, nothing may get communicated. Alita's fear of hurting Krista results in her hinting around, which, rather than sparing Krista's feelings, only frustrates her. Krista is happiest with clarity. Krista's former manager used to address problems by saying to her: "Do not EVER do that again." Krista loved this. She got it. No harm, just help.

But now think about what happens when the Krista types give the Alita types critical feedback. Krista may be oblivious to how sensitive Alita is. Her tough, direct feedback aimed at helping Alita improve—"These three things? Never do them again"—may devastate Alita, setting her back rather than helping her grow. In Krista's mind, her unvarnished approach is no big deal—just giving a little advice. But for Alita, it's scarring. No help, just harm.

If Alita approaches Krista about how upsetting this is for her, their tendencies replicate themselves in this next exchange. Alita would be tentative and vague in describing the real extent of the devastation caused by Krista's harshness. Krista wouldn't hear something this indirect, and would brush it off with a "Buck up, kid" or "Don't take it so personally" or "Sorry, were you saying something?" Krista doesn't see a problem, and is shocked when Alita jumps ship to a competitor six months later: "But I invested so much in her development!"

Of course, there are other variations on the theme of how disposition affects our style of giving feedback. People who worry a lot often give an abundance of feedback as a way to gain a sense of control over their environment. People who have impossibly high standards for themselves can also hold impossibly high standards for others, resulting in a steady stream of coaching and negative evaluation, and a conspicuous silence around appreciation. And people who have trouble with impulse control are often "direct" in ways that are sometimes helpful and sometimes less so. All these variations can result in individuals with the unexpected combination of being insensitive as givers while being hypersensitive as receivers. This is why when you are a giver, asking your receiver to coach you as their coach is so important.

WHAT RECEIVERS CAN DO

A few final words for receivers as we work to adapt to the organization, community, and family we live in. First, a reminder: Regardless of context or the company you keep, you are the most important person in your own learning. Your organization or team or boss might support or stifle feedback. Either way, they can't stop you from learning. You don't have to depend on your annual review or your boss's willingness to mentor. You can watch, ask questions, and solicit suggestions from co-workers, customers, partners, and friends. You don't have to wait around for someone to train you to sell more shoes. Observe whoever sells the most and try to figure out what they're doing differently. And ask them to watch you. Whatever they suggest, try it on. Experiment with the advice, and if the shoe fits, wear it.

Whatever you do in your organization—whether it's selling shoes or saving souls—you're surrounded by people you can learn from.

■ ■ ■

Like the tension between learning and acceptance for each of us as individuals, the tensions at the heart of organizational feedback are a permanent condition. The ideas in this chapter and in the rest of the book can help us manage these tensions, and get us talking to one another.

But while learning is a shared responsibility, in the end, it comes down to you.

Printed by permission of the Norman Rockwell Family Agency Copyright © 1965 the Norman Rockwell Family Entities, Norman Rockwell Museum Collections.

ACKNOWLEDGMENTS

If you want an extra helping of criticism in your life, tell people you are writing a book about how to receive feedback.

Typical comments to Sheila sounded like this: "Interesting. Remember your wedding day?" *Yes, twenty years ago?* "Well anyway, I always thought your dress was . . ." Comments to Doug tended in this direction: "Wait, *you* are writing a book about receiving feedback? That's a little ironic, don't you think?" *Yes, a little, sure.*

So, we've got people to thank—lots of them.

First, we are grateful to everyone who shared their stories and struggles with us. The examples in this book are based on the experiences of real people—clients, colleagues, neighbors, friends, family. Identifying details have been changed, and in some cases we've created composites, but we've tried to maintain the emotional truth of each story.

For many years it was our privilege to work at the Harvard Negotiation Project with Roger Fisher. Roger is a grandfather of the field of conflict management and was one of its most passionate practitioners. *Getting to Yes*, written with William Ury and Bruce Patton, spread the word on interest-based negotiation. Originally published in 1981, it is a masterpiece—among the best things ever written about how human beings should deal with differences. Roger died on August 25, 2012, at the age of ninety. As a friend said at his memorial service, "It's up to us now." Indeed.

Our friend and *Difficult Conversations* coauthor Bruce Patton lives Roger's legacy daily—in the intellectual rigor he brings to any analysis and in the tireless optimism with which he approaches some of the world's toughest conflicts. His contributions to the theory, practice, and pedagogy of negotiation are far reaching, and his generous colleagueship over the past twenty years has been invaluable.

The work of Chris Argyris, Donald Schön, Diana McLain Smith, Bob Putnam, and Phil McArthur form another pillar in our thinking.

Although we don't use the term, the "ladder of inference" helps organize chapter 3, and ideas on contribution and defensive routines inform our thinking throughout. Chris, thanks for your life's work, and for the many lifetimes' worth of ideas you have given the world.

Huge props go out to negotiation theorist and educator John Richardson, who teaches at MIT's Sloan School of Management. It was John who introduced us to the foundational differences among appreciation, coaching, and evaluation. The original formulation of those ideas can be found in *Getting It Done,* which John wrote with Roger Fisher and Alan Sharp. It's a hidden gem in the communication canon.

Over the past twenty years, Bob Mnookin of Harvard Law School has gone from being our (slightly intimidating) mentor to our close colleague and friend. Teaching with you and teammates Erica Ariel Fox, Kathy Holub, Alain Lemperer, Linda Netsch, Frank Sander, and Alain Laurent Verbeke has been one of the most reliably satisfying experiences in our professional lives.

At the Program on Negotiation, we thank Susan Hackley, James Kerwin, Jessica MacDonald, Jim Sebenius, Dan Shapiro, Stephan Sonnenberg, Guhan Subramanian, William Ury, and the small cadre of gifted students who have worked with us as teaching assistants over the years. A special thanks to Michael Wheeler, of Harvard Business School, who came up with the title for this book on his first try.

In the fields of psychology and organizational behavior, we are indebted to the research and writing of Aaron Beck, Carol Dweck, Amy Edmondson, Dan Gilbert, Marshall Goldsmith, John Gottman, Lee Ross, and Martin Seligman. Deep thanks as well to Jeffrey Kerr, Rick Lee, Sallyann Roth, and Jody Scheier for their often uncanny insights into relationship dynamics. Their ideas are all over this book.

Informing our understanding of neuroscience and behavior is the work of Richard Davidson, Cate Fornier, Jonathan Haidt, Steven Johnson, and Sophie Scott. Neuroscientist Cate helped us skate along the cliff's edge of simplification, without (we hope) ever toppling off.

Our friend psychologist Robin Weatherill has walked alongside us on the entire journey, offering incisive comments, stories, observations, and ideas. Thank you, Robin, for your willingness to be an honest mirror and for the wide-ranging conversations during so many Friday-night dinners. You've supported us in more ways than you know.

Many people have busy schedules, but our pal Adam Grant's schedule is *really* busy. The Hardest Working Man in Academia, Adam read a draft while on book tour for his splendid *Give and Take,* passing along studies, thoughts, and ideas we had missed.

Feedback from Scott Peppet at the University of Colorado was delivered with such grace, precision, and wit that we wondered if he was somehow making fun of us. Everyone should make such fun. Michael Moffitt, dean of the School of Law at the University of Oregon, was the first person we entrusted with a draft of the manuscript. Michael pushed us to simplify and shorten. Well, we tried. Bob Bordone at Harvard Law School offered incredibly useful feedback on the first half of the book, so if things deteriorate halfway through, you know whom to blame.

Rob Ricigliano, Judy Rosenblum, and Linda Booth Sweeney are the only three occupants of the intersecting Venn diagram sets formed by people who (1) understand systems thinking, and (2) like us. Given the tight quarters, it's odd that they've never met. Thanks to each for their careful reading and suggestions.

Erica Ariel Fox was too busy writing her own book, *Winning from Within,* to help us with ours. Or was it we who were too busy to help her? Anyway, no one helped anyone. And yet it was an extravagant luxury to have such a close friend writing a book at the same time we were. Thank you, Erica, for the love and encouragement from one who knows.

For their stories, editing, and unbounded willingness to discuss these ideas, thanks to Jennifer Albanese, David Altschuler, Lana Proctor Banbury, Stevenson Carlebach, Sara Clark, Nan Cochran, Ann Garrido, Micah Garrido, Jill Grennan, Jack and Joyce Heen, Barbara and Maland Hoffmann, Kathy Holub, Stacy Lennon, Rory Van Loo, Susan Lynch, Celeste Mueller, Lea Ellermeier Nesbit, Andrew Richardson, Susan and Bob Richardson, Tom Schaub, Angelique Skoulas, Anna Huckabee Tull, Jim Tull, and Karen Vasso.

Our profound thanks to our colleagues at Triad: Sarah Seminski, creative, industrious, and omnivorously talented; Elaine Lin, whose intelligence and humanity so awe clients that they lose their ability *not* to send her baked goods in the mail; Heather Sulejman, Triad's heart and soul, the one who keeps everyone sane but herself, and who appears almost normal despite her frightening devotion to Depeche Mode. And our partner Debbie Goldstein, the most universally loved person we know—Debbie, through life's ups and downs there's no one we'd rather have beside us for the long haul. (By the way, Taylor, we found Georgette. She was in her office.)

Thanks also to those who shared their insights and ideas at the 2013 Triad retreat: Emily Epstein, Sharon Grady, Michele Gravelle and Sam Brown, Peter Hiddema, Audrey Lee, Ryan Thompson, Gillien Todd, and Rob Wilkinson; and to our colleagues and friends who have helped in so many ways: Jeremy Ahouse, Lisle Baker, Eric Barker, Chris Benko, Richard Birke, Robin Blass, Dawn Buckelew, Cecile Carr, Laura and Dick Chasin and colleagues at the Public Conversations Project, Jared Curhan, John Danas, Phil Davis, Alan Echtenkamp, Jac Fourie, Amy Fox, Mike Garrido, Jim Golden, Eric Henry, David Hoffman, Bernardus Holtrop, Ted Johnson, Dee Joyner, Ismail Kola, Susan McCafferty, Liz McClintock, Jamie Moffitt, Monica Parker, Brenda Pehle, Jen Reynolds, Grace Rubenstein, Danny and Louise Rubin, Gabriella Salvatore, Joe Scarlett and Mary Fink, Jeff Seul, Olga Shvayetskaya, Linda Silver, Hill Snellings, Scott Steinkerchner, Laila Sticpewich, Wojtek Sulejman, Don Thompson and Joshua Weiss. BK Loren of the Iowa Writer's Workshop, along with classmates from the summer of 2012, provided invaluable guidance and companionship as the project took shape; Angelique Skoulas generously shared the quiet of her pied-à-terre in Cambridge during the homestretch; mother-in-law Susan Richardson and husband John Richardson cheerfully picked up the slack at home; and the staff of the Carlisle Public Library embodied the ideal combination of "welcome back" and "we won't bother you" all along the way.

We have been collaborating with the folks at Duke Corporate Education for more than a decade. They are invaluable partners in testing what is useful to executives and organizations facing global challenges and change. Holly Anastasio, Dennis Baltzley, Jonathan Besser, Laurie Beyl, Christina Bortey, Jane Boswick-Caffrey, Nedra Bradsher, Cindy Campbell, Mike Canning, Cindy Emrich, Pete Gerend, Monica Hill, Leah Houde, Robin Easton Irving, Nancy Keeshan, Tim Last, Mary Kay Leigh, Pat Longshore, Steve Mahaley, John Malitoris, Liz Mellon, Maureen Monroe, Carrie Painter, Bob Reinheimer, Judy Rosenblum, Michael Serino, Blair Sheppard, and Cheryl Stokes have become trusted friends as well as colleagues.

A big thanks to agent Esther Newberg and the team at ICM. You took us on when we were pups, and over the years, our appreciation for your talent, wisdom, and support has only deepened.

This is our second project with the team at Viking Penguin, and it's been just as gratifying this time around. Susan Petersen Kennedy and Clare Ferraro were all in from the start, and we are deeply grateful for their confidence in us. Cover designer Nick Misani hit a home run on his very first swing. Nick, remember us in your acceptance speech at the industry awards. Carla Bolte created a design that is fresh and inviting. The publicity team—Carolyn Coleburn, Kristin Matzen, and Meredith Burks—along with the marketing team—Nancy Sheppard, Paul Lamb, and Winnie De Moya—shared our conviction that this was both a business book and psychology book, and had great ideas for how to get it out to organizations and individuals alike. Nick Bromley kept everything moving and everyone on track.

We wrote several appreciative paragraphs about our editor, Rick Kot, but Rick deleted them and in their place inserted this: "Rick is awesome, full stop." We'll go with that and add this: Your clear-headed questions and (endless) wise edits have made this a far better book, and the humor embedded in your comments had us laughing out loud. Rick, we would walk on gilded splinters for you. We're hoping it doesn't come to that, but if it does, give us a call.

Doug wishes to acknowledge the incredible support of his closest friends: Don, Syl, Kate, Annie, and Emma; Jimmy, Louisa, Susannah, and Allyson; Wynn, Phyllis, Sophia, Alexa, and Nadia; Matt, Luann,

Faulks, Holly, Bloss, Manuela, and the Krausens, and all the guys over at the Sports Barn and Monkey Down. For whatever reason, I won the friendship lottery and I know just how lucky I am.

And family. Such a good-looking bunch. Rand, when we were growing up, I thought of you as Superman, and I still do; Robbie, you have this amazing ability to make everyone around you feel safe and happy (and I'm sorry for trying to sell you tap water when we were little); Julie, you are the quickest, funniest person I know, and I'm including myself in that assessment; Dennis, Alana, and David, thanks for loving those first three and for being such awesome in-laws. And to all of you, thanks for the biggest gift of all, my niece and nephews—Andy, Charlie, Caroline, Colin, Daniel, Luke, and Matty. Mom, I'll catch up with you and Dad in the dedication.

"Appreciation" doesn't quite express Sheila's indebtedness to her husband, John Richardson, and kids, Ben, Petey, and Addy. They each put up with a consuming project and pretended they weren't keeping that favors ledger I found behind the sofa. My amazing parents, Jack and Joyce, bestowed a lifetime's worth of acceptance and appreciation as well as a healthy skepticism about others' opinions of you, both good and bad. And my grandmother Christine, who passed away at age 105 partway through this project, demonstrated daily the gift of being able to laugh at yourself. Robert and Susan, Jill and Jason, Stacy and Dan, Jim and Susan, Fred and Jessica, Andrew and Amanda—each seemed to know just the right time to inquire or encourage. It's the feedback from each of you that is most important to my own sense of self, and you have been compassionately sparing, always.

A couple of words about grammar and names. We often use the gender-neutral "they" in place of "he or she." Though grammatically incorrect, it's a simple and clear way of describing those who are giving us feedback. We wish to pre-thank those readers who refrain from sending complaints to Viking Penguin. Such complaints would give them one more reason to say, "We told you so."

Though the names in the book represent a range of cultures and traditions, we comment on culture only indirectly. Culture, of course, can have a profound impact on the way feedback is given and heard; even so, it's our observation that the fears, frustrations, and triggered reactions we have when receiving feedback are deeply human and universal.

And finally, our heartfelt appreciation to all those whom we've met and will meet, who have the courage, curiosity, and commitment to seek out and take in feedback when it matters most.

NOTES ON SOME RELEVANT ORGANIZATIONS

THE PROGRAM ON NEGOTIATION (PON) AT HARVARD LAW SCHOOL

When Roger Fisher, Bill Ury, and Bruce Patton founded the Harvard Negotiation Project (HNP) in 1979, they couldn't have anticipated how quickly the negotiation field would grow. In 1983 HNP gave birth to PON, an umbrella organization and interuniversity consortium focused on negotiation, mediation, dispute systems, and conflict resolution. Today PON brings together a multidisciplinary community of researchers and practitioners, and includes HNP and nine other projects focused on theory building, social science research, and excellence in teaching and clinical education.

HNP

Under the leadership of Director Professor James Sebenius, current HNP projects include the Great Negotiator Study Initiative and the China Negotiation Initiative. Past projects have included work on process that contributed to the Camp David Accords of 1978; a training for all parties to the negotiation process before the constitutional talks that ended apartheid in South Africa; and a joint workshop for U.S. and Soviet diplomats among many others. HNP is perhaps best known for the development of the theory of "principled negotiation," as presented in *Getting to Yes,* first published in 1981 (Penguin, 2011—third edition). Other books by the HNP team include *Difficult Conversations* (Penguin, 2010—second edition); *Getting Past No* (Bantam, 1993); *Getting It Done* (HarperBusiness, 1998); *Beyond Reason* (Penguin, 2006); and *3D Negotiation* (Harvard Business Review Press, 2006).

PON

Led by Professor Robert Mnookin and Executive Director Susan Hackley, PON seeks to nurture the next generation of negotiation teachers and scholars. Through a variety of lenses, including law, business, government, psychology, economics, anthropology, the arts, and education, members of the PON community seek to illuminate the causes of conflict and offer prescriptive advice for managing conflict skillfully and efficiently. Why did a deal fail that would have benefited both companies? Why did one country resolve differences peacefully, while another fought a bloody civil war? Why are some divorcing couples able to mediate their separation amicably, while others fight painfully and expensively in court? PON is working to push the theory forward and to help disseminate these competencies around the world.

THE CLEARINGHOUSE

As part of its commitment to conflict management and negotiation education, PON has developed a wealth of negotiation simulations, teaching notes, videotaped demonstrations, and interactive video and electronic lessons. These are available through PON's Clearinghouse and Harvard Business School Publishing.

EXECUTIVE EDUCATION

HNP pioneered the Negotiation Workshop course in the Harvard Law School curriculum and HNP and PON offer executive education through the Harvard Negotiation Institute (HNI) and PON's Executive Seminar series. Sheila Heen, Bruce Patton, and Douglas Stone offer an advanced course on Difficult Business Conversations for executives through both HNI and the PON Exec Ed series. For more information, see www.pon.harvard.edu.

TRIAD CONSULTING GROUP

Founded by Douglas Stone and Sheila Heen, Triad is a global consulting and corporate education firm based in Harvard Square in Cambridge, Massachusetts.

Whether you're rolling out a major change initiative or seeking to improve the day-to-day management skills of senior executives, we can help. We work with clients to strengthen individual and organizational capacity in a range of areas, including

Difficult Conversations
Negotiation and Problem Solving
The Influence Equation
Making Teams Work
Enhancing Impact Through the Systems Practice
Feedback and Learning

Typical consulting engagements include coaching an executive team to function effectively when stakes are high and stakeholders divided; helping to improve collaboration within and across functions; using systems mapping to guide resource deployment and to optimize the impact of key initiatives.

We offer executive coaching, team intervention, mediation and facilitation, and keynote presentations and retreat experiences. We partner with clients to design programs that respond to their context and challenges, ensuring that the approach is relevant and realistic. Triad harnesses connection and humor to enable senior executives to be honest with themselves and one another about what they are up against. We know a lot of this is tough stuff, and we're in it with you.

Our clients span a dozen industries and six continents. They include BAE, BHP, Capital One, Capgemini, Citigroup, the Educational Testing Service, the Federal Reserve Bank, Genzyme, Hess, Honda, HSBC, Johnson & Johnson, Massachusetts General Hospital,

Merck, Metlife, Novartis, Prudential, PwC, Shell, TimeWarner, Unilever, and Verizon.

In the public sector, we have worked with the White House, the Singapore Supreme Court, the Ethiopian Parliament, UN/AIDS, The Nature Conservancy, the Arctic Slope Regional Corporation, and New England Organ Bank. Members of our team have taught and mediated in South Africa, the Middle East, Kashmir, Iraq, Afghanistan, and Cyprus. Our consultants teach at Harvard Law School, Georgetown Law School, Dartmouth's Tuck School of Business, Tufts Fletcher School and School of Medicine, Boston College, the University of Wisconsin, and MIT's Sloan School of Business. We have authored dozens of popular and scholarly books and articles in the field.

Feel free to e-mail us at info@diffcon.com; call us at (617) 547-1728; and visit Triad on the Web at www.triadconsultinggroup.com.

It all starts with a conversation.

ABOUT THE AUTHORS

Douglas Stone is a Lecturer on Law at Harvard Law School and a founder of Triad Consulting Group (www.triadconsultinggroup.com). In addition to corporate clients such as Citigroup, Honda, Johnson & Johnson, Shell, and Turner Broadcasting, Stone has worked with journalists, educators, doctors, diplomats, and political leaders in South Africa, Kashmir, and the Middle East, and in Geneva with the World Health Organization and UN/AIDS. He has trained senior political appointees at the White House and was a keynote speaker at the World Negotiation Conference in São Paulo. His articles have appeared in publications ranging from the *New York Times* to *Real Simple* and the *Harvard Business Review,* and he has appeared on *Oprah,* NPR, and many other television and radio shows. He is a graduate of Harvard Law School, where he served as Associate Director of the Harvard Negotiation Project. He can be reached at dstone@post.harvard.edu.

Sheila Heen is a Lecturer on Law at Harvard Law School and a founder of Triad Consulting Group (www.triadconsultinggroup.com). Her clients span five continents and include TimeWarner, the Federal Reserve Bank, HSBC, Metlife, Novartis, PwC, and Unilever. Heen often works with executive teams to engage conflict productively, repair working relationships, make sound decisions, and execute change in complex organizations. In the public sector she has consulted for the New England Organ Bank, the Singapore Supreme Court, Greek and Turkish Cypriots, and the Arctic Slope Regional Corporation in Barrow, Alaska. Heen has worked with theologians struggling with disagreement over the nature of truth and God, and with senior political appointees for the White House. She has published in the *New York Times* and the *Harvard Business Review,* and appeared on shows as diverse as *Oprah, Fox News,* CNBC's *Power Lunch,* and NPR. A graduate of Harvard Law School, she is schooled in negotiation daily by her three children. She can be reached at heen@post.harvard.edu.

For more about Doug and Sheila and free downloads to help yourself, visit us at www.stoneandheen.com.

NOTES

Introduction: From Push to Pull

1. **every schoolchild will be handed back as many as 300 assignments, papers, and tests:** American schoolchildren between the ages of 6 and 17 spend an average of 3 hours and 58 minutes on homework daily (www.smithsonianmag.com/arts-culture/Do-Kids-Have-Too-Much-Homework.html), and the average school year is 180 days (www.nces.ed.gov/surveys/pss/tables/table_15.asp). If we assume one or two daily assignments, and add term papers, pop quizzes, midterms, finals, and standardized testing, 300 is a conservative estimate, particularly for high school students. **Millions of kids will be assessed as they try out for a team or audition to be cast in a school play:** Thirty-five million children in the United States play organized sports each year (www.statisticbrain.com/youth-sports-statistics); there are 98,817 public schools in the United States (www.nces.ed.gov/fastfacts/display.asp?id=84), and 19 percent of those schools (18,775) offer drama programs (www.nces.ed.gov/surveys/frss/publications/2002131/index.asp?sectionid=3). Many of the 33,366 private schools also have drama programs. **Almost 2 million teenagers will receive SAT scores** (www.press.collegeboard.org/sat/faq) **and face college verdicts thick and thin** (www.statisticbrain.com/college-enrollment-statistics). **At least 40 million people will be sizing up one another for love online, where 71 percent of them believe they can judge love at first sight** (www.statisticbrain.com/online-dating-statistics); **250,000 weddings will be called off** (www.skybride.com/about), and **877,000 spouses will file for divorce** (www.cdc.gov/nchs/nvss/marriage_divorce_tables.htm): Centers for Disease Control numbers include annulments but exclude data from California, Georgia, Hawaii, Indiana, Louisiana, and Minnesota. U.S. Census Bureau records suggest that the annual divorce numbers run around 1.1 million (www.census.gov/compendia/statab/2012/tables/12s0132.pdf).

2. **Twelve million people will lose a job:** Census records show that there were 12,645,000 job losses in the private sector in 2010 (the last year for which data is available). This excludes nonprofits and the self-employed. www.census.gov/compendia/statab/2012/tables/1250635.pdf. **More than 500,000 entrepreneurs will open their doors for the first time, and almost 600,000 will shut theirs for the last:** The Small Business Administration shows 533,945 small

business "births" and 593,347 "deaths" for the year 2009-2010. (www.sba.gov/advocacy/849/12162).

3. **between 50 and 90 percent of employees will receive performance reviews this year:** Statistics range widely, from those reported by the CEB that 51 percent of companies conduct formal reviews annually (reported here: www.westchestermagazine.com/914-INC/Q2-2013/Improving-Performance-Review-Policies-for-Managers-and-Employees) to the 91% of HR professionals surveyed who reported that their organization has a formal performance-management program (www.worldatwork.org/waw/adimLink?id=44473). Organizations with an HR function would be more likely to have a formal system; those that don't may have informal performance practices. **825 million work hours . . . are spent each year preparing for and engaging in annual reviews:** According to the International Labor Office's LABORSTA database, the global labor pool consists of approximately 3.3 billion workers (www.laborsta.ilo.org/applv8/data/EAPEP/eapep_E.html). If even half of them receive some sort of review, and we estimate those reviews take 30 minutes to prepare for and execute on, that comes to 94,178 years. The managers who are conducting the reviews would of course do multiple reviews, so this is probably a conservative estimate.

4. 360-degree feedback is a process by which feedback is solicited from colleagues who are above you, below you, and who are your peers. This input, often scrubbed of identifying details so that it is anonymous, is collected into a report and provided to the recevier.

5. *Merriam-Webster's Collegiate Dictionary,* 9th ed. (1986).

6. **Fifty-one percent . . . said their performance review was unfair or inaccurate:** 2011 survey from Globoforce, www.bizjournals.com/boston/news/2011/04/29/survey-majority-hate-performance.html. Cornerstone on Demand survey puts the statistic at 51 percent. See www.getworksimple.com/blog/2012/01/20/4-statistics-that-prove-performance-reviews-don't-work-for-the-modern-worker. **One in four employees dreads their performance review:** See 2011 Globoforce survey, above.

7. Results of the 2010 Study on the State of Performance Management, survey of 750 HR professionals by Sibson Consulting and World at Work, Fall 2010. Only 20 percent report that when corporate performance is poor, individual ratings go down, indicating poor correlation between individual performance and organizational performance. And just 40 percent say their leaders model performance management through evaluation and coaching of direct reports. http://www.sibson.com/publications/surveysandstudies/2010SPM.pdf.

8. For an overview of feedback-seeking behavior, see Michiel Crommelinck and Frederick Anseel, "Understanding and Encouraging Feedback-Seeking Behavior: A Literature Review," *Medical Education* 2013; 47: 232–241, doi:10.1111/medu.12075. The connection between negative-feedback seeking and performance reviews is explored in Z. G. Chen, W. Lam, J. A. Zhong, "Leader-Member Exchange and Member Performance: A New Look at Individual-Level Negative Feedback-Seeking Behaviour and Team-Level Empowerment Climate," *J Appl Psy-*

chol 2007;92 (1):202–12, and in S. J. Ashford, A. S. Tsui, "Self-Regulation for Managerial Effectiveness—the Role of Active Feedback Seeking," *Acad Manage J* 1991;34 (2):251–80. Studies that show a link between feedback-seeking behavior and creativity include J. Zhou, "Promoting Creativity Through Feedback," in J. Zhou, C. E. Shalley, eds *Handbook of Organizational Creativity*. New York, NY: Lawrence Erlbaum Associates 2008; 125–46, and DEM De Stobbeleir, S. J. Ashford, and D. Buyens, "Self-Regulation of Creativity at Work: The Role of Feedback-Seeking Behavior in Creative Performance," *Acad Manage J* 2011;54 (4):811–31. Exploration of feedback seeking and adaptation can be found in E. W. Morrison, "Longitudinal Study of the Effects of Information Seeking on Newcomer Socialization," *J Appl Psychol* 1993;78 (2):173–83; C. R. Wanberg and J. D. Kammeyer-Mueller, "Predictors and Outcomes of Proactivity in the Socialization Process," *J Appl Psychol* 2000;85 (3):373–85; and E. W. Morrison, "Newcomer Information-Seeking—Exploring Types, Modes, Sources, and Outcomes," *Acad Manage J* 1993;36 (3):557–89.

9. S. Carrere, et al. "Predicting Marital Stability and Divorce in Newlywed Couples," *Journal of Family Psychology* 14(1)(2000): 42–58. See generally: www .gottman.com. We note that Gottman's research relates specifically to the correlation between a husband's openness to input from his spouse and the health of the marriage. Whatever Gottman's particular findings, it's our view that openness on anyone's part will likely improve the health of a relationship.

10. Thomas Friedman, "It's a 401(k) World," *New York Times*, May 1, 2013.

Chapter 2: Separate Appreciation, Coaching, and Evaluation

1. The appreciation, coaching, and evaluation distinctions were introduced to us by John Richardson, and are described in a book Richardson wrote with Roger Fisher and Alan Sharp called *Getting It Done: How to Lead When You're Not in Charge* (HarperBusiness, 1999).

2. Marcus Buckingham and Curt Coffman, *First Break All the Rules: What the World's Greatest Managers Do Differently* (Simon & Schuster, 1999), 28, 34.

3. Gary Chapman, *The 5 Love Languages: The Secret to Love That Lasts* (Northfield Publishing, 2009).

Chapter 3: First Understand

1. This diagram (the Feedback Arrow) and the concepts that follow are based in part on the "ladder of inference," a tool developed by Chris Argyris and Don Schön.

2. Roger Schank: http://www.rogerschank.com/artificialintelligence.html. See also Schank's *Tell Me a Story: Narrative and Intelligence* (Northwestern University Press, 1995).

3. The confirmation bias describes our propensity to notice information that conforms with our preexisting views. See Raymond S. Nickerson, "Confirmation Bias: A Ubiquitous Phenomenon in Many Guises," *Review of General Psychology* (Educational Publishing Foundation) 2(2) (1998): 175–220.

4. The self-serving bias describes our tendency to attribute our successes to our own abilities, and our failures to external factors. This can lead to an inflated sense of our own abilities in relationship to the abilities of others. For the driving example, see O. Svenson, "Are We All Less Risky and More Skillful Than Our Fellow Drivers?" *Acta Psychologica* 47(2) (Feb. 1981): 143–48. The managers' inflated sense of their own performance comes from a 2007 *BusinessWeek* poll of 2000 U.S. executives (www.businessweek.com/stories/2007-08-19/ten-years-from-now-and).

5. David Foster Wallace, *This Is Water: Some Thoughts, Delivered on a Significant Occasion, about Living a Compassionate Life* (Little, Brown and Company, 2009).

Chapter 4: See Your Blind Spots

1. Steven Johnson, *Mind Wide Open: Your Brain and the Neuroscience of Everyday Life* (Scribner, 2004), 31–32. For a fascinating discussion of human iris size and the evolution of cooperation, see Michael Tomasello, "For Human Eyes Only," *New York Times,* January 13, 2007.

2. For an overview of theory of mind see Alvin I. Goldman, "Theory of Mind," in *Oxford Handbook of Philosophy and Cognitive Science,* ed. Eric Margolis, Richard Samuels, and Stephen Stich (Oxford University Press, 2012), 402.

3. See, for example, Simon Baron-Cohen, Alan M. Leslie, Uta Frith, "Does the Autistic Child Have a 'Theory of Mind'?" *Cognition* 21 (1985) 37–46.

4. Johnson, *Mind Wide Open,* 31–32.

5. Albert Mehrabian, *Nonverbal Communication* (Aldine Transaction, 2007). Mehrabian, an emeritus professor at U.C.L.A., claims that tone of voice accounts for 38 percent of our message, body language 55 percent and the actual words spoken, only 7 percent.

6. Jon Hamilton, "Infants Recognize Voices, Emotions by 7 Months," National Public Radio, March 24, 2010: http://www.wbur.org/npr/125123354/infants-recognize-voices-emotions-by-7-months. Also, Annett Schirmer and Sonja Kotz, "Beyond the Right Hemisphere: Brain Mechanisms Mediating Vocal Emotional Processing," in *Trends in Cognitive Sciences* 10(1) (Jan. 2006): 24–30.

7. Atul Gawande, "Personal Best," *New Yorker,* October 3, 2011.

8. Sophie Scott, Institute of Cognitive Neuroscience, University College, London, interview on *Science Friday* with Ira Flatow, May 29, 2009: http://m.npr.org/story/104708408.

9. See, for example, Paul Ekman, *Emotions Revealed: Recognizing Faces and Feelings to Improve Communication and Emotional Life* (Holt Paperbacks, 2007). Ekman argues that due in part to involuntary movement of certain facial muscles, we are not as good at disguising our emotions as we think we are.

10. This is known as the actor-observer asymmetry (Jones and Nisbett, 1971). The actor tends to attribute their behavior to the situation, while the observer tends to attribute the actor's behavior to the actor's character. A related concept is the

fundamental attribution error (Lee Ross, 1967), which states that when we describe the behavior of others, we overemphasize character and underemphasize situation.

11. Robert I. Sutton, *Good Boss, Bad Boss: How to Be the Best . . . and Learn from the Worst* (Business Plus, 2010), 211.

12. Alex Pentland, *Honest Signals: How They Shape Our World* (MIT Press, 2008). For an overview of research and applications, see Pentland, "To Signal Is Human," *American Scientist* 98 (May–June 2010), http://web.media.mit.edu/~sandy/2010-05Pentland.pdf.

13. In a *New York Times* article titled "I Know What You Think of Me" (June 15, 2013), writer Tim Kreider discusses the negative effects of receiving an e-mail from a friend about himself that was intended for another friend: "I've often thought that the single most devastating cyberattack . . . would not be on the military or financial sector but simply to simultaneously make every e-mail and text ever sent universally public . . . the fabric of society would instantly evaporate. . . . Hearing other people's uncensored opinions of you is an unpleasant reminder that . . . everyone else does not always view you in the forgiving light that you hope they do, making all allowances, always on your side."

Chapter 5: Don't Switchtrack

1. "Flowers for Kim," *Lucky Louie,* Episode 6 (2006). Dialogue is slightly edited for language.

2. The fundamental attribution error was coined by Lee Ross in 1977. L. Ross, "The Intuitive Psychologist and His Shortcomings: Distortions in the Attribution Process," in L. Berkowitz, *Advances in Experimental Social Psychology* (1977).

3. We like people who like us, and are like us. See Robert Cialdini, *Influence: The Psychology of Persuasion* (HarperBusiness, 2006), especially chapter 5, "Liking: The Friendly Thief."

4. For more on autonomy in negotiation, see Roger Fisher and Daniel Shapiro, *Beyond Reason: Using Emotions as You Negotiate* (Penguin, 2006).

Chapter 6: Identify the Relationship System

1. Interview with John Gottman by Randall C. Wyatt in 2001 on psychotherapy .net, http://www.psychotherapy.net/interview/john-gottman.

2. For a useful elaboration on relationship systems in business, see Diana McLain Smith, *The Elephant in the Room: How Relationships Make or Break the Success of Leaders and Organizations* (Jossey-Bass, 2011).

3. Peter M. Senge, *Fifth Discipline Fieldbook: Strategies and Tools for Building a Learning Organization.* Crown Business; 1 edition (1994). "Accidental Adversaries" is described by Jennifer Kemeny, based on her work in the 1980s, on pages 145–48.

4. Robert Ricigliano has explored the value of a systems perspective in conflict. See Robert Ricigliano, *Making Peace Last: A Toolbox for Sustainable Peacebuilding* (Paradigm Publishers, 2012).

5. Daniel Kim, Michael Goodman, Charlotte Roberts, Jennifer Kemeny, "Archetype 1: 'Fixes That Backfire,'" in Peter M. Senge, *The Fifth Discipline Fieldbook: Strategies and Tools for Building a Learning Organization* (Doubleday, 1994).

Chapter 7: Learn How Wiring and Temperament Affect Your Story

1. Enormous appreciation goes to neuropsychologist Dr. Cate Fortier for her review of this material, and to Dr. Robin Weatherill for her insight and overview.
2. For a classic article introducing the idea of adaptability and subjective well-being, see: P. Brickman and D. T. Campbell, "Hedonic Relativism and Planning the Good Society," in *Adaptation-Level Theory,* ed. M. H. Appley (New York: Academic Press, 1971), 287–305. Adaptability is also referred to in the literature as "set point theory," the "hedonistic treadmill," and "adaptability theory."
3. D. Lykken and A. Tellegen, "Happiness Is a Stochastic Phenomenon," *Psychological Science* 7 (1996): 186–89. Lykken suggests that 50 to 80 percent may be genetic; other studies suggest closer to 50 percent. See S. Lyubomirsky, K. Sheldon, and D. Schkade, "Pursuing Happiness: The Architecture of Sustainable Change," *Review of General Psychology* 9(2) (2005): 111–31.
4. Piece compared lottery winners and those with spinal cord injuries: P. Brickman, D. Coates, and R. Janoff-Bulman, "Lottery Winners and Accident Victims: Is Happiness Relative?" *Journal of Personality and Social Psychology* 36 (1978): 917–27. Other research, however suggests that the matter is more complicated. See, for example, *The Effects of Winning the Lottery on Happiness, Life Satisfaction, And Mood,* by Dr. Richard J. Tunney, (Nottingham: University of Nottingham, 2006).
5. A number of researchers have suggested that happy individuals react more strongly to pleasant stimuli and that unhappy individuals react more strongly to unpleasant stimuli. See R. J. Larsen and T. Ketelaar, "Personality and Susceptibility to Positive and Negative Emotional States," *Journal of Personality and Social Psychology* 61 (1991): 132–40.
6. For an overview of Jerome Kagan's work, see Robin Marantz Henig, "Understanding the Anxious Mind," *New York Times,* September 29, 2009. See also Jerome Kagan and Nancy Snidman, *The Long Shadow of Temperament* (Belknap Press, 2009).
7. C. E. Schwartz, et al., "Structural Differences in Adult Orbital and Ventromedial Prefrontal Cortex Predicted by Infant Temperament at 4 Months of Age," *Archives of General Psychiatry* 67(1) (Jan. 2010): 78–84.
8. Jonathan Haidt, *The Happiness Hypothesis: Finding Modern Truth in Ancient Wisdom* (New York: Basic Books, 2006), 29.
9. The limbic system is believed to have evolved with the first mammals, more than 100 million years ago. For an excellent overview of the evolution of the brain, see "The Evolutionary Layers of the Human Brain," http://thebrain.mcgill.ca/flash/d/d_05/d_05_cr/d_05_cr_her/d_05_cr_her.html.
10. Richard J. Davidson, Ph.D., with Sharon Begley, *The Emotional Life of Your Brain: How Its Unique Patterns Affect the Way You Think, Feel, and Live—and How You Can Change Them* (Hudson Street Press, 2002), 41 and 69.

11. Ibid., 24–39.

12. A separate 2012 review of fMRI and PET scan studies done between 1990 and 2007 concluded that a "locational" theory of distinct emotions is less supported than the "conceptual" theory—i.e., that different parts of the brain are involved in interpreting emotions and events. K. Lindquist, et al., "The Brain Basis of Emotion: A Meta-Analytic Review," *Behavioral Brain Sciences* 35 (2012): 121–43.

13. Two primary studies: R. J. Davidson, "What Does the Prefrontal Cortex 'Do' in Affect: Perspectives in Frontal EEG Asymmetry Research," *Biological Psychology* 67 (2004): 219–34. On the differences in white matter, see: M. J. Kim and P. J. Whalen, "The Structural Integrity of an Amygdala-Prefrontal Pathway Predicts Trait Anxiety," *Journal of Neuroscience* 29 (2009): 11614–18.

14. In *The Resilience Factor: 7 Keys to Finding Your Inner Strength and Overcoming Life's Hurdles* (New York: Broadway Books, 2002), Karen Reivich and Andrew Shatté talk about resilience having four uses—to overcome obstacles in childhood, to steer through everyday frustrations, to bounce back from major setbacks, and to reach out to achieve all you can. We are using it in the biological sense here, but the impact would affect all of these, which we refer to at various times throughout the book.

15. Davidson with Begley, *Emotional Life of Your Brain*, 83–85.

16. Richard Davidson has created questionnaires that can help you get a handle on your profile with respect to both the time it takes you to recover from negative feelings, and your ability to sustain positive feelings. See Davidson and Begley, *Emotional Life of Your Brain*, 46–49.

17. See S. Lyubomirsky, K. Sheldon, and D. Schkade, "Pursuing Happiness: The Architecture of Sustainable Change," *Review of General Psychology* 9(2) (2005): 111–31. See also Martin E. P. Seligman, *Flourish: A Visionary New Understanding of Happiness and Well-being* (Atria Books, 2012), 157 and 159.

18. Seligman, *Flourish*, 157 and 159.

19. Mihaly Csikszentmihalyi, *Flow: The Psychology of Optimal Experience* (Harper Perennial, 2008).

20. Haidt, *Happiness Hypothesis*, 30–31.

21. Variations on what we are calling "snowballing" have also been referred to as catastrophizing. See David D. Burns, *Feeling Good*. Harper (reprint edition 2009), p. 42. Chris Argyris refers to the phenomenon as the "doom zoom" in "Teaching Smart People How to Learn," *Harvard Business Review* May–June 1991, p. 104.

Chapter 8: Dismantle Distortions

1. Our ideas on the relationship between thoughts, feelings, and story, and how to "contain the feedback" are informed by work in the fields of cognitive and narrative therapy. See, for example, Martin E. P. Seligman, *Authentic Happiness: Using the New Positive Psychology to Realize Your Potential for Lasting Fulfillment* (Atria Books, 2004); Aaron T. Beck, *Love Is Never Enough: How Couples Can Overcome Misunderstandings,*

Resolve Conflicts, and Solve Relationship Problems Through Cognitive Therapy (Harper Perennial, 1989); and Michael White and David Epstein, *Narrative Means to Therapeutic Ends* (W. W. Norton & Company, 1990).

2. Daniel Gilbert, *Stumbling on Happiness* (Vintage, 2007), 167.

3. People's tendency to overestimate the extent to which anyone else is paying attention to them is referred to as the "spotlight effect" or egocentrism. For more on the spotlight effect, see Thomas Gilovich and Kenneth Savitsky, "The Spotlight Effect and the Illusion of Transparency: Egocentric Assessments of How We Are Seen by Others," *Current Directions in Psychological Science* 8(6) (Dec. 1999).

Chapter 9: Cultivate a Growth Identity

1. There is evidence that Western cultures—American and European—are more likely to describe self in abstract trait terms (I'm honest, I'm smart), while Asian cultures—Chinese, Korean, Indian—are more likely to describe self in contextual and relational terms (I'm a student, I'm a brother). For more on cultural differences in self-concept and character, see Incheol Choi, Richard E. Nisbett, and Ara Norenzayan, "Causal Attribution Across Cultures: Variation and Universality," *Psychological Bulletin* 125(1) (1999): 47–63.

2. Leon Festinger first proposed the idea that we measure ourselves against our peers, called social comparison theory. See L. Festinger, "A Theory of Social Comparison Processes," *Human Relations* 7 (1954): 117–40.

3. This observation was made by our colleague Jeffrey Kerr in conversation.

4. From Carol S. Dweck, *Mindset: The New Psychology of Success* (Ballantine Books, 2006) 3.

5. Ibid., 4.

6. Ibid.

7. Dweck, *Mindset*, 11, describing research conducted with Joyce Ehrlinger.

8. Jennifer A. Mangels, Brady Butterfield, Justin Lamb, Catherine Good, and Carol S. Dweck, "Why Do Beliefs About Intelligence Influence Learning Success? A Social Cognitive Neuroscience Model," *Soc Cogn Affect Neurosci.* 2006 September; 1(2): 75–86.

9. Carol Dweck, "Brainology: Transforming Students' Motivation to Learn," *NAIS Independent Schools Magazine*, Winter 2008, www.nais.org/Magazines-Newsletters/IS Magazine/Pages/Brainology.aspx, accessed September 18, 2013. Article contains a helpful summary of key research on fixed- and growth-mindset responses to struggle or failure.

10. This Identity chart is an adaptation of Dweck's chart in *Mindset*, 245.

11. The ability to distinguish assessment and judgment may help explain why people with fixed mindsets are notoriously poor at assessing their own abilities. People with growth mindsets more accurately assess their current abilities, perhaps because they don't have the same sense of judgment about where they stand. Where they stand is only a momentary stop on the journey to where they are going.

Chapter 10: How Good Do I Have to Be?

1. Anne Lamott, *Bird by Bird: Some Instructions on Writing and Life* (Pantheon, 1994), 44.
2. For helpful advice on how to say no, see William Ury, *The Power of a Positive No: Save the Deal, Save the Relationship and Still Say No* (Bantam, 2007).

Chapter 11: Navigate the Conversation

1. The first short film using computer animation and keyframing was the 1974 film *Hunger.* ("Keyframing" is spelled as one word, as is "inbetweening.") Thanks to John Hughes and Pauline Ts'o at Rhythm & Hues for showing us firsthand how computer animation works.
2. Jared R. Curhan and Alex Pentland, "Thin Slices of Negotiation: Predicting Outcomes from Conversational Dynamics Within the First 5 Minutes," *Journal of Applied Psychology* 92(3) (2007): 802–11.
3. John Gottman and Nan Silver, *Seven Principles for Making Marriage Work* (Three Rivers Press, 2000), 22, 27, 39–40. See also J. M. Gottman and R. W. Levenson, "Marital Processes Predictive of Later Dissolution: Behavior, Physiology, and Health," *Journal of Personality and Social Psychology* 63 (1992): 221–33; and J. M. Gottman and C. I. Notarius, "Decade Review: Observing Marital Interaction," *Journal of Marriage and the Family* 62 (2000): 927–47.
4. T. Singer, et al., "Empathy for Pain Involves the Affective but Not Sensory Components of Pain," *Science* 33(5661) (Feb. 20, 2004): 1157–62. Watching another's pain does not activate the entire "pain matrix," but only the part of the brain associated with its affective qualities (bilateral anterior insula, rostral anterior cingulate cortex, brainstem, and cerebellum), but not its sensory qualities (posterior insula/secondary somatosensory cortex, sensorimotor cortex, and caudal anterior cingulate cortex). You don't feel physical pain, but you feel the emotions correlated with physical pain. Of note: People who scored higher on two empathy questionnaires also had stronger mirror neuron brain activity.
5. T. Singer, et al., "Empathic Neural Responses Are Modulated by the Perceived Fairness of Others," *Nature* 439 (Jan. 26, 2006): 466–69. Interestingly, it was overwhelmingly men who had the revenge reaction; it is yet unclear whether this holds generally across studies or is a function of this particular cohort.
6. The interpretation of interruptions varies across cultures. If you are operating in a culture with implicit (or explicit) rules against interrupting (a superior, or an elder, for example), you might instead write down key points and your questions as you listen, letting them know that you are taking notes in order to best understand what they are saying. After they finish, you can ask questions at an appropriate time and place. The goal is to be respectful and engaged, and to work with them to clarify their feedback. Linguist Deborah Tannen has an interesting discussion of culture and interruption in *Conversational Style: Analyzing Talk Among Friends* (Oxford University Press, 2005).

7. Roger Fisher, William Ury, and Bruce Patton, *Getting to Yes: Negotiating Agreement Without Giving In*, 3rd ed. (Penguin, 2011). For an application of these ideas specifically to law and business, see Robert H. Mnookin, Scott R. Peppet, and Andrew S. Tulumello, *Beyond Winning: Negotiating to Create Value in Deals and Disputes* (Belknap Press, 2004), and David A. Lax and James K. Sebenius, *3-D Negotiation: Powerful Tools to Change the Game in Your Most Important Deals* (Harvard Business Review Press, 2006).

Chapter 12: Get Going

1. See this original study at R. F. Baumeister, et al., "Ego Depletion: Is the Active Self a Limited Resource?" *Journal of Personality and Social Psychology* 74(5) (1998): 1252–65. The participants asked to refrain from eating cookies were asked to eat radishes instead. The cookie eaters made an average of 34.29 attempts and persisted for 18.9 minutes, while the radish eaters made an average of 19.4 attempts while persisting for 8.35 minutes. It's reasonable to wonder whether the different amounts of sugar intake and resulting blood glucose levels might have increased the cookie eaters' energy. The researchers did not find a correlation between glucose levels and willpower. For an expanded discussion of willpower, see Roy Baumeister and John Tierney, *Willpower: Rediscovering the Greatest Human Strength* (Penguin, 2012).

2. Atul Gawande, "Personal Best," *New Yorker,* October 3, 2011.

3. Chuck Leddy, "Coaching Tips from Gawande: Surgeon-Author Sees Gain for Teachers in On-the-Job Guidance," *Harvard Gazette,* October 25, 2012.

4. T. C. Schelling, "Egonomics, or the Art of Self-Management," *American Economic Review,* 68 (1978), 290-294. See also, Thomas C. Schelling, *Strategy of Conflict* (Harvard University Press, 1981).

5. Nick Paumgarten, "Master of Play," *New Yorker,* December 20, 2010.

6. The term "gamification" was coined by Nick Pelling in 2002. The concept and approach has moved into mainstream use since about 2010, with the business world using it to increase customer engagement and loyalty, Wikipedia using it to increase contributions (by 64 percent!), and education using gamification principles to find ways to increase student participation in learning. The movement also has its vociferous critics. See blog post by Ben Betts at http://www.astd .org/Publications/Blogs/Learning-Technologies-Blog/2013/03/Gamification-Meet-Gamefulness, and for a more general critique, Alfie Kohn, *Punished by Rewards: The Trouble with Gold Stars, A's, Praise and Other Bribes* (Mariner Books, 1999).

7. For a slightly different take on this, see Seth Godin, *The Dip: A Little Book That Teaches You When to Quit (and When to Stick)* (Portfolio Hardcover, 2007).

8. For an overview of feedback-seeking behavior, see Michiel Crommelinck and Frederick Anseel, "Understanding and Encouraging Feedback-Seeking Behavior: A Literature Review" in *Medical Education* 2013; 47: 232–41, doi:10.1111/medu .12075. The connection between negative-feedback seeking and performance

reviews is explored in Z. G. Chen, W. Lam, and J. A. Zhong, "Leader-Member Exchange and Member Performance: A New Look at Individual-Level Negative Feedback-Seeking Behaviour and Team-Level Empowerment Climate," *J Appl Psychol* 2007;92 (1):202–12; and in S. J. Ashford, A. S. Tsui, "Self-Regulation for Managerial Effectiveness—The Role of Active Feedback Seeking," *Acad Manage J* 1991;34 (2): 251–80.

Chapter 13: Pull Together

1. *Results of the 2010 Study on the State of Performance Management*, survey of 750 HR professionals by Sibson Consulting and World at Work, Fall 2010. Only 20 percent report that when corporate performance is poor, individual ratings go down, indicating poor correlation between individual performance and organizational performance. And just 40 percent say their leaders model performance management through evaluation and coaching of direct reports; http://www.sibson.com/publications/surveysandstudies/2010SPM.pdf.
2. Susan Heathfield, "Performance Appraisals Don't Work," *Human Resources,* available at www.humanresources.about.com/od/performanceevals/a/perf_appraisal.html. Accessed February 2013.
3. Brené Brown, October 2012, from her presentation at the Linkage Global Institute for Leadership Development Conference, Palm Desert, CA.
4. Dick Grote, 12:17PM September 12, 2011, "The Myth of Performance Metrics," *Harvard Business Review* blog post, at www.blogs.hbr.org/cs/2011/09/the_myth_of_performance_metric.html?cm_sp=blog_flyout-_-cs-_-the_myth_of_performance_metric. Grote is the author of *How to Be Good at Performance Appraisals: Simple, Effective, Done Right* (Harvard Business Review Press, 2011).
5. *Results of the 2010 Study of Performance Management* (Fall 2010) 4. When asked who the biggest champions of the performance management system are, 73 percent report it's the top HR executive; 30 percent say the CEO (totals equal more than 100 percent because they could select more than one response).
6. Ibid., 5.
7. For an in-depth examination of psychological safety in the workplace, see Amy Edmondson, *Teaming: How Organizations Learn, Innovate, and Compete in the Knowledge Economy* (Jossey-Bass, 2012).
8. For more analysis and advice on appreciation in the workplace, see Gary Chapman and Paul White, *The 5 Languages of Appreciation in the Workplace: Empowering Organizations by Encouraging People* (Northfield Publishing, 2011).
9. The concept of multitrack diplomacy is presented in William D. Davidson and Joseph V. Montville, "Foreign Policy According to Freud," *Foreign Policy* 45 (Winter 1981–82): 145–57. These principles are at the philosophical core of ongoing work done by the Institute for Multi-Track Diplomacy, founded by John W. McDonald and Louise Diamond.
10. Robert Cialdini, *Influence: The Psychology of Persuasion* (HarperBusiness, 2006).

ROAD MAP

TRUTH TRIGGERS

  ONE DAD, TWO REACTIONS   29

  THERE ARE THREE KINDS OF FEEDBACK   30

    APPRECIATION   31

    COACHING   32

    EVALUATION   33

  WE NEED ALL THREE   35

    EVALUATION SHORTFALLS   35

    APPRECIATION SHORTFALLS   36

    COACHING SHORTFALLS   38

  BEWARE CROSS-TRANSACTIONS   38

    A COMPLICATION: THERE IS ALWAYS EVALUATION IN COACHING   40

  WHAT HELPS?   42

    GET ALIGNED: KNOW THE PURPOSE AND DISCUSS IT   42

    SEPARATE EVALUATION FROM COACHING AND APPRECIATION   43

3. **FIRST UNDERSTAND   46**
    Shift from "That's Wrong" to "Tell Me More"

  WE'RE GOOD AT WRONG SPOTTING   46

  UNDERSTANDING IS JOB ONE   47

    FEEDBACK ARRIVES WITH GENERIC LABELS   48

    GIVER AND RECEIVER INTERPRET THE LABEL DIFFERENTLY   50
      Play "Spot the Label"   52

    WHAT'S UNDER THE LABEL?   52
      Coming From and Going To   53

    ASK WHERE THE FEEDBACK IS COMING FROM   54
      They Observe Data   54
      They Interpret the Data   54
      They Confuse Data and Interpretation (We All Do)   55

RELATIONSHIP TRIGGERS

IDENTITY TRIGGERS

FEEDBACK IN CONVERSATION

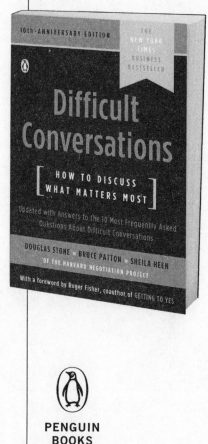